Four Island Utopias

BEING
Plato's Atlantis
Euhemeros of Messene's Panchaia
Iamboulos' Island of the Sun
Sir Francis Bacon's New Atlantis

FOUR ISLAND UTOPIAS

BEING
PLATO'S ATLANTIS
EUHEMEROS OF MESSENE'S PANCHAIA
IAMBOULOS' ISLAND OF THE SUN
SIR FRANCIS BACON'S NEW ATLANTIS

With a Supplement
UTOPIAN PROTOTYPES, DEVELOPMENTS,
AND VARIATIONS

Diskin Clay
Andrea Purvis

The Focus Classical Library
Series Editors • James Clauss and Albert Keith Whitaker

Hesiod's *Theogony* • Richard Caldwell • 1987
The Heracles of Euripides • Michael Halleran • 1988
Aristophanes' *Lysistrata* • Jeffrey Henderson • 1988
Sophocles' *Oedipus at Colonus* • Mary Whitlock Blundell • 1990
Euripides' *Medea* • Anthony Podlecki • 1991
Aristophanes' *Acharnians* • Jeffrey Henderson • 1992
Aristophanes' *The Clouds* • Jeffrey Henderson • 1992
The Homeric Hymns • Susan Shelmerdine • 1995
Aristophanes: *Acharnians, Lysistrata, Clouds* • Jeffrey Henderson • 1997
Euripides' *Bacchae* • Stephen Esposito • 1998
Terence: *Brothers* • Charles Mercier • 1998
Sophocles' *Antigone* • Mary Whitlock Blundell • 1998
Aristophanes: *Birds* • Jeffrey Henderson • 1999

The Focus Philosophical Library
Series Editor • Albert Keith Whitaker

Plato's *Sophist* • E. Brann, P. Kalkavage, E. Salem • 1996
Plato's *Parmenides* • Albert Keith Whitaker • 1996
Plato's *Symposium* • Avi Sharon • 1998
Plato's *Phaedo* • E. Brann, P. Kalkavage, E. Salem • 1998
Empire and the Ends of Politics • S. D. Collins and
D. Stauffer • 1999
Liberty, Equality & Modern Constitutionalism • G. Anastaplo • 1999

Cover: The columns of the Temple of Poseidon at Sounion, looking out to the Sea
Photo: Diskin Clay

Book Team:

Publisher: *Ron Pullins*
Production Assistant: *Andrea Bickum*
Editorial Manager: *Cynthia Zawalich*

Frontispiece, i.
The Course of Empire: Pastoral or Arcadian State (second of a series), by Thomas Cole, oil on canvas, ca. 1836.
© Collection of the New York Historical Society.

Atlantis

Frontispiece, ii.
The Course of Empire: Consummation (third of a series), by Thomas Cole, oil on canvas, ca. 1835-1836.
© Collection of the New York Historical Society

Frontispiece, iii.
The Course of Empire: Destruction (fourth of series), by Thomas Cole, oil on canvas, ca. 1836.
© Collection of the New York Historical Society

Table of Contents

Preface

This book began with teaching and is meant primarily for students and teachers. Over the last many years Diskin Clay has taught a course on Utopias: Ancient and Modern. *Four Island Utopias* grew out of the need to provide students and teachers with translations of three Greek texts which are of great importance to the ancient segment of this course: Plato's description of the island of Atlantis in the Prologue to his *Timaeus* and in its sequel, the *Critias*; Euhemeros of Messene's Panchaia; and finally Iamboulos' Island of the Sun. Francis Bacon's *New Atlantis* had always been one of our readings and now makes the fourth of four island utopias. We begin, therefore, with one of Plato's last works and end with one of Bacon's last works; we move in space from the Atlantic to the mid-Pacific and from the 350s BC to the third decade of the seventeenth century.

This course may never assume a final shape, but the book we present here comes from the course Diskin Clay offered in the spring of 1999 and the collection of texts we prepared for the undergraduates of this course. For this Andrea Purvis supplied the translations, brief introductions, and annotations of the Supplement on "Utopian Prototypes, Developments, and Variations." The Introduction to these texts and to Greek utopian writing is the product of our close collaboration.

The reader might well want to read the texts presented here before turning to the Introduction. Each of the texts selected has its own brief foreword and essential annotations. In the Introduction and in our presentation of the texts that are included in this volume we have had in mind the student and reader interested in our themes (and these themes are many and varied) and the teacher. Thus, we have severely limited our range of references and attempted to focus attention on the primary sources. For the reader who will begin with our texts, our use of the term "utopia" requires some warning and apology. Our working definition of the term is justified in the Introduction (§1, "What is a Utopia?") and illustrated by almost all of the texts we include, with the possible exception of Bacon's *New Atlantis*. A work of utopian literature does not present an ideal society as a model for social reform: it works rather by indirection in directing the reader's critical gaze away from the society created by the utopian author onto his or her own society. Its focus is not the ideal but the real. Its object is to open up possibilities usually excluded by the sheer familiarity of the reader's and author's own society. We occasionally use the term "utopia" literally to refer to utopian places that can be found "nowhere." This is the literal meaning of the Greek words Thomas More combined to produce the name of his fictive island, Utopia. Rarely is the term "utopia" used to describe a society regarded as perfect by its author and the model for the reformation of existing societies. In the case of Francis Bacon's Bensalem and its governing scientific guild (or House of Salomon), the term (also coined by Thomas More) "eutopia" (an excellent place) might serve as well. But we express some doubts about just how seriously Bacon took his *New Atlantis* in our Introduction (§10).

This book is dedicated to our students, the happy few who have discovered the islands presented here even as we have discovered and rediscovered them in their company.

Acknowledgements

We thank first and foremost Thomas Elliott and Professor Richard Talbot: Thomas Elliott for his expert work in providing maps and illustrations for this volume, and Richard Talbot for his great generosity in making the facilities of The Classical Atlas Project at the University of North Carolina at Chapel Hill available to us. We also thank Linda McCurdy who made it possible for us to exploit the resources of the Special Collections of the University of Minnesota Libraries, as well as the Fogg Art Museum and the New York Historical Society for providing us with photographs and the permission to publish them. Finding illustrations for a book like ours is not difficult, but finding photographs and the permission to publish can be a time-consuming task. We are delighted to be able to thank Joanne Lorah for making this task easier and producing the drawing that illustrates an episode from Iamboulos' Island of the Sun (Figure 16).

Illustrations

The British Museum, Figure 10; The Classical Atlas Project and Thomas Elliott, Figures 1-3, 5-7, 11; Duke University Libraries, Special Collections, Figure 12; Thomas Elliott, Figures 13-15; The Fogg Art Museum, Harvard University Art Museums, Figure 8; Joanne Lorah, Figure 16; The New York Historical Society, frontispieces; The New York Public Library, Figure 17; Routledge, London & New York, Figure 4; The University of Minnesota Library, Figure 9.

Maps and Illustrations

Introduction

Texts

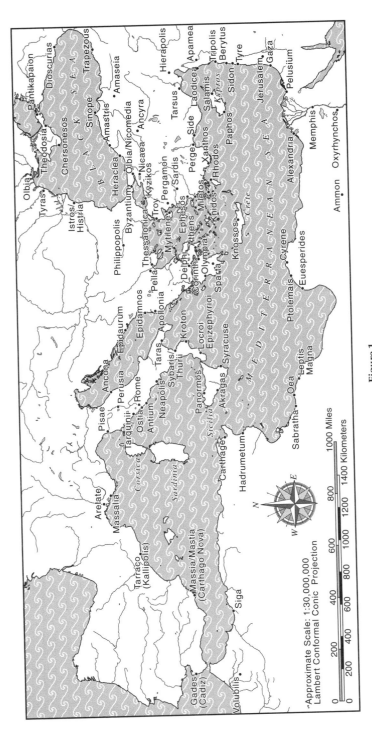

Figure 1
Map of the Mediterranean. Thomas Elliott.

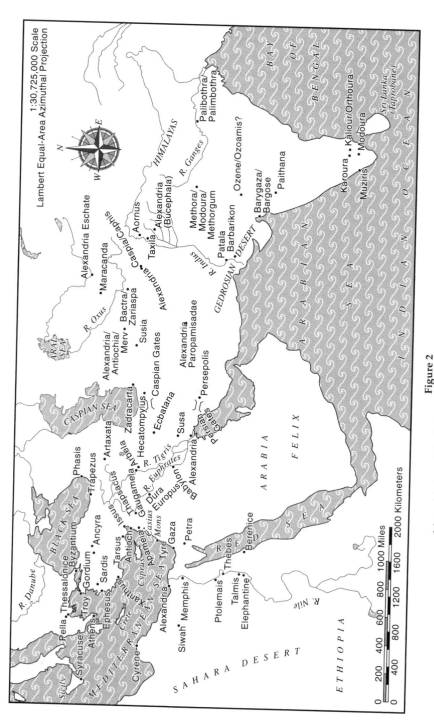

Figure 2

Map of Asia and the Indian Ocean. Diskin Clay and Thomas Elliott.

Figure 3
Utopian map of the Mediterranean world, with Ocean and the utopian islands and people who appear in the book. Diskin Clay and Thomas Elliott.

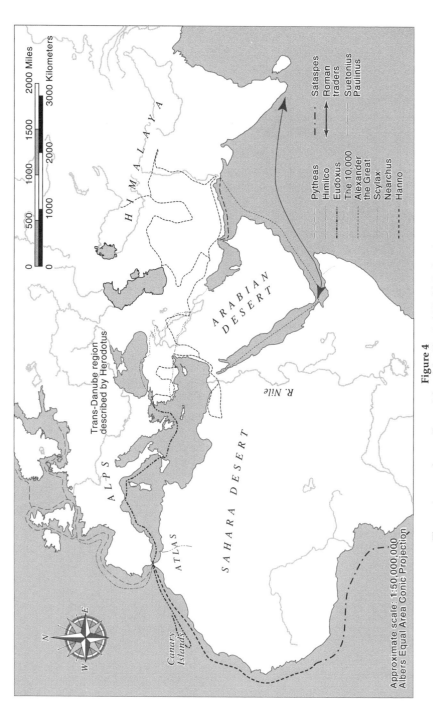

Figure 4

The ancient explorers. From *Atlas of the Classical World*, Richard J. A. Talbert (Routledge, London & New York, 1993). Revised by Thomas Elliott.

Figure 5

Ancient O-T map of the Mediterranean. Reconstruction of Hecataeus' map of the oikoumene. Diskin Clay and Thomas Elliott.

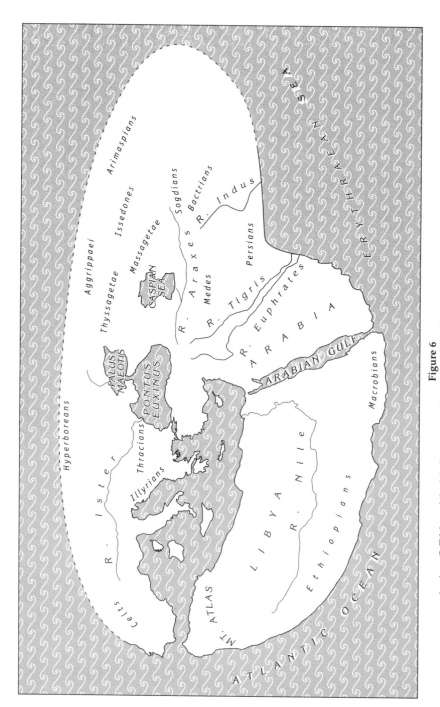

Figure 6

Ancient O-T Map of the Mediterranean. Reconstruction of Herodotus' view of the world, ca. 450 BC.
Diskin Clay and Thomas Elliott.

Figure 7
Theopompos' conception of the world and its "True Continent."
Diskin Clay and Thomas Elliott.

Four Island Utopias

Introduction
Islands in the History of Greek Utopian Writing

§ 1 WHAT IS A UTOPIA?

The word utopia is Greek, but utopia is not a Greek word. The elements of this invented place-name are *ou*, the Greek negative, and *topia*, from *topos*, place. Utopia is Nowhere. Until 1516, there was no such place as Utopia and no such thing as utopian literature. But when Thomas More published his *Utopia*, a new genre of literature was created that has had a profound and defining influence not only on the works that recognized it by imitation but on our understanding of works long written. Later works look back to it as their charter document, and earlier works that had seemed to belong to very different genres become recognizable as utopian. And so, both in prospect and retrospect, works as dissimilar as the book of Genesis, Aristophanes' *Birds*, and Aldous Huxley's *Brave New World* have been bound together in one volume.[1]

More himself recognized some Greek predecessors to his *Utopia*. It is these that concern us in this presentation of Greek utopian literature, and in particular the Greek literature of island utopias. We begin with Plato's Atlantis (**I**). Plato's account of the prehistoric societies of Athens and Atlantis answers in one essential respect to a utopia as More conceived it: it directs its readers' critical gaze from the imaginary societies described to the real societies of author and reader. Plato and his successors depended in various degrees on earlier accounts of idealized peoples, some of which are included in the Supplement (**V**) and are reflected in the later works presented throughout this book. But Plato in particular seems to have shaped More's conception of utopian writing.

The common but unexamined conception of a utopia as a model for an ideal society is inadequate to an understanding of the utopias of More, Plato, and most of the works presented here. In fact, only one of the island utopias presented in this book represents the author's serious view of an ideal and attainable society. This is Francis Bacon's *New Atlantis* (**IV**). All of

---

[1] As they are in a much curtailed collection of utopian literature, *Utopian Literature: A Selection*, ed. J. W. Johnson (New York 1968).

the other islands (Plato's Atlantis, Euhemeros' Panchaia, Iamboulos' Island of the Sun) and remote places described in detail by our authors should not remain the real focus of our attention as readers. Rather, these inaccessible places on the edges of the Greek world were invented in order to direct the reader's critical gaze back on his or her own society.[2] This conception of the Greek utopian islands and places conforms to the larger definition of a utopia that has gained some currency:

> A utopia should describe in a variety of aspects and with some consistency an imaginary state or society which is regarded as better, in some respects at least, than the one in which an author lives. He does not ordinarily claim that the fictitious society and its people are perfect in all respects and that he is propounding a total ideal or model to strive toward or imitate: most utopias are presented not as models of unrealistic perfection but as alternatives to the familiar, as norms by which to judge existing societies ....[3]

There is, in fact, a Greek equivalent for our term "utopian." Aristotle chose it to describe the utopian schemes of Plato's *Republic* and *Laws*: they are created *kat' euchen*—as answers to the political philosopher's impossible prayers.[4] The term applies equally well to the project of Aristophanes' *Birds*, in which the comic poet stages the fulfilled fantasy of a wish for escape and a new supremacy outside of Athens.

We can draw artificial lines that produce an anatomy of the works we are considering in this Introduction. Four main categories suggest themselves: 1. retrospective utopias; 2. utopias of discovery; 3. utopias of foundation; and 4. utopias of the inaccessible present. The myth of the Golden Age (below) and Plato's myth of prehistoric Athens and Atlantis (**I**) fall under the first heading; Euhemeros' Panchaia (**II**), Iamboulos' Islands of the Sun (**III**), Lucian's *True History* (**III** Appendix), and Bacon's *New Atlantis* (**IV**) under the second; Plato's *Republic* (considered in connection with the *Timaeus/Critias*, **I** and § 6 below) and Aristophanes' *Birds* (§ 5) under the third; the Islands of the Blest and the Elysian Fields (**V** and §3 below) and most of the works of the Supplement (**V**) under the fourth. The Supplement's selections are not utopian in the strict sense of the word; they were generally not written with the sole purpose of effecting a critical gaze on the author's society, but do often contain descriptions presenting an ideal of piety and justice in the eyes of the Greeks (as, for example, the

---

[2]   This is true too of the historical inquiry of Herodotus in which the observer is observed and the questioner questioned, in the formulation of Hartog (1980) 19.
[3]   From Gibson (1961) 293. See also Negley (1977) xi-xiv.
[4]   Aristotle *Politics* IV 1288[b]33; cf. IV 1295[a]29. The conception is due to Plato; cf. *Republic* II 499C and 550D.

Figure 8 *The Golden Age,* by Jean-August-Dominique Ingres, oil on paper mounted on wood panel, 1862. Courtesy of the Fogg Art Museum, Harvard University Art Museums, Bequest of George L. Winthrop.

accounts of the Hyperboreans and Ethiopians) or a reversal of societal customs (as, for example, the accounts of the Amazons). Although it is possible to distinguish between Plato's and More's aim of social reform and the various aims of earlier authors of utopian literature, moral and religious implications are present in Greek traditions of imaginary or exotic places from the very beginning.

The first "heaven on earth" in Greek mythology is retrospective. This is the Golden Age of Hesiod's *Works and Days* (109-120), when men lived in peace and the earth provided sustenance spontaneously. The people of this age were "dear to the blessed gods" (120), who granted them a painless life and death and an afterlife as spirits guarding the earth (121-126). The other earliest utopian lands are the realms of the dead, which exist in the present but are inaccessible to most. One could reach the Elysian fields or the Islands of the Blest only after death and by appointment of the gods, although these places are assigned a distant location on earth (see **V 1** and §3 below). The absence of war and evil in these early utopias presents an attraction dependant on principles of both pleasure and morality—war is undesirable because it is painful to many and therefore evil. The image of these utopias could not, therefore, fail to reflect a critical gaze on contemporary society. Idealization of distant people occurred as early as Homer's *Iliad*, as, for example, that of the Abioi from Thrace or Scythia, "the most just of humans" (XIII 6). A more direct critical gaze is illustrated by Hesiod, who moves from the Golden Age and the Age of Heroes to inveigh against his own society in *Works and Days* (174-201).[5] Herodotus, whose account of the Ethiopians may have been used by More (see **V 3 A**), reports several remote peoples whose customs resemble those of the guardian class of Plato's *Republic* and the inhabitants of More's Utopia.[6] Herodotus may have used sources now lost that were the real precursors of utopian literature, written long before Plato.[7]

§ 2   More and the Discovery of Utopia

To understand More's attitude to his Greek predecessors, we must understand how they are recognized in his *Utopia*. More presents his *Utopia* as the faithful record of a conversation involving himself, as ambassador of Henry VIII to Flanders, and a Portuguese sailor he and his party had met at Antwerp. The name of this sailor is Raphael Hythlodaeus. *Utopia* is introduced by a letter to Peter Giles in which More worries that he had not thought to inquire of the exact location of Utopia.[8] So circumstantial is his record of this conversation that one of More's first readers faulted him for being no more than a stenographer to the conversation he recorded.[9] In the literary form and utopian stategies of his Utopia, More is expressing an unacknowledged debt to Plato: for book I of *Utopia* he chose the dialogue form so familiar in Plato. His worry over corroborating details replicates the anxious circumstantial details we find in Plato's account of prehistoric Athens and Atlantis; and, like Atlantis, More's Utopia is an island of no return. (See further below and §6.)

---

[5] See Dodds (1973) 3-4 on the Golden Age and Hesiod's motive of criticism.

[6] For example, sharing of wives (IV 104) and acting as arbiters for others while avoiding war (IV 23). See Hadas (1935) esp. 118, 120-121.

[7] Hadas (1935) *passim*. It has been suggested that this type of writing began in earnest after the Peloponnesian War, due to social and political upheavals giving rise to anxiety and discontent; see Dodds (1973) 13 and Dillery (1995) 43-45. But it is possible that factors influencing readership and the survival of literature are responsible for the impression that this type of literature was first written in the fourth century; anxiety stemming from political or social conditions was not something new.

[8] I 6/**40**.33-**42**.4. We cite the translation of Surtz (1964), and give the page (in boldface type) and line numbers of the Latin text in the fourth volume of the Yale edition of Surtz and Hexter (1965) (abbreviated as the Yale *Utopia* in the notes).

[9] Evidence for this reading comes from a letter of More to Peter Giles, reproduced in the Yale *Utopia* 249.

Figure 9 Frontispiece to Thomas More's *Utopia* (1518). University of Minnesota Library.

The date of the conversation is 1515. More's companions were John Constable and the humanist, Peter Giles (Petrus Aegidius) of Antwerp.[10] In book I, Hythlodaeus recalls an earlier conversation he had during his one visit to England at the palace of John Cardinal Morton in Canterbury. Thus, in literary character the first book is the narrative of a dialogue and a dialogue framed within a dialogue. Book II, which we know from Erasmus was written first,[11] is almost entirely descriptive and was originally conceived as an impersonal account of the newly discovered island of Utopia: "The island of the Utopians extends in the center (where it is broadest) for two hundred miles and is not much narrower for the greater part of the island, but at both ends it begins gradually to taper" (I 59/**110**.7-19). There is no other voice heard in book II of *Utopia*, except the editorial voice of More recalling what he said as a character at its conclusion. It is only with book I that *Utopia* gained its characters, their dialogue, and, in the dialogue reported within the dialogue in Antwerp, a clear connection to contemporary England. The unevenness of style that struck Erasmus (see note 11) is due in part to the shift from the unbroken narrative of book II to the dialogue of book I. Thus More seems to have adopted the strategy of Plato's Atlantis in two stages: first, the unbroken narrative of the *Critias*, and second, the dialogue of the *Timaeus* Prologue.

The first recognition of the ancient world as it was implicated in Hythlodaeus' discovery of the new island of Utopia comes as More is introduced to Hythlodaeus by his friend, Peter Giles. From Hythlodaeus' appearance, More guesses that he must be a sailor. Giles corrects him. The Portuguese is no ordinary ship's captain,

> for his sailing has not been like that of Palinurus, but rather that of Ulysses or, rather, of Plato. Now this Raphael—for such is his personal name, with Hythlodaeus as his family name—is no bad Latin scholar, and most learned in Greek. He had studied that language more than Latin because he had devoted himself unreservedly to philosophy.
>
> (I 12/**48**.36-50.1)

---

[10] Significantly, Giles (1486-1533) was the editor of Lucian (1518), an author More translated and the author of the most fantastic essay in Greek utopian literature, *The True History*. The importance of Lucian to More will appear in sequel.

[11] In his letter to Ulrich Hutten (July 23, 1519) describing the character of his friend, Erasmus touches on More's *Utopia*: "His *Utopia* was published with the aim of showing the causes of the bad condition of states, but was chiefly a portrait of the British State, which he has thoroughly studied and explored. He had written the second book first in his leisure hours, and added the first book on the spur of the moment later, when the occasion offered. Some of the unevenness of style is due to this," translated in Johan Huizinga, *Erasmus of Rotterdam* (London 1952), 238.

There is nothing philosophical about Palinurus. Palinurus was the unlucky helmsman of Aeneas' ship, who was swept overboard by Neptune as his ship approached Italy (Vergil *Aeneid* V 833-861 and VI 337-383). Ulysses was particularly well known to More and his contemporaries in this age of discovery, as were the opening lines of the *Odyssey*, which describe Odysseus (his name in Greek) as a man of many turns, "who had come to know the cities and mind of many peoples" (Homer *Odyssey* I 3). As for Plato, More must have had in mind the traditions of his travels after the execution of Socrates in 399 BC, and in particular his three voyages to Sicily and the court of Dionysius I, and then of his son and successor, Dionysius II, in Syracuse.[12] Such an interpretation would be congenial to the ambassador of Henry VIII, who was to become his Lord Chancellor (in 1529). In fact, the then popular subject of advice given to princes is debated at length by More and Hythlodaeus.[13] It is a subject on which they are far divided, but in which Plato is often invoked (I 38-52/**84**.30-**102**.20). Both Odysseus and Plato had knowledge of men and their cities, and could thus serve as prototypes for Hythlodaeus (and More).

It could be that More had Plato's writings as well as his travels in mind, for Plato is very much present in the debate between More and Hythlodaeus, and Plato (of the *Republic*) is cited by More as Hythlodaeus' "favorite author" (I 39/**86**.10). Plato used a number of nautical metaphors to describe the course of discussion in his dialogues: the second sailing, the sweet bend (of the Nile), and the three waves or storm of paradoxes of *Republic* V are all metaphors that come to mind of philosophy described as a sailing—or 'le voyage philosophique.'"[14] Plato is one of the few ancient authors known to the Utopians. As we shall see, Hythlodaeus introduced most of his dialogues to the island (II 104/**182**.28), and many Utopian institutions are those of the

---

[12] Described by Plato in *Epistle* VII 323D-352A, which More had no doubt was authentic, and by Diogenes Laertius in *Lives of the Philosophers* III 6-7, 18-22. In his letter to the party of Dion in Syracuse, Plato himself makes a connection with Odysseus by saying that he had thrice crossed the straits of Scylla and Charybdis (345E, quoting *Odyssey* XII 428). More also knew of Plato's relations with the tyrants of Syracuse and his philosophical colleague Dion of Syracuse from Cornelius Nepos' *Life of Dion* and the better-known Plutarch's *Life of Dion*.

[13] In the early sixteenth century, Plutarch's Platonic essay on the necessity of a prince to associate with a philosopher was well known and often cited as an authority for contemporary treatments of politics: "That a Philosopher ought to Converse especially with Men in Power," trans. H. N. Fowler, Plutarch's *Moralia* X (Loeb Classical Library: Cambridge, Mass. 1969) 27-47. In the same year More published his *Utopia*, Erasmus brought out his *Education of a Christian Prince*.

[14] The "second sailing" is proverbial and occurs in *Phaedo* 99D, *Statesman* 300E, and *Philebus* 19C; the "sweet bend" occurs in *Phaedrus* 257D; and Socrates' description of the three proposals he makes in *Republic* V as "waves of paradox" (*Republic* V 457B-C and 473C). A connection between the *Odyssey* and the *Republic* is argued by Howland (1993) especially 32-55 and 150-156.

city Socrates creates in the *Republic*. Plato's seafaring, then, might have as much to do with the exploration of the uncharted cities and conceptions of good societies that we find in the *Republic, Timaeus/Critias*, and *Laws* as with his Odyssean travels to Sicily. It is also significant that More's reliance on Plato was noticed by his contemporaries: in a letter to the Dutch humanist Jerome Busleyden, Erasmus describes More's Utopia is a "Platonic island."[15]

Despite his high estimation of Greek and his correspondingly low estimation of Latin as a philosophical language, More wrote his *Utopia* in Latin, since this was the language in which the humanists of his generation communicated across national boundaries. The subtitle of *Utopia* is *De Optimo Reipublicae Statu deque Nova Insula Utopia Libellus vere Aureus*: "Concerning the Best Form of Republic and the New Island Utopia a truly Golden Book." The conception of the best form of government and society goes back to Plato's *Republic*,[16] and the name Utopia itself might owe something to Plato as well. The first edition of this "truly Golden Book" (a title which reflects the antique conception of the Golden Age of mankind) displayed in its front matter a Latin poem of six lines. It is attributed to the poet laureate of Utopia, Anemolius (Wind Bag), Hythlodaeus' nephew. This short poem gives us an indication of the importance of names in More's *Utopia*:

> Called Utopia by the ancients, because of my isolation,
> Now a rival to Plato's City,
> And perhaps her victor. What he limned
> In letters, I alone produced in fact,
> In men and wealth, and excellent laws.
> Justly I deserve to be called by the name Eutopia.

Eutopia is the Good Place. This name has given us the term dystopia, which is its antonym. More's little poem is the first expression of the now common misconception that utopias are seriously intended by their authors as representing perfect societies. At the same time it calls into question the relation between utopia and eutopia. In antiquity, according to Anemolius' poem, Utopia was called Utopia because of its "isolation" (*infrequentia*). That is, it is no place Europeans can reach. In More's narrative, it is called *Utopia* also because of the allergic reaction it provokes in More's contemporary Englishmen. There is no single principle that explains the names More invented for his *Utopia*, but the most important names seem to anticipate a hostile reaction on the part of the reader.[17]

---

[15] *Platonicam insulam*, in the Yale *Utopia* 20.19. The two Platonic islands are Atlantis of the *Timaeus/Critias* and Crete of the *Laws*.

[16] In *Timaeus* 17C it is said that a state like that of the *Republic* is the best form of government; cf. *Republic* V 449A.

[17] Romm (1991) provides a review of the attempts to fit the nomenclature of Utopia into a coherent system.

The name of Utopia's European discoverer is Hythlodaeus, which in Greek means Knower of Nonsense.[18] He is committed to the society of the island he discovered, although he questions the Utopians' attachment to pleasure. Hythlodaeus left this island after more than five years' residence to convey word of it to the Old World (I 55/**106**.13-18). In Book I, Hythlodaeus commends the Persian people he calls the Polylerites, Talkers of Much Nonsense (I 31-34/**74**.21), who have the wise policy of punishing thieves with penal servitude (rather than execution as was the case in More's England). Hythlodaeus' Achorians, Lacklanders, also seem to fit into this pattern of allegric naming.[19] More liked to style himself Morus, which means Fool in Greek, and Erasmus was fond of playing on the Greek meaning of his friend's name, as he did when he dedicated to him his *Praise of Folly* (*Moriae Encomium*).[20]

More might well have had a Platonic inspiration for the name Utopia. In the *Republic*, just after Socrates has referred to his city as Kallipolis (Fair City), he tells his companion, Glaucon, that those who agree with his proposals for the education of the philosopher king "will think that you speak surpassingly well. But those who have no inkling of this (truth) will think that you are talking nonsense" (*Republic* VII 527E). Socrates expresses himself in the Greek idiom: *ouden legein,* to say nothing, is to talk nonsense.

We find exactly the same kind of reaction in Shakespeare's *Tempest* as the shipwrecked Gonzalo imagines himself as king of the seemingly deserted island on which he and his companions have been shipwrecked. This passage bears quotation, since it provides a thesaurus of the most prevalent themes of utopian literature.

GONZALO
I' th' commonwealth I would by contraries
Execute all things; for no kind of traffic
Would I admit; no name of magistrate;   145
Letters should not be known; riches, poverty,
And use of service, none; contract, succession,
Bourn, bond of land, tilth, vineyard, none;
No use of metal, corn, or wine, or oil;
No occupation; all men idle, all;   150
And women too, but innocent and pure:
No sovereignity; —

---

18 From Greek *hythlos*, "nonsense," and the verb *daio*, "perceive." This is the interpretation of the Dutch humanist, Gerhard J. Vossius, *Opera* IV (Amsterdam 1695-1701) 340-341.
19 These people are situated on the mainland southeast of the island of Utopia (I 42/**88**.25).
20 *The Praise of Folly*, trans. H. H. Hudson (Princeton 1941) 1-4.

SEBASTIAN
                    Yet he would be king on't.
ANTONIO
    The latter end of the commonwealth forgets
    the beginning.
GONZALO
    All things in common Nature should produce   155
    Without sweat or endeavour: treason, felony,
    Sword, pike, knife, gun, or need of any engine,
    Would I not have; but Nature should bring forth,
    Of its own kind, all foison, all abundance,
    To feed my innocent people.
SEBASTIAN
    No marrying 'mong his subjects?   160
ANTONIO
    None, man; all idle; whores and knaves.
GONZALO
    I would with such perfection govern, sir,
    T'excel the Golden Age.
SEBASTIAN
                    'Save his Majesty!
ANTONIO
    Long live Gonzalo!
GONZALO
                    And,—do you mark me, sir?   165
ALONSO
    Prithee, no more: thou dost talk nothing to me.
                            (*Tempest* Act II, scene 1)

    King Alonso's reaction to Gonzalo is the reaction More expected to
his *Utopia*, and Socrates, to his Kallipolis. More's *Utopia* is No Place, No
Thing, and, as he liked to describe it, a Nowhere, a Never Never Land—
Nusquama.[21] Perhaps, to cite the Book of Proverbs, the wisdom of God is
the folly of men. In anticipating a hostile and allergic reaction to
Hythlodaeus' account of the society of Utopia, More is characterizing the
insularity of English society. As Hythlodaeus says explicitly, the discovery
of a new world is greeted with contempt by the old (I 56. **108**.11-19.).

    But Hythlodaeus could not have predicted the reception of More's
Utopia. Nor could More have predicted its literary success, but he does
recognize his Greek forerunners. Hythlodaeus, the discoverer of this "new
world" (*novus orbis*, I 55/**106**.16), has a predilection for Greek, as do the
people he has discovered. It appears that Hythlodaeus has not only discov-

---

[21]   Erasmus, *Epistle* 2.339, 346, 357, and 372; cf. Plato *Republic* 9. 592 B.

ered an unknown island at the antipodes; he has discovered vestiges of Greek antiquity. As he moves beyond the equator in space, he moves backward in time.[22]

In the names and institutions of Utopia, Hythlodaeus discovers something Greek.[23] The ease with which the Utopians learn Greek is another indication of their affinity with ancient Greece. If we follow the hints of the account of Hythlodaeus' voyage to Utopia, we learn that the Portuguese adventurer made three voyages with Amerigo Vespucci (whose account of "the last four voyages which are now universally read of" first appeared in 1507).[24] This circumstantial detail might betray still another reference to a Greek author. There is an obvious discrepancy between Vespucci's notorious four voyages and the three voyages on which Hythlodaeus was his companion. More's literal reader would set this discrepancy down in the ledger of truth; his more congenial reader might recognize that Hythlodaeus, like Plato, is known for three voyages of exploration.

Providentially, Hythlodaeus thought to provide himself with books on his third voyage with Vespucci. He never hoped to return to Europe again, but he carried with him European books, or books made European as Greek literature was rediscovered and printed in Europe. Hythlodaeus gives a list of the books that he brought on board with him as he discusses the literary tastes of the Utopians. He brought to Utopia works significant to the history of utopian literature, among others, "most of Plato's works" (II 104/**182**.28). The works that most attract the Utopians are those of Plutarch and Lucian: "They are very fond of the works of Plutarch and captivated by the wit and pleasantry of Lucian" (II 105/**182**.2-3). Poetry too is admitted into this ideal state. Aristophanes comes first in this list, then Homer (acknowledged especially for his *Odyssey*).[25] In introducing Greek poets to Utopia, More seems more generous than was Plato, who has Socrates in the *Republic* exile poets from his state. Hythlodaeus did not, however, think to bring the Bible. This omission may well find its parallel in Plato's deliberate exclusion of the poetry of Homer, his own society's repository of wisdom, from his ideal state.

---

[22] Just so Montaigne in his essay "On Cannibals." The discovery of "France Antartique" moves backward in time precisely as Montaigne moves away from Europe in space. In Bacon's *New Atlantis* (**IV**), the discovery of the island of Bensalem entails a natural history of the continent of America (Plato's Atlantis) as it existed 3,000 years earlier (§26-§29).

[23] The pattern of naming is to give an aboriginal name and its Greek equivalent: the aboriginal Abraxa, for example, becomes renamed Utopia.

[24] This description occurs in *Utopia* I 12-13/**50**.4-6. Vespucci's account of his voyages was published in Martin Waldseemüller's *Cosmographiae Introductio* (St. Dié in the Vosges 1507).

[25] *Utopia* I 12/**48**.31; 13/**50**.5; **52**.31-32, allusions picked up by Erasmus in his letter to Busleyden as he calls Hythlodaeus superior to Ulysses, the Yale *Utopia* **20**.28.

The newly discovered island of Utopia is the counterpart of these newly discovered works.[26] Of these authors, three will especially figure in this introduction: Aristophanes of the *Birds* and the floating island of Cloudcuckcooland (§5); Plato of the *Republic, Timaeus/Critias*, and *Laws* for the states of Kallipolis, prehistoric Athens and island of Atlantis (**I** and §6), and the City of the Magnetes reestablished on Crete (§6); and Lucian for his apparent "island" of the Moon and his Island of the Blest, both of which he describes in his *True History* (**III** Appendix and **V 1 E**). But first, Plutarch, one the Utopians' favorite authors, must be acknowledged for both the Utopians' enjoyment of his works and for his particular significance to More's account of Utopia.

Plutarch was best known for his *Lives*, which expressed moral, social, and political ideals in dramatic and entertaining biographies of Greek and Roman statesmen. The Utopians thus found attractive literature that was both amusing and wholesome, blending recreation with edification. Plutarch's *Life of Lycurgus* has long been entered in the registry of utopian literature as a utopia of foundation. It gives the foundation of the Spartan state and constitution, long admired by anti-democratics such as Critias and Socrates.[27]

In his *Life of Agis*, Plutarch introduces us to an experiment in communism that was soon doomed to failure in the Peloponnesus. But More recognized this work of Plutarch in *Utopia* itself. The *Life of Agis* explains one of the two precise dates in the history of the island of Utopia. According to Plutarch, in 244 BC Agis IV became king and co-regent (with Cleombrotus) of Sparta and attempted to return Sparta to the constitution it had known from its legendary foundation by Lycurgus until the age of Agesilaus (444-360 BC). Hythlodaeus says that the annals of Utopia go back 1,760 years (I 66/120.26-28). By this reckoning, King Utopus founded Utopia in the year 244 BC, the same year as Agis' ascension to the throne.[28] Agis was opposed by the ephor, Leonidas, and, after three years of rule, was murdered along with his mother and grandmother in prison. Like King Utopus, he left no heirs. Perhaps there is one other philosophical life by Plutarch that would have interested the Utopian: Plutarch's *Life of Dion*, on the Syracusan who was the close friend and associate of Plato, records Plato's attempts in Syra-

---

[26] Grafton (1992) provides a broader characterization of the relation between the expansion of Europe with the discovery of the New World and the discovery of antiquity.

[27] Plutarch's *Life of Lycurgus* easily becomes confused with the actual society of Sparta, as it does in Ferguson (1975) chapter 4. The characterization of this society as "utopian" by Rawson (1969) 171, is both accurate to Sparta as an ideal for non-Spartan societies and inaccurate to the strict conception of utopian writing that we employ in this Introduction.

[28] This is the plausible suggestion of Schoeck (1956).

cuse to assure that, if a philosopher could not become king, a king—or the son of a king—might become a philosopher. Lucian, an author the Utopians esteemed for his "wit and pleasantry" (II 105/II **182**.2-3) held the same charms for the Utopians as More holds for us. Both More and Erasmus had translated him into Latin,[29] and Peter Giles was his editor. Lucian's *True History* is a brilliant reflection of the utopian themes that we will discover in earlier Greek utopian literature, which begins with Homer and Hesiod. In his first-person narrative of his travels, Lucian recognizes the main Greek works of many distinct genres that More's *Utopia* allows us to describe as utopian: Homer's *Odyssey*, the myth of the Golden Age and the Islands of the Blest in Hesiod's *Works and Days*, Aristophanes' *Birds*, Plato's *Republic* (and *Laws*), and Iamboulos' Island of the Sun. Lucian explicitly recognized Iamboulos in the Preface to his *True History* as an author of "wit and pleasantry" (*True History* I 3). We have included an excerpt of Lucian's description of the inhabitants of the Moon (*Selenitai*) as the Appendix to Iamboulos' narrative of his travels in the Indian Ocean in **III**. Excerpts from Lucian's description of the Island of the Blest are given in the Supplement, **V 1 E**.

First and last in this list of books, let us name Plato. More recognized the communism of the *Republic* and made it the foundation of the Utopian constitution, not merely for a single class (as is the case of Kallipolis) but for all of Utopian society. But perhaps the *Republic* fascinated More most of all for Plato's genius in indicting the vices of Greek society and Athens most sharply by indirection. Like Gonzalo of the *Tempest*, Plato and More work "by contraries." More's method is implicitly identified as Platonic in the exchange between More and Hythlodaeus in the first book of *Utopia*. The fundamental disagreement between More and the outspoken Hythlodaeus is whether, as in the title of Plutarch's essay, philosophers should address themselves especially to princes.

More's description of his own method of dealing with princes is worthy of an ambassador of Henry VIII and reflects his understanding of both Plato and of himself as an author and statesman. Hythlodaeus' position is blunt and inflexible: "To sum it all up, if I tried to obtrude these and like ideas on men strongly inclined to the opposite way of thinking, to what deaf ears should I tell the tale!" (I 48/**96**.29-31). As an alternative to Hythlodaeus' deep pessimism, More offers the approach of Platonic philosophy: "[But] there is another philosophy, more practical for statesmen, which knows its stage, adapts itself to the play at hand, and performs its role neatly and appropriately.... If you cannot pluck wrongheaded opinions out by the roots, if you cannot cure according to your heart's desire

[29] C. R. Thompson, *The Translations of Lucian by Erasmus and More* (Ithaca, New York 1940).

vices of long standing, yet you must not on that account desert the commonwealth." And, adopting the Platonic metaphor of the ship of state (*Republic* VI 488A-489A), he adds: "You must not abandon the ship in a storm because you cannot control the winds" (*Utopia* I 49-50/**98**.11-30).

The alternative More offers in this dialogue is the indirect approach of Plato's *Republic*, which he in fact adopts as author of his own *Utopia*:

> On the other hand, you must not force upon people new and strange ideas which you realize will carry no weight with persons of opposite conviction. On the contrary by the indirect approach you must seek and strive to handle matters tactfully. What you cannot turn to good you must make as little bad as you can. For it is impossible that all should be well unless all men were good, a situation I do not expect for a great many years to come.
>
> (*Utopia* I 50/**98**.30-**100**.3)

"By the indirect approach" translates *obliquo ductu*, literally, "by drawing obliquely," which refers to the author's drawing his reader toward his point of view, as well as the motion of the pen across the page.

The obliqueness of More's approach, already obvious from his use of names and the dialogue form to introduce Hythlodaeus' unbroken narrative, is also indicated by his geography. More forgot to ask Hythlodaeus just where the island of Utopia is located. Yet we are provided with some clues to its location in the southern hemisphere. Hythlodaeus' omission (I 13/**50**.5-6) is telling, for it forces us as curious readers to rediscover the island, with only a few clues as to its location. Like most of the utopian islands we present here, Utopia lies just beyond any map. From hints dropped by Peter Giles and Hythlodaeus we can locate it somewhere in the newly discovered temperate zone in the southern hemisphere—between Cavo Frio on the south coast of Brazil reached by Vespucci on his third voyage, and the island of Taprobane (Sri Lanka) in the Indian Ocean. From here Hythlodaeus returns to Portugal by way of Calcutta (I 13-14/**50**.3-**52**.24).

What emerges from More's narrative is that, as one passes the equator through the torrid zone of the southern hemisphere, he discovers a temperate zone, with a climate and civilization similar to those of Europe. Utopia, if it is to be placed on a map at all, must be plotted in a stretch of sea in the southern hemisphere as equidistant from the equator as is England in the northern hemisphere. Were it mapped, it would be on the same degree of latitude as England. It is antipodal to England and, despite the negations that describe it (Utopia, Amaurotum, Anhydrus),[30] it is the counter-image of England. More has "worked by contraries." He recognized that he was not original in this oblique tactic; as we shall see, Plato had already

---

[30]   Nowhere, the City of Darkness (London), the River without Water (the Thames).

created in Atlantis the distant image of the doomed and imperial Athens at the end of the fifth century. Before leaving the island that gave its name to a complex and varied genre of literature, we should recall that Utopia was not always an island and that its eponymous founder, King Utopus, was not always a Utopian. He invaded the land first known as Abraxa and created the island Utopia by excavating a canal of sea fifteen miles wide, about the width of the English channel, to separate it from the mainland (I 60/**112**.1-15). This feat of engineering challenges that of the kings of Atlantis, who created a great system of canals linking the central royal city and plain with the sea. And the founding act of separating what was aboriginally a promontory from the mainland evokes the ambiguous conception of all utopian islands: they are both open and closed to the outside world.

§ 3   ISLANDS AT THE "SACRED EXTREME" IN GREEK LITERATURE

There is something in the utopian craving for islands that both contradicts and confirms John Donne's "No man is an island unto himself, each man is a part of the main." Latin *insula* gives us the words isolation and insulation. But the sea that surrounds and isolates islands also opens them to strangers reaching them by ship. Thus islands are ambiguous: they are at once secluded and accessible.[31] This simultaneous potential for isolation and contact is paralleled in the origins and functions of Greek utopias. Idealized civilizations are set at the distant edges of the world,[32] but they are described at what is conceived as the center of a society and reflect the values of the center, often by way of contrast.

Greek utopias are located at what we might call a "sacred extreme." The Greeks are not the only society to have these extremes. In the Babylonian map of the world of about 600 BC (Figure 10) a "salt sea" encompasses Mesopotamia, the Euphrates, and Babylon. Beyond the circumambient Ocean jut out eight wedges. The cuneiform text inscribed into this tablet mentions the strange creatures that inhabit the extreme wedges and the daring mortals that reach them. One wedge contains a land "where the sun never shines."[33] In the earliest surviving Greek literature, the edges of the world are reserved for the gods and the Blest, and are equated with the river called Ocean, which, in the *Iliad*, is origin of the gods and of all things (XIV 201, 302, 246). A common (though not the only) model for the islands sighted in this book would set the Hyperboreans in the extreme north, the Ethiopians and the Islands of the Sun to the extreme south, Atlantis to the extreme west, and Euhemeros' Panchaia to the extreme east (see Figure 3). These islands are washed by the currents of a circumambient Ocean (*Okeanos*).[34] Ocean marks the division between this world and the otherworld, life and death, human and mortal. It is entered by the dead and the Sun (Helios), which Ocean seems to reanimate by its power.[35] Thus

Figure 10 Babylonian map of the world, ca. 600 BC. British Museum Cuneiform Texts BM92687.

an island at the edges of the world next to Ocean is the logical location of a perfect life or afterlife.

Utopias occur at chronological as well as geographical extremes. Hesiod's Golden Age marks the first human habitation of earth as well as the first perfect society. The life of this race is assigned no specific location,

---

[31] Gabba (1981) speculates on the Greek fascination with islands. He attributes this first to the natural interest in islands as geological formations, then to the role of the sea as a divisive factor (55-60).

[32] On which in general, see Ferguson (1975) and Romm (1992).

[33] Discussed and illustrated in A.R. Millard, "Cartography in the Ancient Near East," in Harley and Woodward (1987) 111-113, figure 6.10 (p. 114).

[34] For the early Greek conception of the world, see Clay (1992).

[35] On Ocean, see Nagy (1973) 149-153, 161; Nagy (1979) 196; Clay (1992) 136-137, 149-152.

is now extinct, and thus inaccessible. The afterlife utopia (on which see **V 1**), however, has both a physical location (though often ambiguous) on earth and a kind of accessibility through human hope. Before Hesiod, Homer had described an afterlife utopia called the Elysian Fields. In the *Odyssey*, which is filled with sacred islands, the sea god Proteus reveals to Menelaos that he will not die at home in Argos; he will be taken to the Elysian Fields at the end of the world near Ocean, a place where no snow or rain ever falls, but the gentle and fecund Zephyr (West Wind) refreshes the chosen few (**V 1 A**, *Odyssey* IV 561-569). The climate of the Elysian Fields has much in common with Homer's description of the home of the gods, Olympus (*Odyssey* VI 41-47), and Hesiod's description of the Islands of the Blest (**V 1 B**, *Works and Days* 168-173) within his account of the five Ages of Mankind (*Works and Days* 109-201). These are the successive ages of Gold, Silver, Bronze, Heroes, and Iron. Placed between the Age of Bronze and the Age of Iron (in which Hesiod lived) is the age of the heroes who fought at Thebes and Troy (156-173). To these warriors Zeus grants a life "at the edges of the earth," where they are to live, like the men of the Golden Age, without a care "alongside Ocean with its deep currents."

The locations of afterlife utopias differ from source to source, as does their situation on a mainland, single island, or a group of islands. We find them set variously west, southwest, and northeast of the Greek world, as well as in Hades (see **V 1**). The traditions about the afterlife of the most famous Greek hero of the Trojan War, Achilles, display the most numerous variants. He is sometimes said to have been transported to the White Island (also known as Leuke).[36] White Island was generally thought to be located in the Black Sea, at the mouth either of the Ister (Danube; see Figure 3) or the Borysthenes (Dnieper), and its accessibile location in the known world has been seen as representing the northern counterpart of the place where another famous warrior, Memnon, was buried to the extreme south in Ethiopia.[37] In other accounts Achilles is said to dwell in the Islands of the Blest,[38] often located far west of the Greek world. Elsewhere the equation between the White Island and the Islands of the Blest is explicit, for example, Pliny says: "Achilles' island is the same as that called the White Island and [the Island] of the Blest" (*Natural History* IV 93). Although visitors to the island brought back reports of epiphanies of the hero there, the place was uninhabited by the living.

---

36 In the epic poem *Aithiopis*, perhaps seventh century, summarized in Proclus *Chrestomathia* II (in T. W. Allen, *Homeri Opera* V [Oxford 1912] p. 106.12-15). On the various locations of Leuke, see Rohde (1925) 565-567 n. 102. On islands as dwellings of heroes after death, see Rohde (1925) 536-538, 541, 571-572 nn. 130-134; Nagy (1979) 167-172, 179, 189-190, 206-208; and Hedreen (1991).

37 Pindar *Nemean* IV 49-50; Pausanias III 19.11-13; Hedreen (1991) esp. 319-322.

38 Pindar *Olympian* II (see **V I C**) and Plato *Symposium* 179E-180B.

The far west, however, seems to be the most commonly mentioned location of utopian islands of the departed. Souls of the dead were thought to descend to Hades from the western edge of the earth just as the sun did each evening, giving light to the Underworld as it crossed over to rise in the east.[39] Pindar describes a section of Hades where the sun shines during night on earth, red roses bloom in meadows, frankincense and golden fruit flourish, and the pious enjoy horses, games, and music; a lovely scent pervades the place and the inhabitants offer continual sacrifices.[40] The conflation of the Underworld's separate quarters for the most pious or virtuous of souls (and mystic initiates) with Elysion or the Islands of the Blest is common especially in later epitaphs,[41] perhaps because of a common belief that there was no significant land mass beyond the Pillars of Heracles (the Straits of Gilbraltar) and that there lay the ends of the earth.

But in the map of Asia and Africa that can be extracted from the text of Pomponius Mela's Latin *Geography* (*Chorographia;* Figure 11),[42] a group of islands located off the west coast of Africa beyond the Pillars of Heracles have sometimes been identified as the Islands of the Blest, in Latin, the *Insulae Fortunatae.* These islands were said to be visited by sailors, especially in the Roman period, and have been identified with the Canary Islands as well as Madeira.[43] The powerful and acquisitive Carthaginians allegedly sent some colonists to at least one of these islands at a much earlier period, but then forbade its habitation and barred access to the sea out of greed and fear.[44] The political policies of the Carthaginians (no longer in force in the Roman period) are mirrored in this region's appearance in poetry as the object of an impossible "escape wish." For example, in Euripides' *Hippolytus* (741-751), the chorus longs to escape to where the Pillars of Heracles are guarded by "an Old Man of the Sea" who allows no one to pass farther, confirming the "holy boundary of the sky" (*ouranos*) held up by Atlas; nearby are the apple groves of the "singing Hesperides," where "sacred life-giving earth augments the bliss and happiness of the gods."[45]

---

[39] See Nagy (1973) 160-161.

[40] Fragment 129, translation available in *Pindar II. Nemean Odes, Isthmian Odes, Fragments*. Ed. and Trans. William H. Race. Loeb Classical Library 485 (Cambridge, Mass. 1997) 365-367.

[41] Rohde (1925) 541, 571 nn. 132, 133. Mystic initiates have a special place in the Underworld in the the *Homeric Hymn to Demeter* (480-482) and in Aristophanes' *Frogs* (see esp. 454-459).

[42] See his comments on the Hyperboreans, **V 2 F**, and the recent translation by Romer (1998).

[43] See especially Plutarch *Life of Sertorius* 8-9, Pliny *Natural History* VI 199-205, Konrad, 106-110, and *OCD³* s.v. "Islands of the Blest."

[44] See Pseudo-Aristotle *On Marvelous Things Heard* 84 (836ʙ 30-837ᴀ 6) and 136 (844a), Diodorus Siculus V 19-20, with Romm (1992) 126-127, and nn. 12 and 13.

[45] See on this and other similar passages W. S. Barrett, *Euripides Hippolytos* (Oxford 1964) 300-306; Mace (1996) 244 with notes.

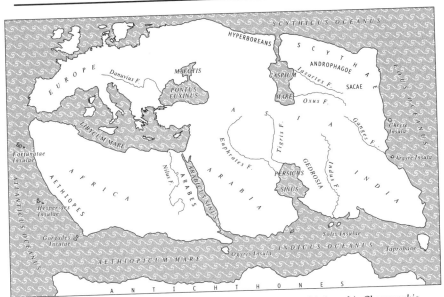

Figure 11 Reconstruction of Pomponius' Mela's Map of the World, from his *Chorographia*. Diskin Clay and Thomas Elliott.

The difficulty in locating or reaching utopias enforces their inaccessibility. The sacred character of barriers is implied not only in the sanctity of the natural boundaries, but is sometimes made explicit in their imposition by divine force directly. Divine force is exerted on potential visitors, as in the case of the afterlife utopias which can be reached only after death and with permission of the gods. Divine force can also be applied to the inhabitants themselves, as in the case of Homer's Phaeacians, who are punished by Poseidon for conveying outsiders in their ships (*Odyssey* XIII 149-183). Poseidon sets a mountain on their island, thus rendering it unrecognizable and barring all possibility of a return there, just as the island of Atlantis sank in a night of deluge and earthquake and filled the Atlantic with the mud that made it impassable (*Timaeus* 25C-D). Often we hear that the residents of a utopia, for example, Herodotus' Ethiopians, choose to be isolated, a choice that implies their aloof superiority from the rest of mankind and makes them similar to the gods (see **V 3 A**). The chronological barrier blocking access to the Golden Age utopia of Hesiod may also be considered divine, since the gods both produced that race and brought it to an end. Philosophical barriers could replace or augment sacred ones. For his Atlantis, Plato employs chronological as well as geographical inaccessibility, perhaps partly to help illustrate a philosophical concept of the limits of humans to perceive "truth" in the everyday world.[46]

---

[46] Romm (1992) 124-26.

Figure 12 The Old and New Worlds of Claudius Ptolemy, from *Geographia Universalis* (Basel 1540). Duke University, Special Collections.

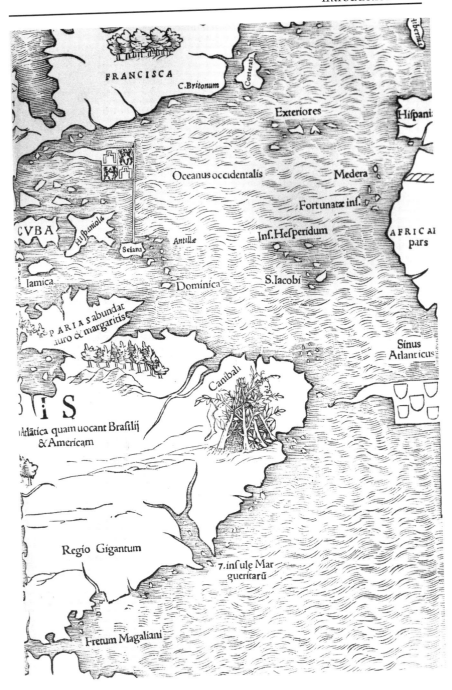

FRANCISCA

C.Britonum

Corterat

Exteriores

Hispania

Oceanus occidentalis

Medera

Fortunatæ inf.

CVBA

Hispaniola

Inf.Hesperidum

AFRICAE
pars

Seiana

Antillæ

Iamica

Dominica

S.Iacobi

PARIA S abundat
auro & margaritis

Sinus
Atlanticus

Canibali

BIS

Atlãtica quam uocant Brasilij
& Americam

Regio Gigantum

7.infulę Mar
gueritarũ

Fretum Magaliani

One function of barriers to utopias is to mark off their inhabitants as distinct from ordinary humans. Barriers symbolize the essential distance and differences of utopians from others: they are frequently blessed or rewarded with fertile soil, abundance of food, longevity, and painless death. These themes seem to revolve around the popular fourth- and fifth-century antithesis of *nomos* (man-made law and custom) and *physis* (nature). Utopian cultures, through their self-restraint in practicing justice and piety (*nomos*), implicitly or explicity receive the reward of control over nature (*physis*), equivalent to divine favor manifesting itself in a pleasant climate, fertility, long life, and freedom from pain.

These moral and religious connotations occur in Hesiod's description of the gods' favor for the humans of the Golden Age, who lived peacefully, without wars or other evils (*Works and Days* 109-120). Pindar (*Olympian* II = **V 1 D**) and Plato (*Gorgias* 523-524) are explicit in their descriptions of the Islands of the Blest as the dwelling reserved for only the just. Thus, those dwelling at the sacred extreme often seem to have earned their blissful existence by their piety and are privileged in their access to the gods. Descriptions of utopias also often include paradigms of worshippers. The Hyperboreans are comparable to the inhabitants of Bacon's New Atlantis in their reception of a religion even before those of the society writing and reading about them; the Hyperboreans are hosts to Apollo before the god comes to the Greeks (**V 2 A**), just as the Bensalemites receive the New Testament before it has been written for others (**IV §17-20**). Similar principles are illustrated in the tales of the land of the Ethiopians and of the Atlanteans as origins of the gods (**V 3 B** and **V 5 A**).

It should be noted, however, that emphasis on religion has different connotations in antiquity than it does in Judaeo-Christian societies. In ancient Greece, worship entailed most often gaiety, revelry, and entertainment. A society devoted to continual worship such as that of the Hyperboreans was admired not only for divine favor but also for its leisure, resources, and predisposition to enjoy a perpetual holiday. This is true too of Lucian's rendition of the Island of the Blest, where spring and festival are both eternal (**V 1 E**).

Barriers to utopias also serve to express a doctrine similar to that of "Original Sin," whereby curiosity, exploration, and exploitation are followed by corruption and suffering.[47] Nature is equated with the will of the gods and forbids humans to transgress their allotted boundaries, even if the worlds beyond are inhabited by ideal and pious societies that humans would do well to imitate. Thus, Pindar in *Pythian* X (**V 1 B**) recognizes that ancient heroes, but not humans of his age, can visit the Hyperboreans.[48]

---

[47] See Romm (1992) 73-76 on this and for literary examples of the "noble savage" criticizing the Greeks.

[48] Similar statements of Pindar are translated and discussed by Romm (1992) 17-18.

The Phaeacians' direct divine punishment by Poseidon portends the indirect vengeance of the gods acting through natural forces on those who dare to match themselves with the power of the sea. Poseidon in the *Odyssey* circles the earth (XI 241), as though representing Ocean, reminding humans of their limits. In his travels, Odysseus often oversteps his bounds, apparently motivated by what might be considered the "sins" both most attractive to and feared by Greeks in antiquity: curiosity and hunger for fame and honor. Odysseus is made to atone by being appointed Poseidon's missionary and being fated to die at sea (XI 121-135). Alexander of Macedon became a paradigm of a hero who could cross previously unexplored regions, provoking both ambition and anxiety for later imperial expansionists at Rome.[49] In addition, the dangers and fearsome aspects of unfamiliar places could be exaggerated or invented and thus deter further exploration. Tales of savages and monsters appear often in descriptions of India and the East.[50] Figure 12 illustrates a similar anxiety attached to the discovery of the New World in the Renaissance. Cannibals and Giants await the explorers of South America and those who venture beyond that continent face shipwreck and the "Island of the Damned." The anxiety of discovery also characterizes the ancient explorers, but the new is seen in terms of the old and known. New regions beyond those discovered appear in our sources when the once unfamiliar becomes familiar, as, for example, tales of Thule, said to be several days sail away from Britain, follow familiarization with Britain.[51]

The interactions between utopian and other peoples are necessarily perceived as rare, but they are instrumental in effecting a critical gaze back toward the central society of author and reader. The islanders' awareness of the outside world varies according to the context and function of the utopia: some utopian islands barely know of other peoples, even as they are discovered by them. This is true of More's Utopia and the Crete in Plato's *Laws*, a dialogue occupied by the refoundation of the City of the Magnesians in a location half-way between Phaestus and Cnossus in Crete. The Spartan and Cretan founders of this city are unaware of the world known to the Athenian visitor to the island of Crete. But Francis Bacon's Bensalemites (**IV** §15) and Homer's Phaeacians know the world across the seas that surround them even as they are unknown to the outside world.

Religion and morality are prominent factors in utopians' relations with, as well as awareness of, the outside world. The Hyperboreans, for example, journey to Delphi, the very center of the Greek world, to build

---

[49] Romm (1992) 137-39. Roman expressions of anxiety or disapproval of exploration and expansion occur in Cicero (Romm [1992] 133-35), Tacitus' *Germania* XXXIV (Romm [1992] 147-49), Horace, Pliny, and Seneca (Romm [1992] 162-71).

[50] Romm (1992) 82-120.

[51] See Romm (1992) 156-162.

the oracle of Apollo (Pausanias X 5.8), and bring (or later, send) gifts to Apollo at Delos, an island in the center of the Cyclades (**V 2 C**, Herodotus IV 33-35). While these visits reflect piety, Homer's Phaeacians are perceived as impious because of their interactions with the outside world, perhaps reflecting anxieties of the culture that imagined them and projecting these anxieties onto the divine world. The warlike Atlanteans and Amazons venture out of their lands to conquer and acquire new territory, and can perhaps be viewed as antitheses to the Hyperboreans, whose contacts with the Greeks are motivated solely by a peaceful will to present gifts.

Reported visits by those from the center to the periphery are, of course, more common, as a necessary pretense for the narrators' knowledge of the utopian worlds. In the earliest and most mythical varieties of utopias, however, this pretense is absent (the Muse is the source of the poets' knowledge) and the identity of the visitors is significant. Heroes and humans in some ways central to Greek ideology and events are said to have reached the Hyperboreans: Heracles (Pindar *Olympian* III 13-18, 31-34); Perseus (**V 2 B**, Pindar *Pythian* X 29-46); Croesus, king of the Lydians and patron of Delphi (Bacchylides *Ode* III 58-62). The distinctions, barriers, and interactions of central and utopian peoples reveal the roots and developments of utopian themes, especially justice, religion, foreign policy, food and hospitality, and death, and reflect the ideology underlying them.

§ 4   The Islands of the *Odyssey*

> When you find the cobbler who stitched up Aeolus' bag of winds, you will discover the course of Odysseus' wanderings.
>
> (Eratosthenes)[52]

> Man is by nature an animal who lives in a polis.
>
> (Aristotle *Politics* I 2.1253a)

The age of the Homeric epics was characterized by colonization and the developments of the polis and panhellenism, as society emerged from the "Dark Age" with its scattered habitations and absence of political consolidation and community organization. Although Greeks were as yet united neither under one name nor one government, they had begun to see themselves as a people who shared language (despite their several dialects), religion, and social and political institutions such as hospitality and assemblies. In this context, when we acknowledge one of the most important achievements of Homeric epic as the definition of "Greek cultural self-consciousness,"[53] the seemingly unrelated comments of Eratosthenes and Aristotle can be read together as clues to the function of the *Odyssey*'s is-

---

[52]   As quoted by Strabo (in defense of Homeric geography), *Geography* I 2.15.
[53]   Hurwitt (1985) 83.

lands. The first quotation alerts us that the islands Odysseus encounters are imaginary; the second states succinctly what the *Odyssey*'s islands, in their contradictions to Greek society, express by contrast: the nature of humans to live in a *polis*, a community united by shared language, religious rites, policies towards outsiders, and social and political institutions.

The *Odyssey* is an epic of returning home (a *nostos*) to Greek society and, in the process, of defining and appreciating it. It traces the long voyage and the painful nostalgia of Odysseus on his way home from the Trojan war to the island of Ithaca, where he had lived and governed twenty years earlier. The action of the *Odyssey* opens on Ithaca without Odysseus, who is at that time stranded on the divine island of Ogygie with its sole inhabitant, the goddess Calypso. The several fantastic islands and their inhabitants that he encounters as obstacles to his return encompass a wide range of types of habitation and existence: potential (deserted), sub-human, human, and divine. Implicitly these possibilities reflect the norms of Greek society to which Odysseus longs to return. The contrasts of these islands with Odysseus' own island, Ithaca, as he had left it and the threats that the islands' inhabitants pose to his return throw into relief and clarify the image of his desired destination.

The third line of the *Odyssey* describes Odysseus as a man of many turns, who "came to know the cities and minds of many men." This line introduces the first work of anthropological literature in Greek. The *Odyssey* itself is not a work of utopian literature, although, in his curiosity about other peoples and places, Odysseus prepares for the work of Herodotus as well as the Greek utopian literature surveyed here. It is sometimes claimed that, in his elaborate description of Scherie, the island of the Phaeacians, Homer created the first Greek utopia.[54] But Scherie is not a utopia in our sense of the word. It was not Homer's purpose to shift his hearers' critical gaze back onto a society he deemed imperfect, but rather to elicit a reflective gaze, helping to define and delineate the values of the developing *polis*.

The home of these values is Odysseus' goal, Ithaca, but Ithaca is in fact a place of great ambiguity. It is a small but familiar island in the Ionian Sea (modern Ithaki). As a point of departure and return it is located at the center of the *Odyssey*. It is first described as anarchic and without the authority of its absent king or his son, Telemachus, who is just coming of age. It has fallen under the control of local lords, who have come to claim Odysseus' wife Penelope in marriage. The suitors who occupy Odysseus' palace offend against hospitality and religion. Athena, disguised as a guest-friend (*xenos*) of Odysseus, is ignored by the suitors, who feast on oxen and

---

[54]   As did Finley (1965) 100-102; Ferguson (1975) 14 ("the first surviving Utopia in European literature"); and Gabba (1981) 58.

drink wine without libation or sacrifice (I 105-124). But there is another Ithaca; it exists in the memory of the island as it was once ruled by Odysseus and is recalled as Telemachus holds the first assembly since Odysseus' departure (II 25-34). In the past, the island and its inhabitants held regular assemblies and flourished under the benevolent and paternal rule of Odysseus (II 234).

Ithaca is not the most fertile land. It has no plains or meadows, but is rough and mountainous and fit only for pasturing goats and raising strong men, as described by Telemachus as he rejects a gift of horses from Menelaos (IV 605-608),[55] and then by Odysseus in the court of Alcinous, king of the Phaeacians (IX 21-28). As Odysseus describes his home to his host, it is "rocky but produces strong sons" (IX 27). Odysseus adds that his island is the sweetest sight under the sun. As we have seen (§3 above), there is in Greek thought a strict association between human justice and god-given fertility. This is illustrated in what Odysseus tells his wife in his first interview with her. He deflects Penelope's direct inquiry about this identity and speaks in flattering and epic terms about her fame "reaching broad heaven,"

> Like [the fame of] some king without fault,
> Who rules over many strong men like a god
> And upholds strict justice. His land produces
> Barley and wheat; its trees are laden with fruit;
> It sustains sturdy flocks. The sea about it
> Teems with fish, all because of his good leadership.
> Under his rule his people thrive and are strong.
>
> (*Odyssey* XIX 109-114)

Ithaca provides a contrast to the image of fertility, and yet still represents an ideal. It may not be an agricultural paradise, but it is capable of supporting an orderly society. The roughness of the land and the hardiness of the people who work it are integral elements of the Greek identity that Odysseus seeks to return to, as are order and justice.

If the status of Ithaca is ambiguous, it is, at least, a definite place. By contrast, the islands of the *Odyssey* are uncharted and beyond the limits of the known world. In the order of their sighting they are: Pharos (described by Menelaos), Ogygie and Scherie (described by Homer as narrator), the island that lies across from the land of the Cyclops, the floating island of Aeolus, Circe's island of Aiaia (or Aia), the island of the Sirens, and the Island of the Sun (all described by Odysseus in the court of Alcinous on Scherie). Finally, Eumaeus describes Syrie, his native isle. The islands are literally "utopian": they can be located nowhere. But they can all be plot-

---

[55] The ideal of a rough land as the home for tough men is perhaps best described in Herodotus *Histories* IX 122.

ted on the coordinates of a complex conceptual map that reveals Homer's exploration of the possibilities and values of human society.

The last known landmark between Odysseus' departure from Troy and his return to Ithaca is Cythera, an island that lies between Cape Malea and Crete. After he passes the island of Cythera, we and he lose our bearings (IX 80-81). The passion for identifying the *Odyssey*'s islands began in antiquity and continues today,[56] but in fact the islands Odysseus reaches in his wanderings before Ithaca can be located on no map of the Mediterranean. For example, the Island of the Sun (also called Thrinacia) was identified as Sicily (called Trinakria) in antiquity[57] but, like Circe's Aiaia, it is probably imagined as lying to the east at the rising of Helios. When Odysseus finds himself on the island of Circe, he addresses his companions:

> Listen to what I say, my companions, you who have suffered
> Many hardships. My friends, we know neither where lies the dusk
> To the west nor the light of Dawn, nor the path of the Sun
> That brings light to mankind when he descends beneath the earth.
> (IX 189-192)

GOAT ISLAND, THE LAND OF THE CYCLOPES, SCHERIE

The places of Odysseus' landfalls divide into sub-human, human, and divine. Goat Island, the land of the Cyclopes (IX 106-566), and Scherie present together the extremes of levels of habitation below the divine level. An unihabited island lies offshore of the Cyclopes' land, where Odysseus spends the night before he crosses over to the land of the Cyclopes. Let us call it "Goat Island."[58] Odysseus describes it with the eye of a colonist (IX 116-151).[59] It has a deep, protected harbor and is densely wooded. It offers all the possibilities of human exploitation; but it bears no sign of human cultivation. Odysseus describes its promise in negative terms: there are no hunters on it, no shepherds or farmers, and no crops; nor are there shipwrights or ships, "which make their voyages to the cities of men" (IX 127-129). The working

---

[56] His voyages have often been mapped. The fold-out map in Bérard (1971) vol. 3 represents one of the most commonly ambitious itineraries; it takes Odysseus as far as the Straits of Gibraltar. An itinerary much less ambitious than the ancient traditions that identify the island of Helios as Sicily is that taken by Severin (1987), who has Odysseus hug the coasts of Greece.

[57] By the historians Thucydides (*The Peloponnesian War* VI 2) and Polybius (Strabo I 2.15-16).

[58] As did Jenny Clay (1980).

[59] There is an uncannily similar account of the uninhabited island described in William Dampier's account of the rescue of a "Moskito Indian" marooned over three years on Juan Fernandez Island (from *A New Voyage around the World*, fifth edition, London 1703) 84-88 reproduced in Daniel Defoe, *Robinson Crusoe*, Michael Shinagel, ed. (New York 1975) 245-248.

of trees into ships and the contacts seafaring makes possible help to define the boundaries between civilized (Greek) and primitive or sub-human existence. The lush meadows of the island and the natural springs they betoken attract the eye of the settler, as, in 1492, the deep green of the Caribbean island attracted Columbus when he reached it on October 12.[60] Odysseus' admiration before the natural beauty of this island recalls the wonder Hermes experienced when he reached Calypso on the island of Ogygie (IX 153; cf. V 75-76). "Goat Island" could become a "marvelous possession"—a fine human settlement, with unfailing crops and vines (IX 130). But it is uninhabited save for the nymphs who haunt its summits.

Opposite "Goat Island" lies the land of the Cyclopes—"not too near and not too far" (IX 117). The island off-shore is of no interest to the Cyclopes, who have no ships and no need to cultivate its land. Without plowing or seeding, their own land provides crops and grapes for them spontaneously, and Zeus brings them rain (IX 106-121). "Goat Island" and the mainland of the Cyclopes are locked in opposition. The uninhabited island is ripe for human cultivation; the land of the Cyclopes produces crops without cultivation and evinces one of the characteristics of human life in the Golden Age (see §1). The Cyclopes do not live in a society, but they are nonetheless close to the gods. As Aristotle observed in his *Politics* (I 2.122^{b}20-27), only the gods and Cyclopes live outside of the society of a polis. The Cyclopes live in caves in the company of their families and flocks and have no settled traditions to bind them; nor do they have assemblies (IX 112-115). They do not sacrifice to the gods nor do they fear the Zeus who protects strangers. They offend against the norms of civilized life by eating flesh raw. Perhaps their worst offense against civility is that they have no knowledge of the Homeric epic; Polyphemus has never heard of Agamemnon, "whose fame reached high heaven" (IX 264).

The land of the Cyclopes is remote from, yet closely related to, another island, Scherie, the island of the Phaeacians. The Cyclopes and Phaeacians were once close neighbors, when the Phaeacians lived in Hyperie (VI 4, the land or island "beyond" or "above") and until the violence of the Cyclopes drove Nausithous (Swift Ship) to found a new city on Scherie (VI 4-5). It could well be that Hyperie, the original home of the Phaeacians, was the deserted "Goat Island" visited by Odysseus.[61] Scherie might seem to lie at an extreme from the land of the Cyclopes, but it is best understood in its connection to the land of the Cyclopes in a system of meaningful oppositions. The Cyclopes and the Phaeacians appear to represent respectively the lowest and highest forms of societies; Odysseus rejects both.

---

[60]   Described in his journal of October 13, *Christopher Columbus: Journal of the First Voyage (Diario del primer viaje) 1492*, B. W. Ife, trans. (Warminster 1990) 32.
[61]   As Jenny Clay (1980) suggests.

The speaking names we find on Scherie correspond to its geographical abstraction: Rhexenor (Manbreaker), Nausithous (Swiftship), and Arete (Object of Prayer) are the counterparts of the abstract geography of the *Odyssey*. Alcinous (Saving Intelligence), Odysseus' host, is one of the chief rulers on the island, and by his name signals the sophistication and highly civilized nature of his society, in contrast to the barbarity and lawlessness of the Cyclopes.[62]

Both Polyphemus and Nausithous are the sons of Poseidon, and both islands enjoy the favor of the gods, but unlike the Cyclopes, the Phaeacians devote themselves to worship of the gods. At the harbor of the island is a precinct of Poseidon (VI 267); Zeus is honored by libations (VII 179-181); and the gods in general by sacrifice (VIII 59-61). Nausithous' city bears clear markings of the Phaeacians' close proximity to the gods. The most evident sign of this proximity is that the gods join the Phaeacians openly at their feasts. Alcinous tells Odysseus: "we are close to them, as are the Cyclopes and the savage tribe of Giants" (VII 205-206). Another sign of the favor of the gods is the god-given fertility of the island (VII 112-130).[63] In Alcinous' gardens stand tall shade trees and rows of fruit trees bearing pears, pomegranates, apples, figs, and olives, brought to ripeness by gentle Zephyr (West Wind).[64] All are, as Homer describes them, "the radiant gifts of the gods" (VII 132). Such are the gifts of the gods to the land of the just king, as Odysseus describes this to Penelope (XIX 109-114, quoted above).

The island of the Phaeacians has the look of a utopia (in the unexamined sense of this word) and closely resembles Greek society in some aspects, but is rejected by Odysseus. On the one hand, in addition to Greek religious practices, poetry and athletic contests mark Scherie as a place of panhellenic values (VIII 62-82; 256-94). The city of the Phaeacians is walled and contains a place of assembly, as does Ithaca.[65] But Scherie is not presented as the best form of human society for Odysseus. The Phaeacians live in intimate relations to the gods, yet they evince a strain of xenophobia (VI 273-284). Hephaestus has fashioned the king's palace of gold, silver, and bronze (VII 81-94). Odysseus, who comes from the poor island of Ithaca, is astounded by its radiant beauty (VII 133-134), but the Phaeacians are too gaudy for Odysseus. When offered the king's daughter's hand in marriage, he refuses it, intent on returning to his own Greek Ithaca, wife, and family. The island

[62] On the contrasts between the Phaeacians and the Cyclopes, see Hurwitt (1985) 77-78.
[63] A fertility replicated and deliberately recalled in Iamboulos' Island of the Sun: III, 56.7.
[64] This is the wind that blows upon the Elysian Fields and the Islands of the Blest (V 1).
[65] The agora is mentioned in VI 266 and VII 44-45, yet the palace and not the agora is the place of assembly on Scherie.

of the Phaeacians is not a society given to warfare; rather it is devoted to sea-faring, foot-races, feasting, hot baths, and changes of clothing (VI 270-272; VIII 245-255). (Later in antiquity, the Epicureans were compared to the Phaeacians.) The Phaeacians are unable to defend themselves from outsiders, and do not have the qualities needed to work the rough land of Ithaca.

SYRIE

Syrie is perhaps the island that most closely resembles Ithaca in the *Odyssey*, but it is not one that Odysseus finds on his voyage home. After Odysseus reaches Ithaca, his swineherd Eumaeus describes it to him as his home. He locates it at "the turning point of the sun"—at one of the tropics:

It possesses no great abundance, but is a fertile place,
With much grazing land, many flocks, and is covered with vines
    and barley.
Hunger never comes upon its inhabitants,
Nor does any other disease that afflicts unhappy humankind.
But... Apollo comes upon them with Artemis
And they bring them death with their sacred arrows.

(XV 405-411)

As is the case of the men of the Golden Age and some of the other utopian places we present in this collection and Introduction, an easy death is a mark of a condition that lies beyond the human experience. So is the absence of hunger and illness, but the qualification "no great abundance" and the implication that the islanders must labor for their sustenance pulls this island back towards the Greek center of things. With this touch of realism, the sacred extreme becomes slightly more accessible and moves towards Ithaca as well as later utopias.

THE DIVINE ISLANDS OF THE ODYSSEY

Some of the islands discovered by Odysseus (and Menelaos) are "divine" in that they are the habitations of divinities. They attract our attention for two reasons: first, humans cannot stay for long in these divine islands; they must leave them to return to their own mortal condition, which is seen anew as it is defined by the divine; and second, divine as they are, these islands prepare for the utopian islands at the sacred extreme that are in fact inhabited by humans. As one sights them in the narrative of the *Odyssey*, it becomes clear that they exhibit a scale of divine civilization, as the islands of the *Odyssey* that are inhabited by humans exhibit a scale of human civilization.

The first of these divine islands is described by Menelaos, who, like Odysseus, has gained a knowledge of "the intelligence and character of many noble men" in his travels (IV 267-268). He says that he was blown off course on his return to Argos and has travelled to many lands considered exotic by Greeks: Cyprus, Phoenicia, Egypt, Ethiopia, and Libya (IV 83-85). The island which he was compelled to visit to find out how he could finally return to Sparta bears the name Pharos (Flare or Light). It is a day's sail off shore. (This is, therefore, not the island on which Ptolemy II constructed the lighthouse that was one of the wonders of the ancient world, which was a few minutes away from shore.) Menelaos describes his voyage to Egypt and Pharos at great length (IV 351-586). Pharos is lowest on the scale of divine islands, for it has no permanent inhabitants either human or divine, and lacks natural resources to sustain life. It is visited only by Proteus, the Old Man of the Sea, and his daughter (Eidothea). When he reached it, Menelaos learned from Proteus that he must sacrifice to the gods in order to return home, that gods will eventually transport him to the Elysian Field,[66] and that his companion Odysseus is stranded on Calypso's island (IV 555-560). Pharos, then, is a site of transition and revelation of knowledge, but not suitible for habitation. Menelaos' human status is clarified as he learns that he must now propitiate the gods, but will later receive their reward.

With Ogygie Odysseus finds a divine island that posseses divine abundance. It has a single divine inhabitant and it is described in more detail than any other landscape in the Homeric poems (V 55-86). Clouds of sea birds are Calypso's only companions before Odysseus arrives. This solitary goddess lives in a cave draped with tendrils of vine. Four springs well up in her domain. They feed a meadow lush with violets and parsley. The sight of this marvelous island entrances even Hermes, who is sent by Zeus to free Odysseus after seven years there (V 73-74). Gold and silver are present on this island (V 63, 230, and 232). The fire of cedar wood in the hearth of Calypso's cave makes the island fragrant, but its smoke is not the smoke of sacrifice (V 123).

Calypso's name means She Who Hides. Her name is a speaking name: so long as he remains on the island, Odysseus remains "hidden," and one important aspect of his mortality and Greekness is suppressed: recognition by other mortals in the forms of honor and fame (*time* and *kleos*). Thus human and immortal goddess cannot dwell together on this island as both "immortal and ageless forever" (V 35-136; cf. 218). At the "sacred extremes" of the *Odyssey* the worlds of mortals and immortals can never coincide: Odysseus' mortality is confirmed by his desire for recognition and his nostalgia for Ithaca and his mortal wife, although, as we have seen, Ithaca has none of the divine grace or fertility of Ogygie.

There are four other divine islands discovered by Odysseus: the island of Aeolus, Circe, the two Sirens, the god of the Sun (Helios).

---

[66] See §3 above and **V 1 A.**

Odysseus describes all these islands in the court of Alcinous, on Scherie, the last island he visits in his long-delayed return to Ithaca. His long narrative of his travels (Books IX-XII) was notorious in antiquity as "the tale told to Alcinous"—meaning an audacious piece of fiction.[67] Aeolia is the realm of Aeolus, King of the Winds (X 1-27). A wall of bronze surrounds it. Its remoteness from human society is indicated by the fact that Aeolus, his wife, their seven sons and seven daughters are its only inhabitants. Sons are married to daughters and the island is turned inward upon itself and upon a single endogamous family sufficient unto itself.[68] But the island also betrays the tell-tale signs of Greek civilization and is thus closer to the utopias of the pious that emerge later in Greek literature. Aeolus is "dear to the gods immortal" (X 2). His palace is filled with the smoke of sacrifice (knise, X 10). And, unlike any of Odysseus' island hosts save Alcinous, Aeolus is spell-bound by Odysseus' epic recitation, rendered over a full month, of "Troy, the ships of the Achaeans, and their return home"—that is, the themes of the *Iliad* and *Odyssey* (X 15). Neither Calypso nor Circe (although she directs Odysseus home) are interested in Odysseus' travels (or the epic of the *Odyssey*). Again, as on Scherie, we encounter a speaking name: Aeolus (*aiolos*) means "darting," "quick moving," "changeable," like the wind. Aeolia is not an island Odysseus can remain on. It is a floating island and has no fixed place on the sea. And, although the Homeric epic is welcome here, Aeolia's bronze walls and single closed family indicate that it is not open to the outside world.

After his visit, and a forced return to and departure from Aeolus, Odysseus lands on the island of Circe, in the middle of the vastness of the sea (X 135-574). Aiaia is imagined as lying far to the east at the rising of the Sun (cf. XII 3-4). As ever, Odysseus looks for signs of human civilization and cultivation—the "works of men" and the human (meaning Greek) voice (X 145). He recalls the "hospitality" he received at the hands of the Cyclops Polyphemus and the Giant cannibal Antiphates, in the land of the Laestrygonians (X 200). On the island of Aiaia he sights smoke and eventually the divine Circe, whose great house is filled with gold and silver. The singing goddess is attended by four serving women. On her densely wooded island with its palace, Circe rises a step above the isolation of the solitary cave-dwelling Calypso in the scale of divine civilization.

Circe turns Odysseus' men into swine and keeps them in a pen. Like the Lotus Eaters and the Sirens (XII 39-54; 165-200; see below), and like Calypso who promises to make Odysseus "immortal and ageless forever," Circe

---

[67] Plato treats it as such in *Republic* X 614 B (in introducing his own Myth of Er) and Lucian holds it out as the prime example of the kind of fiction he professes to avoid (yet imitates), *True History* I 3.

[68] As Jenny Clay (1985) has pointed out.

threatens to make her visitors lose all thought of home. That is, just as she can transform the sailors who reach her island into swine, she can rob humans of their mortality by making them forget their human condition and place in the world by mixing "dreadful drugs" in their food (X 234-235). Drugs are required to turn Odysseus' men into swine and to return them to their human form, and to make them remember their home. When they see their captain, they believe they are already back in Ithaca (X 414-416).

The Lotus has the same effect on Odysseus' companions as Circe's drugs. Eating it supresses all nostalgia (IX 82-104). Another narcotic is the song of the Sirens: whoever hears the voices of the Sirens takes no thought of or delight in returning home to his wife and children (XII 41-42). The shore of their island is covered with the rotting bodies of mariners who approached to listen to their song (XII 45-146).

Circe is the daughter of Helios and Perse, a daughter of Ocean and Tethys (X 137-138). On the island of Helios, the Sun (so named at XII 274, XII 261-402), there seem to be only two inhabitants other than the 350 head of immortal heifers of this island. They are other daughters of Helios, Phaethousa (Shining) and Lampetie (Blazing), who guard his cattle. Despite Odysseus' piety and prayers to the gods (XII 333-334), Odysseus and his men are compelled to leave this desolate and sacred island for the sacrilege of Odysseus' crew slaughtering the immortal heifers of the Sun. Again, it is proven that mortal cannot associate permanently with immortal. And, in reaching Ogygie, Aiaia, the island of the Sirens, and the island of the Sun, Homer has reached the "sacred extreme." What is significant for our inquiry is the fact that in later and more truly utopian literature these sacred extremes are inhabited by humans. It is also significant that the contacts between mortals at these sacred extremes return our reflective gaze to the human condition as it defined by the divine. Life on these fertile islands might seem ideal, but it is a life without kinship, society, a *polis*, religion, or human nostalgia.

Homeric anthropology prepares us for Greek utopian literature and especially the literature of island utopias, but Homer's *Odyssey* is not utopian in our sense of this word. The ideal of Odysseus as a just and paternal king of a small, steep, and rocky island hovers over the reality of what Ithaca had become in his absence. Homer holds up no heavenly ideal in order to focus our attention on the sorry reality of contemporary Greek society. Rather he turns our gaze on the possibilities of divine and human society encountered as one of the heroes of the *Iliad* returns home.

§ 5   ARISTOPHANES' CLOUDCUCKOOLAND

Aristophanes' *Birds* is usually entered into the ledger of Greek utopias, with good reason. In Aristophanes' comic fantasy two Athenians join to found a city in the air midway between heaven and earth.

Cloudcuckooland (Nephelokokkygia) offers the dazzling prospect of a human gaining sovereign power over both the gods above and the men below. The names of Aristophanes' protagonists are, not surprisingly, speaking names: Peisthetairos (He who Persuades his Companions) and Euelpides (Optimist). The idea of the project of founding Cloudcuckooland belongs to Peisthetairos alone. The ambition of a single mortal (and significantly an Athenian) wresting power from Zeus to enjoy a life of pleasure is comic, but as we shall see, it is comic in a sense specific to Athens in the year of the play's production, 414 BC, one year after imperial Athens had launched the Sicilian expedition. Aristophanes' comic fantasy is also specific to the context of the play's performance: the Attic festivals of Dionysus, a god called "Freer" (Eleutheros) and "Releaser" (Lyaios). These festivals were the most important periods of relaxation and release from the intense pressures of work, family, and city.

The tragedies performed in the festivals of Dionysus projected their action back into the distant past and focused almost obsessively on the unspeakable actions and sufferings of a few great families, such as the houses of Laios in Thebes and Atreus in Mycene. Attic comedy wore the other mask of this Janus face and looked directly at the civic and cultural present of the city of Athens; one of its difficulties for a modern reader is that it is so topical. Comedies competing in the festivals of Dionysus often presented on stage the possibility of either escaping from the present state of the city or transforming the city to conform to the wishes of an individual. Most of Aristophanes' extant comedies present comic schemes of escape from society by radically transforming society. *Acharnians* (425), *Peace* (421), *Lysistrata* (411), and *Ecclesiazusae* (392) all come to mind. All of these plays have a protagonist who, in the sacred space of the festival of Dionysus, makes the world of the *polis* conform to his or her desire. In this, Attic comedy comes close to the genius of later utopian writing, for the world transformed constitutes—"by indirection"—not a seriously held proposal for political reform but a radical criticism of the world untransformed.

So far as we can judge, earlier Attic comedy had a powerful tendency to evoke dream visions of a Golden Age, and offered for a brief moment on stage a fleeting image of fantasies realized and wishes fulfilled. We know of some comic versions of life in the Golden Age that were staged before Aristophanes' *Birds*, but neither Crates in his *Wild Animals*, nor Telecleides in his *Amphictyons*, nor Pherecrates in his *Miners* conceive of attaining such a life by founding a city. Their visions are all retrospective.[69] They represent nostalgic returns to a lost Golden Age under Kronos in which human desires were fulfilled without labor. Similar to these comic utopias are the

---

[69]   Athenaeus of Naucratis gives a chronological presentation of the themes of these plays and their gastronomic dreams, with some quotations, *Deipnosophistae* VI 267E-270A. Baldry (1953) treats this theme.

poetic wishes focused on the Islands of the Blest (§3 above). Aristophanes' *Birds* is, like Plato's *Republic* and *Laws*, a utopia of foundation. It does not look backwards to a Golden Age.

The *Birds* opens with the two Athenians arriving in Thrace, where they are seeking the advice of the Thracian king Tereus, now transformed into a hoopoe. They need to discover from a bird's-eye view a place where they can find a comfortable life, one free from the intolerable political life and litigation they have left in Athens, flying away "with both feet" (44, 121-127). King Tereus suggests a "blessed city on the Red Sea," but Peisthetairos insists on a Greek city. This must be a new foundation (144-148). On the spur of the moment, the Athenian improvises the fatally flawed project of building a city of baked brick, like Babylon, midway between heaven and earth: his injunction to Tereus and the birds, who had never been confined before, is "Found a city!" (172). This new scheme frustrates his original project of escaping from the irritations of Athens, for a proper Greek city requires all the intolerable citizens Peisthetairos had hoped to be rid of. Driven to Tereus by a "strong passion" (*eros*) for the free life of the birds (412-414), Peisthetairos sees his newly founded city invaded by every profession he wanted to be free of. New blessings attract old curses: a priest, a poet, a prophet, a city planner, an imperial inspector, a peddlar of decrees, all of whom Peisthetairos turns from the gates of his new city.

The triumphant ending of the *Birds* shows Peisthetairos, the new "tyrant" (1708), feasting like a victorious comic poet, with his new bride, Basileia (Queen, or as William Arrowsmith translates it, Miss Universe). The end of the play and the happy (but doomed) expectation of the banquet to celebrate the victory of the comic poet (Aristophanes won only second prize) cannot conceal the failure of both of Peisthetairos' star-crossed projects: to escape from life in Athens and at the same time to found an imperial city to which both gods and men will be subject. In the end, the mid-heavenly city of Cloudcuckooland is subjected to the imperial city from which the two Athenians had sought to escape.[70]

Like all comic fantasies, Aristophanes' Cloudcuckooland can be described in the now familiar term Aristotle chose to describe the "utopian" schemes of Plato's *Republic* and *Laws*: it is created *kat' euchen*—as an answer to the ambitious and disgruntled Athenian citizen's impossible prayers.[71] If wishes were birds, then Athenians could fly. Aristophanes' Athenian refugees, who seek a quiet and secure place to live, where they can be free of the crowding annoyances of life in Athens, have their counterpart in the contemporary figure of Alcibiades. Like Peisthetairos (in 414),

---

70 Konstan (1997) has produced a fine analysis of the utopian projects of the *Birds* and the contradictions that frustrate them. Hubbard (1997) analyzes the utopian themes of other comedies of Aristophanes.

71 See §1 and n4 above.

Alcibiades had been persuasive (in 415): he persuaded the assembly of Athens to undertake an expedition against the powerful maritime city of Syracuse in Sicily—an expedition tacitly recalled in Plato's *Timaeus/Critias* (**I 3**). Aristophanes' protagonist in some ways reflects the ambitions of this statesmen as well as of imperial Athens.

To anticipate our presentation of Atlantis, let us recall that the Sicilian expedition ended in 413 in an unprecedented disaster for the Athenians. In Thucydides' judgment this destruction of the Athenian fleet was the greatest disaster in Greek history (VII 87). In restricting his judgment to Greek history, he must have had in mind the defeat of the two Persian expeditions against Greece in 490 and 480-479. The defeat of the Athenian expedition in Sicily by free Greeks to the west represents a tragic reversal: the Athenian victors over the Mede had become the Greek imperial power[72] and in their turn suffered a fate similar to the Persians they had defeated.

§ 6   PLATO'S ATLANTIS

The first text translated in this collection is Plato's single, ambitious, and incomplete dialogue, the *Timaeus/Critias*. (Despite its separation in later editions of Plato's works the *Timaeus/Critias* constitutes a single dialogue.[73]) Together, the *Timaeus* Prologue and the *Critias* make up the account of the prehistoric civilization of Athens and the island empire of Atlantis (**I 1 and 2**), known in antiquity as the *Atlantikos logos*. The history of prehistoric Athens and Atlantis is told by Critias in the *Timaeus/Critias*. In the *Timaeus*, Critias introduces the long, uninterrupted speech of Timaeus; his own account of the war between the prehistoric states of Athens and Atlantis in the dialogue that bears his name breaks off in mid sentence. No work of ancient fiction has held such a fascination for the human imagination and—in the distracting search for the vanished island of Atlantis—no philosophical project has been so poorly understood.[74] Atlantis has come to be viewed as historical, not fictional; as utopian in the unexamined sense of the word; as a lost continent, not a submerged island. But Plato's fictional island of Atlantis is a part of the main as a utopia that reflects his own society and forms a complex philosophical project that involves the *Republic*, the *Timaeus*, the *Critias*, the promised *Hermocrates*, and the *Laws*.

Critias' account is dubbed an "extraordinary tale, but a tale of absolute truth" (*Timaeus* 20D). The enigmatic nature of the tale's credibility is illustrated by the fact that the description of Atlantis stands at five removes

---

[72]   For this representation of Athenian imperialism, see §6.
[73]   Haslam (1976) has made this argument.
[74]   The career of Atlantis and the coextensive history of credulity has been recently written by Ellis (1998). The visual history of Atlantis is illustrated in Geoffrey Ashe (1992). Diskin Clay (2000) presents the *Timaeus/Critias* as a Platonic fiction.

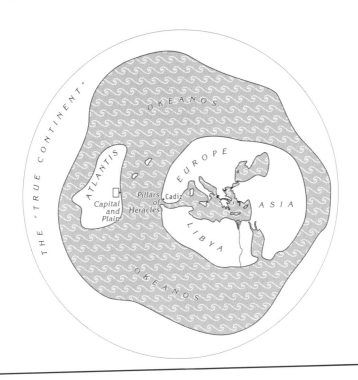

Figure 13 The World of Plato's *Timaeus/Critias*. Diskin Clay and Thomas Elliott.

from its original in a hieroglyphic inscription of Sais. The history from this sacred inscription is passed on to Solon by the Egyptian priest of the temple of Neith in Sais; from Solon to Critias the elder; and from Critias the elder to Amynander and Critias the younger; and from this Critias to Socrates, Timaeus, and Hermocrates. While the alleged sources cited may inspire the reader's confidence, the author's distancing himself from them should provoke doubt. Plato's technique becomes a hallmark of fiction, especially of later utopian fiction: the use of external authorities simultaneously to validate and to call into question the account recorded by the author. In this way, the author entices the complicitous reader to believe his "lies," but recognizes his readers' intelligence and offers as a reward for complicity a kernel of truth within his lies.

Plato's *Atlantikos logos* is not only the first and most striking example of philosophical fiction; it represents a significant stage of Plato's sustained attempt to work out "in words" the best form of human society. This project was initiated in the *Republic* and concludes—or rather is left open for the

reader to meditate upon—with the last sentence of Plato's last philosophical dialogue, the *Laws*. In the course of Plato's meditation of the best form
of human society a number of cities are created "in speech": Kallipolis (so
called in *Republic* VII 527C); prehistoric Athens and Atlantis; and finally
the city of the Magnetes in Crete, which is refounded in the speech of the
Athenian stranger in Plato's *Laws*. This vast philosophical project is advanced in the *Timaeus/Critias*, which appears to promise a "tetralogy" or a
group of four interconnected dialogues.

The *Timaeus* opens as Socrates counts "one, two, three." The numbers
point to the three interlocutors of the dialogue: Timaeus of Locri, Critias of
Athens, and Hermocrates of Syracuse. Critias and Hermocrates are well
known to the historical record, and as we shall see, their identities are crucial
to an interpretation of the plan of the dialogue. In the first stage of this dialogue, Socrates summarizes the speech of the day before. This speech seems—
but only seems—to implicate the *Republic* as the first dialogue of the tetralogy of the four speeches. In many respects this speech does recall the *Republic*.
In both, Socrates distinguishes a class of farmers and artisans from a class of
warrior guardians; assigns to each class the single occupation for which it is
naturally apt; decrees that the guardian class be educated to regard all possessions in common—including women and children, and that women belong to this class; and by this provision abolishes the Greek family. In Socrates'
mention of the proposed equality of some men and women who belong to
the guardian class and in the community of wives and children, we have
two of the three "waves" of paradox that Socrates stirs up in *Republic* V.[75] But
the *Timaeus* Prologue omits distinctive features of the *Republic* and therefore
cannot refer to that work as we have it. The two works occur in two different
chronological frameworks (defined by annual Athenian festivals) and employ two different casts of characters. Even more significant are omissions of
content: the *Timaeus* Prologue has not a word to say about the *Republic*'s
third wave of paradox nor even the philosophical heart of the *Republic*: the
philosopher king and the class of philosophers to which he belongs.[76]

The *Timaeus* Prologue continues with Critias introducing his own (the
third) contribution to the tetralogy, but his speech is deferred as Timaeus
gives a second speech on the creation of the world, its soul, and humankind
by a divine craftsman (*Timaeus* 27C-92C). The agreement among Socrates,

---

[75] 540A-457B and 457C-471C. Perhaps the most useful analysis of these proposals in
    connection with Greek utopian political thought is Dawson (1992) chapter 2.
[76] Set out in *Republic* V 473C. The discussion of the education of the philosophers
    continues to the end of book VII. I state, as have others before me, the very
    deliberate obstacles Plato creates as his reader attempts to link the *Timaeus/
    Critias* with the *Republic* in Clay (1997). For the specific links between Socrates'
    speech of "yesterday" as recalled in the *Timaeus* Prologue and the *Republic*,
    consult the notes to I, *Timaeus* 17A-19A.

Timaeus, Critias, and Hermocrates is that Critias will take the newly created race of humans from Timaeus and Socrates' guardians from Socrates and make them citizens of Athens (*Timaeus* 27A-27B). Hermocrates is expected to contribute a fourth speech, which in fact is never given. But a plausible interpretation of the project intimated by the *Timaeus/Critias* is that the argument of the dialogue will move from the static ideal city of three classes Socrates lays out in the *Republic* to the world of genesis and change described by Timaeus; and from the genesis of the universe to the earliest stages of human history and the war between Athens and Atlantis, which is Critias' subject. Since Critias' speech ends precipitously with the words Zeus did not pronounce before the gods assembled ("And, when he had gathered them together, he said... " *Critias* 121C), we have no sequel in a *Hermocrates*. What would Hermocrates have said on the occasion of the Panathenaic festival in praise of Athens? To answer this question, we must first observe the connections of the dialogue to historical Athens.

Plato, through Critias, speaks in praise of prehistoric Athens, and suggests the similarities between imperial Atlantis and imperial Athens of the fifth century. Athens and the island of Atlantis seem situated at antipodes to east and west. At first, only the oppositions between the two states are apparent. Antediluvian imperial Atlantis stands as the opponent of antediluvian Athens in almost everything that counts. It is a monarchy divided among ten kings and a power intent on enslaving the peoples of the Mediterranean (*Timaeus* 25B); Athens is the leader of the free world and the liberator of the Mediterranean (*Critias* 125D). Atlantis is a sea power and its god is Poseidon; Athens is a land power, apparently without a navy; its goddess is Athena who planted the olive in the soil of Attica. In Periclean Athens, Athena and Poseidon are shown on the west pediment of the Parthenon locked in their struggle for Attica. According to Critias, these two gods received their separate domains (Athena, in Athens; Poseidon, in Atlantis) without quarreling (*Critias* 109B and 113B). But Plato, who could admire the west pediment of the Parthenon, knew that the two gods were still locked in a struggle for mastery over Athens.

There are, however, telling details in Critias' elaborate description of Atlantis that project onto this island the distant image of imperial Athens of the Sicilian expedition. Both peoples claim to be autochthonous—that is, to have sprung from the earth. The name of one of Poseidon's ten sons is Autochthon (*Critias* 114B), and "autochthony" is one of Athens' most notorious historical pretentions.[77] Other details crowd for attention. Both states are organized into ten groups: Atlantis into the domains ruled by the de-

---

[77] For the name Autochthon, see **I 2**, *Critias* 114B. On the Athenians as autochthonous, see *Critias* 113C-D; *Menexenus*, 238D-E; Loreaux (1986) 149-150 and index s.v. "autochthony."

scendants of its ten original kings; Athens, into the ten tribes established by Cleisthenes in 507. Interestingly, nine of the kings of Atlantis are called *archontes* (*Critias* 114A), the term for the nine chief magistrates of Athens. Perhaps the most impressive connection between Atlantis and imperial Athens is Atlantis' harbor, which Critias describes as "teeming with ships and crowds of merchants who had arrived from all over the world and whose voices and bustle produced a commotion and hubbub that could be heard day and night" (*Critias* 117E). There can be no better description of the port of imperial Athens, the Peiraeus.[78] A dramatic passage in Thucydides describes the launching of the Sicilian expedition from the Piraeus in 415 (VI 31-32). From this point, imperial ambitions of Athens moved west. They were doomed to failure as were the Atlanteans' similar ambitions as they penetrated the Mediterannean and moved towards the east.

In answer to our earlier question, perhaps Hermocrates might have said something like what he said as he organized resistance in Sicily against the invasion of Athens.[79] He warns the people of Kamerina that Athens had simply extended the Persian attempt to enslave Greece to the west (Thucydides VI 76.4 and 77.1).[80] His word "enslave" is familiar from Critias' account of the ambitions of Atlantis (*Timaeus* 25B). Hermocrates' taciturn presence[81] in this dialogue might be eloquent for the end of an ambitious Platonic history that began with the origin of the universe and what had become of pristine Athens. The end of this history begins with the Athenians' catastrophic defeat in Sicily in 413 and continues with the final defeat of their fleet at Aegispotami in 405. The presence of the historical Critias represents the final stage. Critias headed the group of oligarchs known as the "thirty tyrants" (404-403), and fell in a battle of civil strife against the exiled democrats in 403. His fate reminds us that the reason Solon could not complete his epic of Altantis was the civil strife he encountered on his return from Egypt to Athens (*Timaeus* 21C). By creating in prehistoric Atlantis the distant image of the sea power he knew as a young man, Plato has turned his reader's critical gaze from the Athens and Atlantis of Critias' Egyptian history to the Athens whose end was commemorated by the tyrannical reign of Critias himself.

---

[78] On the harbors and other correspondences, see Pierre Vidal-Nacquet, "Athens and Atlantis: Structure and Meaning of a Myth," in *The Black Hunter: Forms of Thought and Forms of Society in the Greek World*, trans. Andrew Szegedy Maszak (Baltimore 1986) 263-284.

[79] We translate his two speeches in **I 3**, "What Hermocrates Said."

[80] Plato had already alluded to such imperial ambitions in *Republic* I 351B.

[81] Hermocrates is not completely silent in the *Timaeus/Critias*, but he speaks briefly only twice, first in *Timaeus* 20C-D and then in *Critias* 108B-C.

§ 7   THEOPOMPOS' CONTINENT BEYOND OCEAN

In the early third century, an associate of the Academy named Crantor devoted a commentary to Plato's *Timaeus*. Perhaps more than a generation before, Theopompos of Chios produced his own version of the myth of Atlantis in his history of Philip of Macedon, in one of his dramatic excursions known in antiquity as his "Book of Marvels"[82] (**V 4**). For his account of the vast continent encompassing the *oikoumene* (the world of human habitation), the "islands" of Europe, Asia, and Libya (Figure 7), he produces as his authority the satyr Silenus, who was captured by King Midas of Phrygia and compelled to reveal his semi-divine knowledge of the larger world that lies beyond human ken. The continent seems to have been called "the Meropis land," named after one of the peoples inhabiting this vast continent (Strabo VII 3.6). The cities Silenus first describes are called Eusebes (Pious) and Machimos (Warlike). So far as we can judge from our only report of this passage, Theopompos operates by a series of displacements all of which tacitly recognize Plato's *Timaeus/Critias*. In Theopompos' historical and philosophical fiction, Silenus replaces Plato's Egyptian priest of the temple of Neith at Sais; Midas the Lydian king, Solon; the continental city of Machimos, Atlantis; the city of Eusebes, Athens; and the vast continent embracing the three "islands" that once comprised the O-T[83] map of the known world, the "true continent" of Plato's fiction.[84] Theopompos also recalls the Hesiodic traditions of the Golden Age to convey the peaceful life of the citizens of Eusebes, and of the Bronze Age to convey the nasty, mean, brutish, and short life of the warriors of Machimos. The imperial expedition of Plato's Atlantis is evoked as Silenus describes the invasion (presumably of the three "islands" known to the Greeks) by the Machimoi, who penetrate as far as the Hyperboreans with a force of ten million. Like the Atlanteans, the Machimoi possess gold and silver in abundance. Like the kings of Atlantis, and like the Athenians who invaded Sicily, they too fail in gaining their objectives.

§ 8   EUHEMEROS OF MESSENE'S PANCHAIA

Panchaia is the invention of Euhemeros of Messene. Euhemeros was not a sedentary philosopher—no more than was Plato. But unlike Plato,

---

[82] Felix Jacoby assigns the fragments of this work to Theopompos' *History of Philip*, in his commentary to *FGrHist* 115 F 64-77.

[83] In an O-T (or T-O) map of the world the letter T is inscribed in the circle of the O with its upper bar intersecting the center horizontally and its vertical bar dividing the lower hemisphere into two equal parts (see Figures 5 and 6).

[84] The Egyptian priest describes Atlantis as "greater than Libya and Asia combined" and the continent containing Ocean as a true continent (*Timaeus* 24E-25A). Pierre Vidal-Naquet, (1986) 264-265, establishes the suggestive correspondences between Plato and Theopompos. In this he follows the lead of Rohde (1914) 204-206.

whose travels took him no farther west than Sicily, much less than halfway to the site of his Atlantis, Euhemeros actually reached the Indian Ocean where he situated the islands which were the subject of his utopian project. Diodorus Siculus is the only source to reveal the significant facts that Euhemeros' *Sacred Inscription* was a first-person narration and that he related how he went on many long trips on behalf of Cassander, who became king of Macedon after the death of Alexander.[85] One of these voyages took him from the Red Sea into "Ocean to the South," where he discovered the new world of Panchaia. Diodorus says that he "travelled to remote regions" (*ektopisthenai*). This is, in fact, a technical term, signifying a journey beyond (*ek*) any known place (*topos*), and therefore implies that we cannot retrace his voyage. But the term is also significant for the ancient study of Homeric geography, where it means that Homer took Odysseus beyond the Mediterranean and any place known to mankind. A parallel term, *exokeanismos*, means that Homer took Odysseus beyond the confines of even Ocean.[86]

What we know about these islands comes at two or three removes. For some of Euhemeros we depend on Diodorus; for some of Diodorus' account of Euhemeros we depend on Eusebius. This is an accident of transmission. The transmission of Euhemeros' account as it has come down to us is parallel to his invention of the transmission of information within his work, an invention appropriate to any utopian project following in the wake of Plato's *Atlantikos logos* (see §6 above). As authorities he cites himself as an eyewitness to the island and, for the history of the island and its colonization, its priestly cast and ultimately the Sacred Inscription composed by the first of all Greek historians, Zeus himself. This inscription stands on a golden banquet couch. It replaces the cult statue in the temple of Triphylian Zeus and gives Euhemeros' work its title. On it is inscribed the history of the life of Ouranos and of Zeus as the far-travelled benefactor of humankind (Diodorus V 46.3). This history has its necessary sequel supplied by Hermes, who added to the inscription the history of the next generation of humans become gods, Apollo and Artemis.

The most prominent feature of Panchaia is its sacred character. It is an island once inhabited by humans become gods (Ouranos, Kronos, and Zeus) and it supplies all the aromatic gums (frankincense and myrrh) necessary to the cult of the gods throughout the inhabited world. Its location on the eastern periphery of the Greek world situates it within the fluidity

---

[85] For the Greek penetration into Bactria (Afganistan) and India the classic study is that of Tarn, *The Greeks in Bactria and India* (1951); for the historians (Onesikritos in particular) of this expedition into the east see Pearson (1960). The islands of the Panchaian archipelago are described in III, Diodorus V 41.4-46. Another treatment of these islands occupied book VI, which has been lost. For its contents we rely on Eusebius' *Praeparatio Evangelica* II 2.59B-61A.

[86] For the two terms, see Romm (1992) 186-196.

of the traditions that move on the currents of Ocean at the sacred extreme. Finally, the east has supplied a people to answer to the Hyperboreans to the north, the (most commonly recognized) Ethiopians to the south, and Atlanteans to the west. The sacred character of what was known as Arabia Felix (Saudi Arabia, also known as Arabia Eudaimon)[87] has migrated to three islands of the Indian Ocean.

Piety towards men become gods is characteristic of Euhemeros' age. One thinks of Alexander called Zeus Ammon, the Athenian ithyphallic hymn to Demetrios Poliorketes, "a god now manifest to us," the Ptolemies called *euergetes* and *soter* and the diadochs of Alexander called *eumeneis* and Antiochos *epiphanes*. But the very name Euhemeros is notorious for a new species of impiety. Unlike the first generation of the atheists in antiquity (Diagoras of Melos, Theodoros of Cyrene, Protagoras of Abdera), Euhemeros created a theology—or anthropology. "Euhemerism" reconstructed the origins of the human concept of the gods and the meaning of piety and cult, arguing that the gods worshipped by mankind were once human beings. Like their human votaries they were born and died; but unlike most of their votaries they conferred great benefactions on their fellows and came to be worshipped in gratitude for their extraordinary accomplishments.

For all his innovation and responsiveness to the innovations of his own age, Euhemeros does retain elements of earlier religious sentiments, including those of Plato, for whom only the eternal and supremely intelligible—and therefore intelligent—is divine. Euhemeros seems to recognize Plato's "astral theology," when he distinguishes between the two groups of divinities worshipped on the island of Panchaia and recognizes not only the traditional gods of Greek cult but the eternal divinities of the heavens.[88]

The location of Panchaia cannot be fixed on any map of the *oikoumene* known to Euhemeros at the beginning of the third century. In his island book (V), Diodorus speaks of a group of eastern islands at "the extremity of Arabia Felix that is bound by Ocean."[89] The first is Panchaia, also called the "sacred island." The second is unnamed; the third is certainly Taprobane (Sri Lanka), although Diodorus does not name it. The subcontinent of India is said to be just visible from the easternmost promontory of this vast island (V 42.3, Figure 3).

---

[87] "Blessed" because of its incense, which was used in sacrifice. The fragrance wafting from the coast of Arabia is noted by Herodotus *Histories* III 113; this passage is recalled by Lucian *True History* II 5 (**V 1 E**), in his description of the Island of the Blest; cf. Diodorus II 54.

[88] II, Diodorus V 1. This is actually Eusebius quoting Diodorus, who in turn must be referring to Euhemeros. On "astral theology," see J.-A. Festugière, *Epicure et ses dieux*[2] (Paris 1968, *Epicurus and his Gods*, trans. C. W. Chilton, Oxford 1955) chapter 5.

[89] II, Diodorus V 41.4. These have been prosaically identified as Abd el Kuri and Socotra.

The second island is used for the burial of the dead, since burial is not permitted on the sacred island Panchaia. This is a significant detail and one that reflects the relation between the sacred island of Delos and the neighboring and profane island of Rheneia. The details of Euhemeros' narrative, with their emphasis on the sacred, take on an intelligible shape when they are drawn into the space of earlier utopian writing. As was Theopompos a generation before him, Euhemeros seems well aware of the philosophical fiction of Plato's *Atlantikos logos*.

The sacred inscription for which the work is named is compared to Egyptian hieroglyphics (literally, "sacred writings") in precisely the language that describes the hieroglyphic history of the war between Athens and Atlantis in the *Timaeus*.[90] There is, of course, still another sacred inscription described in Critias' narrative. Poseidon was its author. It is cut into a stele standing in the sacred precinct of Poseidon in the royal capital of Atlantis. It contains the laws Poseidon had established for his ten sons and their descendants (**I 2**, *Critias* 119C-120A).

These inscriptions from Plato's text that occur within the text and title of Euhemeros' fiction reflect a passage in the *Republic* where Socrates announces his project of gaining a view of the soul "writ large" in the larger stele of the state (*Republic* II 368D). Just so, we can keep in mind Plato's *Atlantikos logos* to gain a better view of the text of Euhemeros' *Sacred Inscription*. In turn, Euhemeros' *Sacred Inscription* gives us a new and unexpected view of the project of Plato's successive utopias of the *Republic*, *Timaeus/Critias*, and the *Laws*.

A number of details in Euhemeros' text invite attention. The temple of Triphylian Zeus clearly recalls the temple of Poseidon in the sanctuary at the center of the concentric rings that make up the royal and divine city of Atlantis (*Critias* 116C-117A). Elephants are indigenous to both Panchaia and Atlantis, as is ivory; the use of chariots in warfare on Panchaia reflects the archaic practice of the kings of Atlantis.[91] What is most striking about the island of Panchaia is its tripartite class structure. The distribution of power is not entirely clear as Diodorus reports it. In one place he speaks of a king of some of the districts of Panchaia (**II**, V 42.1); the principal city, Panara, is ruled by three elected archons (**II**, V 42.5). But these political arrangements seem to be a part of a larger class structure that divides Panchaian society into priests (who control the artisan class),[92] farmers, and warriors.

---

[90] **II**, Diodorus V 46.7; cf. **I 1**, *Timaeus* 23E, 27B; and 23A.
[91] Elephants: **II**, Diodorus V 45.1; **I 2**, *Critias* 115A; ivory: Diodorus V 46.6, *Critias* 116D; chariots: Diodorus V 45.1; *Critias* 119A-D.
[92] Who seem to be occupied with the buildings and statues that honor the gods of the island and the magnificent sanctuary of Triphylian Zeus.

The ordering seems strange, since it is not hierarchical. The explanation for this odd order is the fact that Euhemeros has inscribed two texts of Plato in his *Sacred Inscription*. The first is the text of the *Republic*, with its class structure of farmers and artisans, warrior guardians, and guardians of the state, who will develop into philosopher kings. The second is the text of the *Timaeus* and the Saite priest's description of the rigid cast structure of Egypt, which articulates into priests, farmers, and warriors in that order (**I 1**, *Timaeus* 24A)— exactly what we find in Euhemeros. Euhemeros forces us to see the successive transformations of Plato's utopian project in the retrospective light of the early third century.

Piety is not one of the virtues of Plato's Kallipolis; in its place is justice and the rule imposing a single function for each member of society. No temple can be found in Kallipolis. What is missing from Plato's *Republic* becomes evident as Critias describes prehistoric Athens, with its acropolis and its sanctuaries of Athena and Hephaistos. Priests live with the warrior class established on the heights by some "god-like men."[93] The kings of Atlantis are devoted to the cult of Poseidon and, unlike the guardian class of prehistoric Athens, they are lavish in their use of precious metals in their temple and cult statue of Poseidon. The walls of his temple are gold; its roof, ivory inlaid with gold; its acroteria, silver. The statue of Poseidon and his chariot and the hundred Nereids surrounding him must all have been made of gold as well (**I 2**, *Critias* 116D-E).

The temple of Triphylian Zeus is the cult center of Panchaia. The priests who are confined to this vast sanctuary wear gold. The temple is made of silver, gold, and ivory. The banquet couch of Zeus is of gold, as is the table set out before it (**II, V** 46.2-7). In stark contrast to the heavenly,[94] dull, and austere city of Plato's *Republic*, lie two earthly, radiant, and wealthy islands at the "sacred extremes" of the Greek world: Atlantis to the west and Panchaia to the east.

The first word of Plato's last utopian project is *theos*, god (*Laws* I 624A). The cults that have no place in Kallipolis are elaborately reestablished by the anonymous Athenian who joins with the Cretan Kleinias and Spartan Megillos in refounding the City of the Magnetes.[95] The deeply religious character of the *Laws* and the importance of Zeus the lawgiver to Plato's final utopian project might help us understand why Euhemeros has the priests of Panchaia claim that their ancestors accompanied Zeus, when he left Crete, the island of his birth, for the sacred island on the Indian Ocean (**II, V** 46.2). Plato invented the lost island of Atlantis, and thereby created the possibilities of lands and islands still more remote, such as Theopompos' continent that lay beyond Ocean, and Euhemeros' Panchaia.

[93]   **I 1**, *Timaeus* 24A; **I 2**, *Critias* 110C and 112 B-C.
[94]   As it is implicity described at *Republic* IX 592B.
[95]   Especially in *Laws* VI 753A-D; 759A-760A; 761C, 771A-772A, and 778B.

§ 9   IAMBOULOS' ISLAND OF THE SUN

We come finally to Iamboulos, who is named by only two ancient authors—Diodorus and Lucian. Diodorus speaks of the principal island of the archipelago of the Islands of the Sun as "the island that has been discovered to the south in Ocean" (**III**, II 55.1). His credulity is not shared by Lucian, who understands Iamboulos' narrative for what it is: a fiction whose powerful charm is that it clothes itself in the garments of truth and personal observation. Lucian facetiously mentions Homer, Ktesias of Knidos, and Iamboulos as liars whose vice he will avoid in his own *True History* (I 3). It is very likely that Lucian adapted Iamboulos' description of the inhabitants of the Islands of Sun to his "island" of the Moon (Selene) and the Selinitai (**III**, Appendix).[96] As Odysseus in his tales told at the court of Alcinous on Scherie, Euhemeros in his *Sacred Inscription*, and Lucian after him, Iamboulos casts his account of his voyage in a first-person narrative (for which we have only Diodorus' summary in **III**, II 55-60).

Spices are important in Iamboulos' narrative, as is Arabia Felix; both seem to allude to Euhemeros' Panchaia. In Iamboulos' narrative, the Ethiopians on the west coast of the Red Sea are situated to the south of the sacred extremes on the compass of the Greek utopian imagination. Iamboulos and his companions are captured as they attempt to purchase spices in Arabia Felix and are carried across the Red Sea to the Ethiopians, who treat them as *pharmakoi* (scapegoats) in a ceremony of periodic purification. Iamboulos and (it seems) a single companion are put on a small boat with six months provisions and told to head into the Ocean to the south. Up to this point in Greek literature the Ethiopians (or one branch of them) have occupied the southern or eastern extreme of the known world and from Homer on they have been intimately associated with the gods.[97] These pious and just people tell Iamboulos that if he sails south he will "reach a fertile and populated island and discover a virtuous people inhabiting it and live a life of bliss with them" (**III**, II 55.3-4). After four months of sailing south and driven by violent storms, Iamboulos discovers the island the Ethiopians had directed him to.

The island Iamboulos discovers has one extraordinary feature: it is perfectly circular and has a circumference of exactly 5,000 stades. We know of another island of the sun in Greek travel literature. This is the divine island of Helios, which Odysseus reaches before Zeus destroys his ship and companions and he is cast up on the sacred island of Calypso (§4 above). The more remote island that Iamboulos reaches lies on the equator and possesses most of the features of the Golden Age, the Islands of the Blest,

---

[96]   As Werner Fauth persuasively argues in "Utopische Inseln in der 'wahren Geschichten' des Lukian," *Gymnasium* 86 (1979) 39-60.

[97]   *Odyssey* I 22-25; see **V 3**.

and Elysian Fields as we know these from Hesiod and Homer.[98]

We must pass over the incredible things Iamboulos encountered on the Island of the Sun to reflect briefly on the genre of philosophical fiction that Plato invented with his *Atlantikos logos* and its expression in Iamboulos. There is not a single Island of the Sun; rather it is part of an archipelago of seven perfectly round islands of exactly the same size. One asks: Why seven and why round? One possible answer is that Iamboulos has in mind the geometry of Poseidon as Critias describes this in the *Critias*. The circular precinct fashioned by Poseidon on the island of Atlantis is surrounded by six concentric circles of water alternating with land rings (Figure 14, **I** 2, *Critias* 113D-E). There is something divine about the circle and the number seven, which is present in the rings created by Poseidon. The measurement and geometrical perfection of the Islands of the Sun might be explained as a terrestrial reflection of the Greek system of seven planets.

Second, Iamboulos deliberately recalls one of the paradoxes Socrates proposes in the *Republic* and recalls in the *Timaeus* Prologue: the community of wives and children.[99] Indeed, the manner the islanders adopt to test the mettle of their children is deliberately recalled by Iamboulos who mounts them not on horses but on the backs of huge birds who carry them high into the sky (whimsically illustrated in Figure 16, below).[100] Further, the gods worshipped by the Helionesiotai (if we can give them this name) are the "true gods" of the astral theology that Plato introduced in his *Timaeus* and described in his *Laws* and that Euhemeros recognized in his Panchaia. And like the guardians of Plato's Kallipolis, the islanders sing hymns to the gods and (apparently) offer praise to outstanding men.[101]

Iamboulos' stay on the Island of the Sun is ended when the islanders decide that their guests of seven years are incorrigible and expel them from their bliss. Iamboulos and his companion sail for more than seven months and are shipwrecked on the coast of India. The companion perishes, but Iamboulos survives to tell the tale and is rescued by the philhellene King of the state of Palibothra (Pataliputra) on the Ganges. We have lost his account of the marvels of India. Like Sherlock Holmes' "The Great Rat of Sumatra," it is a tale "for which the world is not yet prepared."[102] We do not know if Iamboulos sighted the three islands of the Panchaian archi-

---

[98] These features are manifest in Diodorus II 57.1, where Iamboulos cites the lines describing the spontaneous fertility of the island of the Phaeacians (*Odyssey* VII 120-121); cf. Hesiod *Works and Days* 118-119, 172-173; *Odyssey* XIX 109-114; and **V** 1.

[99] *Republic* II 423E, V 457B-4651C, and **I**, *Timaeus* 18C-D.

[100] **III**, Iamboulos II 58.1 and 5; Plato *Republic* V 476 D.

[101] **III**, Iamboulos II 59.6; cf. *Republic* X 607A.

[102] "The Adventure of the Sussex Vampire," in Sir Arthur Conan Doyle, *The Complete Sherlock Holmes* (Garden City, New York 1905) 1034.

pelago on his voyage to India; but we do know that Panchaia and the Islands of the Sun are washed in the waves produced by Plato's Atlantis sinking into the Atlantic.

§ 10 FRANCIS BACON'S NEW ATLANTIS

In the beginning, all the world was America.

(John Locke)

Bensalem is the last of the four imaginary islands presented in this collection. It is the only island utopia among these four in which the word "utopia" might be taken to designate the literary presentation of a society considered perfect by its author, but the work is not only "not perfected" in its state as a fragment; it is imperfect in many essential details. We shall return to all that is missing and the conception of this work as a work of utopian literature as we conclude.

The voyage to the island of Bensalem takes us 180 degrees around the globe from the middle of the Atlantic Ocean from Plato's ancient Atlantis to the middle of the Pacific Ocean. Bacon wrote his *New Atlantis* sometime between his disgrace and fall from political power in 1621 and his death in 1626. The date usually given is 1624. Like More, Bacon rose to become Lord Chancellor of England; but, unlike More, Bacon was confined to the Tower for only a few days. He was then released to resume his private career as author and scientist. His *New Atlantis* was published in 1626 or 1627 by William Rawley, his chaplain become literary executor. Rawley added the prefatory note included in the Foreword of our text (**IV**) and later turned the work into Latin to assure it the international audience of More's *Utopia*.[103]

It is not our purpose to present the philosophical and scientific background of Bacon's *New Atlantis* and its governing body of scientists who form the House of Salomon (or College of Six Days' Works). The place of his *New Atlantis* in the history of utopian writing concerns us most, particularly its relation to Plato of the *Timaeus*/*Critias*. Bacon was not an admirer of Plato, but he chose to imitate one of Plato's most baffling works.

When he published his *Instauratio Magna* in 1620, Bacon chose for a frontispiece the design of two caravels sailing west out of the Pillars of Heracles (Figure 17). Thereby he directs our attention to the Atlantic, which was closed to the ancients, and beyond the Atlantic and beyond his *Instauratio Magna* to a newly discovered island in the Pacific. Like the accounts of Odysseus, Euhemeros, Iamboulos, and Lucian, Bacon's *New*

---

[103] Printed with the posthumous edition of his *Sylva Sylvarum: or A Naturall Historie* (London 1626 [1627]); no. 170 in Gibson (1950). Rawley's Latin translation was published with Bacon's *Opera Moralia* in 1538 (nos. 196 and 197). Denise Albanese has located what she takes to be the sole copy of the 1626 printing in the Folger Library, "The New Atlantis and the Uses of Utopia," *ELH* 57 (1990) 508n11.

Atlantis is a first-person narrative. The identity of its narrator is never established, but he begins with the words: "We sailed from Peru...." *New Atlantis* also includes within this first-person narrative a dialogue between the Governor of the House of Strangers of Bensalem and the anonymous narrator and his companions. Like the Greek utopias we have passed in review, New Atlantis is an island and an island of exceptional fertility (§29). The island is referred to as "that happy land" and "this happy island" (§16 and §22) and qualifies as an early modern version of the Islands of the Blest. To promote his utopian fiction, Bacon followed More in inventing the place names, titles, and the language of Bensalem. His *New Atlantis* presents not only the marvelous but the miraculous in the cross of flame that announced to this remote island the gospel of Christ before other nations had received his gospel. The Christianity of the island presents a puzzling combination of religious and scientific faith (§17- §20).

There are obvious and deliberate contacts with Plato, the most obvious of which is the title Bacon chose for his work and the location of the newly discovered island far to the west and well beyond the frontiers of the known. Bacon is both a subtle and a critical reader of Plato. The account of the empires of "the great Atlantis," Mexico, and Peru as they existed some 3,000 years before the narrator and his companions reached the island of Bensalem, offers a critical reading of Plato's history of Atlantis.

Bacon is one of Plato's many readers who took Critias' history of the destruction of the island empire of Atlantis seriously as natural history, as did Montaigne before him.[104] In this he was following a venerable tradition of credulity. He gives the Governor of the House of Strangers in Bensalem the responsibility of narrating the history of the island and the histories of the empires Tyrambel (Atlantis, identified as Mexico, the West Indies and North America) and Coya (Peru). The Governor does not take Critias' history to be "absolutely true." He rejects the claim that Atlantis was plunged into the sea by an earthquake, and his dating of the deluge that destroyed its civilization differs radically from what we find in Plato. He places the deluge that overwhelmed the civilization of Atlantis 3,000 years before the date of the anonymous narrator's discovery of the Pacific island of Bensalem—not, as in Plato's *Atlantikos logos*, 9,000 years before Solon's visit to Sais. The engineering works of Poseidon and the kings of Atlantis he deems as "poetical and fabulous." (He might well regard them as allegorical and representing a Jacob's ladder leading to heaven, a *Scala Cœli*.[105]) The Governor of the House of Strangers identifies Atlantis with the new

---

[104] As is evident from his essay "Des Cannibales" (I 31), *Œuvres complètes*, ed. Albert Thibaudet and Maurice Rat (Paris 1962) 200-201. Unlike Bacon, however, Montaigne did not identify the new world with Plato's Atlantis; see *New Atlantis* §24-§28.

[105] See **IV**, §26.

world of Mexico, discovered not six-score years before our narrator arrives on the island of Bensalem. And he follows Plato's account of how civilizations are destroyed by great deluges and arise afresh.[106]

Bacon's reader is reminded not only of Plato, but of Bacon's essay "Of Vicissitudes of Things" (58). In this essay, Bacon presents as an example of vicissitude the peoples of the new world who survived the flood: they are a young and "an ignorant and mountainous people, that can give no account of the time past; so that the oblivion is all one as if none had been left. If you consider well of the people of the West Indies, it is very probable that they are a newer or a younger people than the people of the old world."[107] Bacon's Latin aphroism *iuventas mundi, vetustas saeculi* ("the youth of the world is the old age of this generation") does not apply to the cyclical cataclysms in which peoples are overwhelmed and emerge again as amnesiac and in a state of infancy; the Platonic utopia of retrospect and the remote Golden Age of prehistoric Athens is reversed by the new scientific spirit which could regard the ancient as transformed into the new.

Bacon also recognizes the character of Plato's history of prehistoric Athens and its conflict with imperial Atlantis (§24 - §27). If he was a critical reader of the geology of Plato's Atlantis, he was a subtle reader of the meaning of Plato's *Atlantikos logos*. He suggests that Bensalem is the Pacific counterpart of prehistoric Athens. According to Bacon's fiction (which depended in some part on José de Acosta's history of the New World[108]), the fate of Atlantis and the Divine Vengeance that was its punishment is paralleled by another attempt to invade a utopian society: the American empire of Tyrambel (Mexico) attempted to extend its power into the Mediterranean, just as the empire of Coya (Peru) attempted to extend its power into the South Sea (§26 - §29). What Bacon realizes and replicates in his *New Atlantis* is the fact that prehistoric Athens and not imperial Atlantis is the true counterpart of his island of Bensalem.

Bacon follows Plato in leaving his work unfinished, but unlike Plato he ends inelegantly with a complete sentence. But we are reminded from the details with which More's Hythlodaeus describes the institutions of the island of Utopia how much is missing from Bacon's Bensalem: there is a king; a Governor of the College of Six Days' Works, and a Governor of the House of Strangers. What relation obtains among the king and these corporations remains obscure, as does the relation between politics and science, and religion and science. We know virtually nothing of the educa-

---

[106] **IV §26-§27; I 1**, *Timaeus* 23A-C.
[107] Vickers (1996) 451.
[108] *Historia natural y moral de las Indias*, 1590; *The Natural and Moral History of the Indies, by Father Joseph de Acosta.* Reprinted from the English translated edition of Edward Grimestone, 1604, and edited, with notes and an introduction, by Clements R. Markham (London 1880).

tion of the Bensalemites, or their laws or literature. The fullness of More's *Utopia* reveals the essential respects in which Bacon's sequel in *New Atlantis* remains "unperfected."[109] In his letter introducing *New Atlantis* to its public, Rawley spoke of the work as "a model" for a greater project that would have included a "frame of Laws, or of a commonwealth." It is clear that Bacon contemplated such a project for some thirty years.[110] Here Bacon might have imitated Plato too, for it is often claimed that Plato left his *Atlantikos logos* unperfected to return to the history of Athens and Persia in the *Laws*.[111] But it could be that Bacon, like Plato, knew that any essay in utopian political philosophy must remain imperfect and unperfected, since human nature must remain imperfect and unperfected.

---

[109] The gaps in Bacon's treatment of the society of Bensalem are noted by J. C. Davis in his *Utopia and the Ideal Society: A Study of English Utopian Writing 1516-1700* (Cambridge 1981) 117-118.

[110] As Davis (1981) 123 shows.

[111] The common view is stated by F. M. Cornford, *Plato's Cosmology* (New York 1957) 5-8 and more recently Gerard Naddaf, "The Atlantis Myth: An Introduction to Plato's later Philosophy of History." *Phoenix* 48 (1994) 189-209.

Chronological Table of Authors

800 BC	Homer
700 BC	Hesiod
500 BC	Pindar (518-ca. 445)
	Herodotus (480s-420s)
	Thucydides (ca. 455-400)
400 BC	Plato (ca. 428-349)
	Theopompos of Chios (378-ca. 319)
300 BC	Hecataeus of Abdera
	Euhemeros of Messene (died ca. 280)
	Dionysios Skytobrachion (ca. 250)
	Iamboulos
	Pseudo-Aristotle = student of Peripatetic school (third century BC or later)
30 BC	Diodorus Siculus (completed work ca. 30 BC)
AD 50	Pomponius Mela
AD 250	Pseudo-Callisthenes
AD 1500	Sir Thomas More (1478-1535)
AD 1600	Sir Francis Bacon (1561-1626)

I. Plato's Atlantis

Our sole source for the history of the island of Atlantis is Plato in his *Timaeus* Prologue and *Critias*. Plato, whose *Timaeus* (17A-27B) and unfinished *Critias* combine to give us a narrative of the war between prehistoric Athens and Atlantis, seems to be entirely responsible for a tradition he attributed to Solon and the Egyptian priest who passed the tradition down to Solon. The *Timaeus* has four speakers: Socrates, Timaeus of Locri in southern Italy, Critias of Athens, who became the leader of the "thirty tyrants" in 404 and was killed in 403, and Hermocrates of Syracuse, the general who opposed the Athenian expedition against Sicily of 415-413. It appears from the *Timaeus* Prologue that Timaeus, Hermocrates, and a third unnamed visitor have come to Athens for the great quadrennial festival in honor of Athena, the *Panathenaia*. Socrates' speech, in the tradition of the *Panathenaikos logos* (or display speech delivered during this festival) is not preserved, but from Socrates' rehearsal of its main points (*Timaeus* 17A-19A) he seems to recall his proposal for an ideal form of society in Plato's *Republic*. Apparently, however, his description of what he had said on the day before does not include his proposal, which he argues in the *Republic*, of a philosopher king as governor of his state—the single proposal that would make such a state possible.

In his long speech Timaeus gives a cosmology in the guise of a cosmogony and an account of the manufacture of the world and its soul by a divine craftsman (the *demiourgos*). It is the second speech in the program of four speeches (or "tetralogy") initiated by Socrates the day before. Critias comes third and his speech connects with Socrates' *Panathenaikos logos* in his claim that the citizens of prehistoric Athens were in fact the real embodiments of the guardian class of Socrates' theoretical state. His speech breaks off at 121C in mid-sentence, before the conflict between Athens and Atlantis or the deluge that overwhelms Atlantis, strips Athens of its soil and destroys its warrior class can be described in full. The fourth speech of this program, the *Hermocrates*, was never written and we can only conjecture what its subject might have been from his speeches in Thucydides, *The Peloponnesian War*. We have a version of the two speeches Hermocrates gives to organize opposition to the Athenian invasion of Sicily in the Appendix, "What Hermocrates Said" (I 3).

Page and column numbers of this translation of the *Timaeus* Prologue and *Critias* refer to the edition of the dialogues and letters of Plato in three volumes by Henricus Stephanus (Henri Etienne) of Paris, 1578. Each page of this edition was printed in one column of text divided into five sections (A-E). Stephanus' printed text is the text cited in all modern discussions of Plato.

1. Prologue: the *Timaeus* 17A-26C

Socrates meets all of his guests of the day before, save one, and recalls what he had said then on the occasion of the Panathenaia.

SOCRATES: **(17A)** One, two, three . . . . But, my dear Timaeus, where is the fourth of those who were yesterday guests at our banquet, and who have now invited us to dinner?

TIMAEUS: It so happens that he has fallen ill, Socrates. Otherwise, he would not have willingly been absent from this gathering.

SOCRATES: Well then, is it not your task and the task of your companions to fill in for our absent guest?

TIMAEUS: **(17B)** Absolutely. And we shall leave nothing wanting, at least in so far as we are able. It would not be fair for the rest of us, who were treated to your hospitality yesterday—as was fitting, since we are not Athenians—to fail to offer you a dinner in return, and with good heart.

SOCRATES: Tell me: do you recall all the subjects I assigned you to speak on?

TIMAEUS: Some we remember, but what I have forgotten you will have to remind us of, since we have you here now. Or better, if it is no trouble for you, why don't you rehearse our themes again, beginning with the beginning so that we will have them more firmly in mind?

Socrates recalls for the company his description of the state he deemed best.

SOCRATES: **(17C)** I will do as you ask. Now yesterday the essential points of what I said concerning what in my opinion is the best state: these were the kind of constitution that it is governed by and the kind of men that make it up.[1]

---

[1] This conversation cannot be the conversation reported by Socrates in the *Republic*. In both the *Timaeus* and the *Republic*, Socrates looks back on the conversation of "yesterday." But the occasion of the *Timaeus* trilogy is the festival of the Panathenaia (*Timaeus* 20C and E, and 26E); that of the *Republic*, the introduction of the cult of the Thracian goddess Bendis to the Peiraeus (*Republic* I 327A). Socrates is the only character these dialogues share. The *Timaeus/Critias* and *Republic* differ in their literary form: the *Republic* is a narrative dialogue, the *Timaeus* dramatic. The widest gap separating the two dialogues is Socrates' silence in the *Timaeus* Prologue concerning his notorious proposal of the philosopher king in the *Republic* (V 473C-D, elaborated throughout books V-VII) in the conversation recounted in the *Timaeus*. (See note 13 on *Timaeus* 19A.)

TIMAEUS: Indeed, and the state you described was agreeable to the thinking of us all.

SOCRATES: Now tell me, did we[2] not distinguish the class of farmers and the class of all other artisans as separate from the class of those who would fight for the city?[3]

TIMAEUS: We did.

SOCRATES: **(17D)** And once we had assigned to each class the single occupation, the single craft that is naturally suited to it, we said that those whose duty it was to fight on behalf of all should be the sole guardians of the city, whether a stranger from without or a citizen from within should set about to harm it, **(17E)** and that they should be mild in judging those under their rule and consider them as naturally their kin, but that they should be harsh to the enemies they encounter in battle.[4]

TIMAEUS: That was exactly it.

SOCRATES: I believe that we were saying that in the character of their souls our guardians had to be both exceptionally spirited and at the same time exceptionally philosophical, so that they could be appropriately mild or harsh in their dealings with both groups.[5]

TIMAEUS: We did.

SOCRATES: And what did we say of their education—that they should be trained in gymnastics and "music,"[6] and all the instruction that is proper to them?[7]

TIMAEUS: Exactly.

SOCRATES: **(18B)** And I think that we said that the guardians who have re-

---

2   "We" recalls the fiction and metaphor Socrates maintains in *Republic* II-IX that he, Glaucon, and Adeimantus are the founding fathers (*oikistai*) of their theoretical state; cf. especially *Republic* II 378E and IV 427B.

3   The initial segregation of the warrior class from the single class of artisans and farmers is made in *Republic* II 370 A-D.

4   Two considerations come into play here. First is the conception of performing exclusively the function within a state for which a citizen is suited by nature. This conception of justice is suggested dimly in *Republic* II 370A and then more fully in II 374B-D and IV 433D-E. The seemingly ambiguous temperament of the guardian class is first described in *Republic* II 375C.

5   The "philosophical" characteristic of the guardian class involves their canine ability to distinguish between friends and foes, *Republic* II 375E-377A.

6   That is, education in both poetry and the music that was an integral part of it, *Republic* II 376E. What we consider musical training is taken up in III 398B-409A.

7   Socrates lays out the program for educating his guardian class in *Republic* II 376E - IV 427C.

ceived this education should not consider gold or silver or any other possession as their own personal property, but they should receive a wage from those whose safety they guarantee, as their auxiliaries and defenders, as much as is right for prudent men, and that they should spend this for their community and live their lives in close association, concerned only with their virtue for all of their lives and keeping free of all other occupations.[8]

TIMAEUS: The argument was as you describe it.

SOCRATES: **(18C)** And then we did not leave women out of our account, but we said that we had to bring their characters into harmony to make them as much like the character of men as possible, and that we should assign to all of them activities to be shared with men, both in war and in the other occupations of life.[9]

TIMAEUS: The proposal was what you describe.

SOCRATES: And what was said about their having children, or is this impossible to forget because of the novel character of our proposals? In the matter of marriages and the getting and raising of children we established a community for all and a system in which no father could recognize the offspring of these marriages as his own child; rather the guardians were to recognize all children as part of one family. **(18D)** They should treat as brothers and sisters all children of the appropriate age, and all those who are older by a generation or two as parents and grandparents, and those who are born in the next generations as children and grandchildren.[10]

TIMAEUS: Yes, as you state it now, this is easy to recall.

SOCRATES: And do you not remember that the male and female rulers were to strive to make sure, so far as they are able, that, when it came time to shut a couple up in a wedding chamber, their children should be of the best breed possible and that the rulers should covertly arrange a kind of lottery to assure that superior and inferior parents should be kept apart by having them draw lots that would join them to women who were like them; **(18E)** and that, to avoid any resentment arising from these arrangements, they should lead the couples to believe that Fortune was responsible for their mating?[11]

---

[8] *Republic* II 374B-D and III 415D-417B.
[9] By this he means all women who have the characteristics desired in the guardian class.
[10] This idea, hinted at in *Republic* IV 423E and set out under the provocation of Polemarchus in V 457B-461C, will sweep away the fundamental Greek institution of the family (*oikos*).
[11] *Republic* V 458E-460A.

TIMAEUS: We recall.

SOCRATES: **(19A)** And did we not make the proposal that it is necessary for the rulers to raise the children of superior parents, but the other children of inferior parents should be distributed throughout the rest of the city under the cloak of secrecy. And, as these children of inferior parents grow up, the rulers ought to consider returning to their proper station in life those who are worthy of it; but that they must reduce to the station of those who are to be promoted to the guardian class those among the children of the guardians they find unworthy?[12]

TIMAEUS: Yes, it was exactly as you describe it.

SOCRATES: Now tell me, have we completely covered our argument as we made it yesterday and have we given a summary of our main topics or do we still need to add some details of what we said then?

TIMAEUS: Not at all, Socrates, these were our arguments exactly.[13]

His review of this state ended, Socrates describes to his companions what he would like to hear in sequel, and lays out the difficulties of the project he has in mind.

SOCRATES: **(19B)** Now, if you like, you can hear the sequel to our description of the state and what my reaction to it is. I would describe this reaction by the following comparison. Imagine that you had seen some magnificent animals either rendered in a painting or actually alive, but motionless, and then conceived the desire to observe them in motion and to exercise one of the feats that seem appropriate to their bodies in a test of strength. Such was my reaction to the city we have described. **(19C)** And I would be delighted to hear someone describe as a part of this tale the trials that put this city to the test—trials that pit this city against other cities and, most fittingly, tell us how it engaged in war and gave proper return for its training and education both in the deeds it performs and in the words it employs in its negotiations with each of the other states.

Urge to give life to the image

---

[12] *Republic* V 460E.
[13] Socrates has not mentioned, and Timaeus appears to have forgotten—if he ever heard—the discussion at *Republic* V 473C-D. Here, Socrates proposes that "there can be no end to evils for cities or for the human race unless philosophers become kings in our cities or those who are now styled kings and potentates become true and competent philosophers." Plato repeats this conviction in *Epistle* VII 711D.

(19D) This speech in praise of these men and this city is, Critias and Hermocrates, something that in my verdict I could never deliver properly myself. There is nothing extraordinary about my limitations. I have formed the same opinion about the poets, both those who lived long ago and those of this present age, and my opinion is in no derogation of the race of poets; but it is clear to everyone that the tribe of imitators can imitate best and most easily what it has been reared in. Objects that lay outside the education of these artists prove difficult to imitate accurately in action and still more difficult to imitate in discourse.

(19E) And, as for the tribe of sophists, I think that it has great experience in many forms of discourse and many other fine things. But I fear that because it is a race of vagabonds traveling from city to city and has never settled down in a fixed manner of life, it could never take a proper aim at either philosophers or statesmen and hit accurately what these men might do or say as they engage in war and its battles and associate with others in deed and word. The one alternative remaining is the race of men of your disposition, men who by their nature and their training participate in both philosophy and statesmanship.

Socrates now assigns their speeches to each of his companions.

(20A) Timaeus here is the citizen of a city of excellent laws—the city of Locris[14] in Italy. In wealth and family he is second to none of his fellow citizens and he has served in the highest offices of his city and enjoyed the greatest honors. And, in my opinion, he has attained the heights of all the summits of philosophy. And, as for Critias, all of us who are Athenians know that he is no stranger to the subjects we are speaking of.[15] And there are many witnesses to the fact that the native talent and education of Hermocrates are adequate to all these requirements, and we should trust their

---

[14] Locris is a Greek colony sent out from mainland Greece and founded on the tip of the toe of Italy at the end of the eighth century BC. It was long governed by an oligarchy of one hundred houses, and its lawgiver, Zaleukos, enjoyed a great reputation in antiquity for his severe code of laws. In Plato's *Laws*, the Athenian says of the Locrians that "they have the reputation of being the best-governed state in that part of the world," *Laws* I 638B. "Best-governed" (*eunomotatoi*) is Socrates' word for Locris here in the *Timaeus* Prologue.

[15] This remark can only apply to Plato's relative, Critias (his mother's first cousin), notorious for his part in the rule of the "thirty tyrants" in 404-403. The Critias of Plato's "Atlantis" (to give his epic an epic title) and *Charmides* (ca. 460-403) was the author of a variety of poetic works and an elegiac poem on the constitution of Sparta; for this, cf. DK 88 A 32-37 and B 6-9.

testimony.[16] **(20B)** This explains why it was that yesterday, when you asked me to describe the state, I was happy to oblige. I was well aware, as I considered the matter, that no one other than yourselves could more satisfactorily complete the argument that was to follow, if you were willing to speak. For, once you had brought our city to a state of preparedness for a war worthy of it, you alone, of all men of this age, would better render, if you were willing, fitting conduct for that city. Now that I have given the speech that you assigned to me, I in my turn have assigned to you the theme I have now described. And you agreed, as you had all of you deliberated together how to return the hospitality of my speech. **(20C)** I am here now and dressed in all my finery for this purpose and more prepared than anyone to receive hospitality.

Hermocrates introduces to Socrates the speech that Critias will offer.

HERMOCRATES: And, indeed, Socrates, as Timaeus here said, you will not find that we are lacking in eagerness nor do we have any excuse not to do as you ask. It is for this reason that yesterday, as soon as we arrived here at Critias' house and the guest rooms where we are staying—and even earlier on our way here—we considered our responsibilities. **(20D)** Critias here introduced us to an account of great antiquity. Repeat this account for Socrates, Critias, so that he can determine with us whether it is suitable or not to answer to the task you have set us.

CRITIAS: This is what we must do, if this is agreeable to Timaeus, our third partner, as well.

---

16 Hermocrates of Syracuse was one of the most important leaders in Sicily during the period of the Peloponnesian War. One striking witness to his talent and education was Thucydides, who gives a long account of Hermocrates' organization in Sicily of the opposition to the Athenian invasion of 415-413 and praises his intelligence and courage (VI 72.1). The speeches he gave first at Syracuse and then at Kamerina (VI 32.3-34 and 75.3-80) which might give us a hint of the speech he would have given in the last part of this "tetralogy"—the unwritten *Hermocrates*—are given below (**I 3**, "What Hermocrates Said"). These two speeches suggest the significance of his silence in the Timaeus trilogy. In his speech at the congress in Kamerina, he argues that just as Athens has enslaved the rest of Greece she will now attempt to enslave Sicily (VI 76.4). His strong word "enslave" is the word often used to describe Persia's ambitions on Greece, and the word Critias uses to describe Atlantis' designs on the Mediterranean and Athens herself (*Timaeus* 25C, below); cf. Herodotus 1.27 (of barbarian and Greek) and 1.94 (of Persian and Greek); Plato *Republic* I 351B and *Menexenus* 239D. Comparable in thought is the language of Aeschylus *Persians* 234, 402-405, and 745.

TIMAEUS: Indeed, it is.

Critias introduces the extraordinary tale he had once heard as a boy from his aged great-grandfather, Critias, who had heard it from his father, Dropides, who had heard it from Solon himself.

CRITIAS: Good. Now, Socrates, listen to an extraordinary tale, but a tale of absolute truth, as Solon, the wisest of the seven sages once told it. **(20E)** Solon was a relation of our great-grandfather Dropides,[17] and his great friend, as he himself often states in his poetry. Dropides told Critias, our great-grandfather, that there were great, amazing, and ancient deeds accomplished by this city which have been effaced by time and the destruction of our citizens—as the old man related this to us in turn. **(21A)** One of these was the greatest of all, and it might be fitting for us to recall it as thanks to you and at the same time as a just and truthful hymn, as it were, and speech of praise for the goddess on the occasion of her festival.[18]

SOCRATES: An excellent suggestion. But, tell us Critias, what is this deed, which is not a matter of words, but was accomplished in reality by this city of ours in ancient times and comes from a tradition passed down by Solon?

CRITIAS: **(21B)** I will declare it. I heard the ancient account given by a man who was not then a young man. Now at that time Critias was, as he said, already near ninety years old, and I could not have been more than ten years old. It happened to be the day of the festival

---

[17] In another source Dropides was said to be Solon's brother. By one genealogy, Plato would stand "sixth from Solon," as Diogenes Laertius puts it in his *Lives of the Philosophers*, III 1. Dropides is uncommon as a personal name and he is not mentioned in the remains of Solon's poetry.

[18] This is the festival of Athena or the Panathenaia—the most important of the three festivals mentioned in this "tetralogy." It was a festival that attracted many visitors from all over the Greek world, and it was the occasion for the meeting between the young Socrates and the aged Parmenides in Plato's *Parmenides*. The occasion of the *Republic* was the Bendidea or the new festival held in the Peiraeus in honor of the Thracian goddess Bendis; and the occasion for the aged Critias telling the story of Atlantis to his grandson was the Apatouria. In order to link the *Republic* and *Timaeus*, the Neoplatonist commentator Proclus made a mistake only possible in the fifth century AD: he located the Bendidea just before the Panathenaia in the religious calendar of Athens. Actually, they are months apart. Plato's *Timaeus* is our first piece of evidence for speeches in praise of Athens as part of the Panathenaia; later, in 342 (seven years after Plato's death) Isocrates produced his *Panathenaikos*.

of the Apatouria we call Koureotis.[19] For those of us who were boys the festival followed its usual course, and our fathers set a contest for rhapsodic performances. There were many recitations from the poems of many poets and, since they were new at the time, many of us boys sang the poems of Solon. **(21C)** And one of the people who belonged to our phratry—either because this was his true opinion or because he wanted to please Critias—said that he believed that Solon was a man of supreme wisdom in all other things but in respect to his poetry he was most liberal of all poets. And the old man, who was mightily pleased, smiled and said—I recall his words vividly: "Amynander, if he had not treated poetry as a pastime, but took it seriously as do other poets, and if he had not been compelled by the civil strife provoked by evil citizens and the other disturbances he encountered on his return to put it aside,[20] **(21D)** in my personal opinion neither Hesiod nor Homer nor any other poet you could name would be more famous than he."[21] And he asked: "Critias, what was his theme?" "Well now," he answered, "it concerned the greatest of actions and one that can rightly be called the greatest of all actions—one

---

[19] This was the third day of the festival of the Apatouria (celebrated in October) reserved for the recognition the young men (and infants) who were to be enrolled in their phratries ("brotherhoods"). All male children born since the last Apatouria were introduced to their large kinship group and all young men (*kouroi*) who had grown to be *epheboi* (i.e., reached the age of puberty) were introduced or reintroduced and were made citizens. (The month of the Apatouria, Pyanepsion, fell nine months after the Attic month of Gamelion, the marriage month.) The name for the festival probably derives from Ionia and the kinship term *apatores*, those descended from the same *father* (*pater*, cf. Herodotus I 147), but some Greeks derived it from the word for deception *apate*.

[20] After Solon had served as archon and lawgiver during the social and economic crisis of 594, he left Athens for a period of years so he would not be forced to interpret the laws he had enacted; in his *Life of Solon* 25.4-29, Plutarch describes Solon's travels and the chaos he discovered on his return to Athens. Herodotus also attests to Solon's visit to Egypt (I 30.1) and reports that he derived an Athenian law from Egypt, requiring that each man report his occupation to the government each year (II 177.2).

[21] This statement of the elder Critias seems to explain the unfinished state of the *Critias*. Since both Solon's epic on Atlantis and his failure to complete it are Plato's inventions, it is significant for the interpretation of this projected tetralogy that Solon's "Atlantis" was left unfinished because of the civil discords of historical Athens. The unfinished state of Plato's *Critias* had two explanations in antiquity: the first took the hypothesis of Plato's *Timaeus/Critias* seriously and attributed its unfinished state to Solon's failure to complete it (Plutarch *Life of Solon* 26.1 and 31.6); the second sought the explanation in an illness that prevented Plato from finishing it (Ibid. 32.21).

that our city Athens accomplished then, but which, in the passage of time and the destruction of those who brought it to pass, has no history that has reached our age." Amynander asked him: "Tell it from its beginning: What was Solon's account? How did he tell it? And who assured him of its truth?"

(21E) And he said: "There is in Egypt a district in the region of the Delta at its apex where the current of the Nile divides into two streams; it is called the nome of Sais.[22] In this nome the largest city is Sais. King Amasis came from this very city. Its inhabitants have a principal protector goddess whose name in Egyptian is Neith; but in Greek, according to the account of the people of Sais, it is Athena.[23] The people of Sais are very fond of Athenians and they claim that in some manner they are related to the Athenians.

How Solon visited Sais on his travels to Egypt

"Now, when he had journeyed to this city, Solon said that he was shown very great consideration by its inhabitants. **(22 A)** And he went on to say that on one occasion, when he asked the priests who were most versed in history about the antiquities of Sais, he discovered that neither he nor any other Greek knew anything that amounted to anything about such things. One day, when he wanted to start a conversation with the priests about ancient history, he attempted to discourse on the most ancient events of Athenian history—about Phoroneus,[24] who is said to be the first human, and about Niobe, and then he went on to tell the tale of Deucalion, and Pyrrha and how they survived after the flood, **(22 B)** and to give a genealogy of their descendants. And, as he recalled this history, he said that he attempted to produce a chronology for the history he had given. And one of the priests who

---

[22] *Nomos* is Greek for a "district" of Egypt.

[23] Sais is now actually on the western arm of the Nile which divides near Giza. Amasis (Amosis II) was king of Egypt in the 26th dynasty. He deposed Apries in 570 BC and ruled until 526. One of the reasons for the identification of Neith with Athena was her emblem (a shield) of crossed arrows; like Athena, she could be seen as a warrior goddess.

[24] According to Argive legends Phoroneus was the son of the river Inachos and the first human. The traditions are recalled by Pausanias in his *Guide to Greece* (II 15.5). The mythographer Apollodorus gives a catalogue of his descendants in his *Library* (II.1). Apollodorus' history makes contact with Egypt in the generation of Io, daughter of Inachos. There are a few fragments of an archaic epic, the *Phoronis* (collected in Malcolm Davies, *Epicorum Graecorum Fragmenta* [Göttingen 1988] 153-155).

was a very old man said to him: 'Solon, Solon,[25] you Greeks are eternal children, there is not such thing as an aged Greek.' On hearing this he asked: 'What do you mean by that?' The priest answered: 'Your souls are those of young men. For in your souls you possess no ancient learning that is passed down by venerable tradition nor any knowledge that has grown gray with the passage of time. I shall tell you the reason for this.

The aged priest now explains the archaeology of Greek ignorance.

(22C) "'There have been many destructions of humankind of many kinds, as there will be in the future. Fire and water have produced the greatest of these, but there have been others of shorter duration that have been brought about by countless other causes. Now your own tradition of Phaethon is one example: once Phaethon, the son of Helios, yoked the chariot of his father and, because he was not able to drive along the path of his father, scorched the surface of the earth and perished by being struck by a thunderbolt himself. This legend wears the face of a myth, (22D) but in reality there is a regular alteration in the movement of the heavenly bodies around the earth and this occurs at long intervals and causes devastation of the surface of the earth by great conflagrations.[26] On these occasions all those who live on the mountains, at high elevations, and in dry areas are more readily destroyed than men living in the neighborhood of rivers and the sea.

The providential location of Egypt described

"'But the Nile, which is our savior in many other ways,[27] preserves us on these occasions too by coming into flood. Now when the gods cleanse the earth again by sending a deluge of rains, the cowherds and shepherds survive, but those of you who live in cities are carried out to sea by rivers in flood. (22E) But in our

---

[25] The repetition of Solon's name recalls and reverses the import of the words of Croesus in Herodotus, when, at the point of death, he recalls the wisdom of Solon's counsel ("Count no man happy before he is dead") and calls out "Solon, Solon, Solon" (I 86; cf. I 29-33 on Solon and Croesus).

[26] The priest's description of these cosmic alternations in the movement of the heavens coheres closely with the myth of Plato's *Statesman*. Here the Eleatic Stranger describes two phases in the rotation of the heavenly bodies around the earth: one from west to east; the other from east to west (269D-274E). The first obtained under the age of Kronos, the second after the crime of Atreus, who served his brother the flesh of his children.

[27] The priest is recalling the conception of Egypt as the "gift of the Nile," as Herodotus describes it (II 5.1).

country neither at that time or any other time does water flood from high places down onto the fields, but the opposite phenomenon prevails and waters rise from the valley of the Nile below. These are the reasons why our history reaches back to the most remote antiquity. **(23A)** But in fact, in all regions where neither excessive rains or heat prevent it, the human race always increases in numbers, but in natural calamities it is reduced.

"'All we know by oral tradition that has occurred, either in your country, or in Egypt, or some other place, has been written down and preserved in our sanctuaries in Egypt for ages, if it has proved noble or great or if it is remarkable in some other way. But in your country and in other countries, during each period of recovery the art of writing has been discovered only recently to record these events, as have the other necessities of civilized life. But, once again, a deluge pours down from heaven and comes upon you in fixed intervals like a disease, and leaves those of you who survive without writing and without culture. **(23B)** And so you revert to your origins like young things who know nothing either of our history of ancient times or of your own. The genealogy, Solon, which you just delivered describing your own past is a case in point. It is not much different from a nursery tale. You can remember only a single deluge that covered the earth, although many occurred before that. What is more, you do not know that the noblest and best race to arise among humankind arose in your territory. From these, your ancestors, you, and your entire city came to be what it is now, **(23C)** developing from the tiny seed that survived that deluge. But you have no idea of this race because those who survived over many generations died without a voice, since they did not possess writing.

The priest begins the forgotten story of Prehistoric Athens.

"'Now, Solon, at one time, before the cataclysmic destruction by deluge, the present city of Athens was pre-eminent in warfare and in all respects it was governed better than all other cities.[28] We have received the report of its surpassingly noble exploits and its forms of government which are said to have been the fairest[29] of all cities under the sun.' **(23D)** Solon said that he was amazed when he had heard this, and, with great excitement, he asked the priests to give him an exact and full history of these

---

28   This is the adjective, *eunomotatoi*, by which Socrates had described Timaeus' city of Locris, *Timaeus* 20A.
29   This adjective recalls the name Socrates gave to his perfect city in the *Republic*, Kallipolis (Fair City), *Republic* VII 527C.

ancient states. The priest replied: 'Solon, I have no reason to grudge you this. For your sake and your city's sake I will tell you—and most of all for the sake of the goddess who received your city and this city as her portion, and reared and educated us. Your city came before ours by 1,000 years **(23E)** and her seed came from Earth and Hephaestus.[30] Our city came later. Now, the date for the origins of our civilization, as recorded in our sacred writings, goes back 8,000 years. I will now reveal to you in brief compass the institutions of your citizens some 9,000 years ago and the greatest of the deeds they accomplished. We can examine the written record and go through the precise account of all of this, set out in its proper order, **(24A)** at another occasion, when we have the leisure.

The priest declares that some of the customs of the prehistoric Athenians are to be discovered in the present customs of Egypt.

"'First of all, I want you to compare their institutions with those of our country. If you look, you can discover here in Egypt examples of the kind of life that existed at that time in your country. The first that comes to mind is the fact that the class of priests is segregated from the other classes; the next point of comparison is the class of artisans; each guild performs its own work and does not meddle with the work of other classes. And then there is the class of herdsmen, of hunters, and of farmers.[31] **(24B)** And you have probably noticed that here in Egypt the military class is segregated from all the other classes; their duty has a single command—war and preparedness for war. Consider too the fashion of their shields and lances. We were the first of the peoples neighboring Asia to employ these arms. Our goddess revealed these to us, just as she revealed them to the inhabitants of your country before us. And you can see as well the great attention our law in Egypt has paid from our very beginnings to developing human intelligence concerning the world. **(24C)** In our progress, we have

---

[30] Or from earth and fire. The reference to earth is an acknowledgment of the Athenian tradition of autochthony, expressed dramatically for Athens by Euripides in his *Ion* 275-270. Erichthonios was the first Athenian to spring up from the soil of Athens. The autochthony of the Athenians is matched by the pretension to autochthony of the Atlanteans; see **I 2**, *Critias* 109C-D, 114C and Socrates' mock funeral oration in *Menexenus* 237B.

[31] This reproduces the three-tiered class system of Plato's *Republic*, except that the "true" or philosophical guardians of that polity are represented by the Egyptian caste of priests, and the lowest class of the *Republic* is divided into artisans and farmers. But the conception of justice as "performing one's proper function" remains the same.

made discoveries of all sciences, including divination and medicine, and we have applied these divine arts to health and the world of humans. Our civilization has mastered all the other branches of knowledge that depend upon these.

"'Such in that age was the general frame and ordering of your civilization, a civilization that the goddess created when she founded your city before ours. She chose the location in which you were born, because she appreciated the temperate balance of your seasons, and knew that this land would produce men of great prudence and intelligence.[32] (24E) For the goddess is devoted both to war and to wisdom, and she chose the land which would bear men who resembled her most closely when she founded your city.

"'You lived, then, with institutions such as I have described and a life even better regulated than ours. In comparison with all the rest of mankind you were outstanding in every form of virtue, as one would expect of a people produced and educated by the gods. Many and great are the exploits of your city that are recorded in the writings of our city and these are the objects of our admiration. Now, of all these, one stands out for its magnitude and for its great worthiness.

How the Empire of Atlantis came to threaten ancient Athens

(24E) "'These writings record how mighty was the power that your city brought to a halt as it made its progress in its invasion of all of Europe and of Asia as well, threatening you from beyond the Mediterranean and from the Atlantic Ocean. In that age that Ocean could be crossed. Opposite the straits which you call, as you tell us, the Pillars of Heracles[33] this island was greater than Libya and Asia combined. So the sea was at that time navigable to those who sailed to other islands and from these islands they

---

[32] The notion that climate influences character appeared in the fifth century; harsh climates and soil difficult to cultivate were thought to produce the best warriors and the most skilled and intelligent citizens (Hippocrates *On Airs, Water, Places* 24; Herodotus IX 122). Critias, however, contrasts a fertile prehistoric Athens (whose citizens were competent) with the eroded and barren historical Athens, *Critias* 111B-E.

[33] These are the Straits of Gibraltar and the narrow entrance into the Mediterranean. For the Greek navigators the Pillars of Heracles were the end of the world to the far west (Figure 3). In the geography of the *Phaedo* the eastern and western limits of the known world are the river Phasis to the east and the Pillars of Heracles to the west (Plato *Phaedo* 109A; cf. Strabo III 5.5). The Pillars of Heracles become a metaphor for the limits of human aspiration, as in Pindar *Isthmian* IV 12.

could cross in stages to all parts of the continent that lay opposite and bordered this sea, **(25A)** a sea that can be truly called a sea.[34] The entire interior region within the straits we speak of gives the appearance of a lake with a very narrow entrance for ships. But the land containing that Ocean which is truly an Ocean could be justly called a continent. Now, on this island of Atlantis there arose a great and wondrous and mighty nation of kings whose power extended over the entire island and reached to many other islands and regions of the continent. **(25B)** And in addition to these, the kings ruled over Libya within our Mediterranean up to the borders of Egypt and Europe as far west as Etruria. And the entire power of Atlantis gathered into a single force and at that time attempted to enslave in a single invasion your country and our own country as well as the entire Mediterranean.

"'It was at this time, Solon, that the might of your city displayed itself in its valor and strength to the entire world. In her serene courage she employed all the arts of warfare, as she stood at the head of all the other states. **(25C)** She was leader of all Greek states, but of necessity she was left to stand alone when other nations had abandoned her cause.[35] She faced the most terrible dangers and prevailed. And she set up a trophy of the arms of the invaders, and prevented those peoples who had not yet been enslaved from being enslaved and magnanimously emancipated all the other peoples who lived within the boundaries of Heracles. But afterwards, earthquakes and floods of incredible violence struck, and, in one terrible day and night, your entire warrior class disappeared as one body beneath the earth, **(25D)** and in this same calamity the island of Atlantis sank into the sea and disappeared. This explains why that distant sea cannot be navigated and resists exploration even now, since the mud produced as the island sank covers its surface to a great depth.'"

Critias concludes his brief account of the story he had heard from his grandfather and wonders at the vividness of his childhood memory.

(25E) There, Socrates, you have heard what the aged Critias said on the authority of the report of Solon, as I have given it to you in a brief version. And listening to you speaking yesterday about

---

[34]   See Figure 13, The world of the *Timaeus/Critias.*

[35]   In her heroic isolation, prehistoric Athens resembles the historical Athenians who defeated the Persians on the plain of Marathon in 490 BC. Athens was then abandoned by the states of northern Greece, and the Spartans arrived too late on the day after the decisive land battle (Herodotus VI 120; Plato *Menexenus* 240C-D; *Laws* III 698E).

the state and men you were describing, I was struck by the coincidence, and recalled the story I told now. By an amazing coincidence that was not a coincidence, much of what you said resembled what Solon said. **(26A)** At the time, I did not want to say anything, because I had heard Solon's story so long ago that I could not recover all of it. And I realized that, if I was going to speak as I have now, I would have to review it completely in my mind. This explains why I was so ready to agree to your proposal yesterday. I thought that I could contribute a speech that would meet your requirements and meet the most difficult requirements in all such situations, and I thought that we would have solved our difficulties with this speech. So it was, as Hermocrates has said, that, as soon as I left this place, I recalled all these details to my companions here, and, after I left them, I spent the night reviewing and recovering virtually the entire story. **(26B)** I can report to you that the old wisdom, that children have amazing memories for what they learn, is true. I do not know if I could recall everything that I heard yesterday, but I would be astonished if I have forgotten any detail of what I heard ages ago. **(26C)** For I listened to it then with the enormous delight only a child can feel. The old man too was glad enough to tell me what I wanted to know, since I kept asking him questions. And as a result it has remained fast with me as if it had been branded into my memory and left an indelible picture. And then again at dawn I told this story to our company here so that they would have no lack of inspiration for their speeches as well as I for mine.

So, Socrates, I am now prepared to give my speech, to which all I have said is an introduction, not only touching on the most important topics, but just as I heard it, point by point. We will now transform the citizens and the city which you described to us yesterday as if they were creatures of a myth[36] to a state of reality here in Athens, **(26D)** and we will claim that city of yours was in reality this city, and we will claim too that the citizens you conceived of were those ancient citizens, who were our ancestors and whom the priest spoke of. In any case, they will match your description, and we will not misspeak if we say that your citizens are those who lived in that age. Each of us will join in and take his turn as we attempt as best we can to offer a speech that

---

[36] In the *Republic* (IV 450D and VII 540D) Socrates describes his imaginary state as what he would pray for (*kat' euchen*), in other words, "utopian." This becomes the most common equivalent of our term "utopian" in Greek. For the Greek equivalent of our term "utopian," see Introduction §1.

answers the tasks you have assigned to us. And so, Socrates, you have to consider if this speech we propose suits what you have in mind **(26E)** or if we should look for some other in its place.

SOCRATES: What other argument should we choose rather than this, Critias. It would be wonderfully suitable to this festival of the goddess now being celebrated because of its close connection with her.[37] And the fact that it is not a myth that has been invented but a true argument is, I suppose, a very important consideration. And let me ask you: How and from where else could we find other speeches, if we were to abandon these? There is no way and no where. No, you must invoke Good Luck and deliver your speeches, **(27A)** and I can be repaid for my speech of yesterday and listen in my turn.

CRITIAS: Socrates, consider now the program of entertainment that we have arranged for you. We decided that Timaeus should speak first. He is the most expert astronomer among us and he has devoted by far the most effort to understanding the nature of the universe. He will begin with the origin of the world and end with the birth of mankind. I will follow him, and, as if I were his successor, receive the humans who have come into being in his account. And as your successor, Socrates, I will receive some of those citizens of yours who have been trained in a superior education. And, according to the account of Solon and according to his law, I must introduce our ancestors to you as judges and make them citizens of this city.[38] **(27B)** These were the Athenians whom the report of the sacred inscriptions declared to have vanished from sight. But for the rest of my speech I will speak as if they were our fellow citizens and Athenians in reality.[39]

---

[37] That is, the glory of Athenian history is an eminently suitable theme for the Panathenaia, the greatest festival of the Athenian state. One of the great events of the Panathenaic festival were the speeches delivered in praise of Athens. (See note on *Timaeus* 21A, above). The difference between these speeches and the *Panathenaikoi logoi* of Socrates and Critias is that the former took place at a large public gathering, while Socrates spoke to a company of nine in the house of Cephalus in the Peiraeus, and Critias to an even smaller company of three.

[38] Critias is reenacting on the occasion of the Apatouria the ceremony by which he himself had been recognized as an Athenian citizen and a member of his phratry. (See note on *Timaeus* 21B, above.)

[39] Critias will take up his speech at *Critias* 106B, after Timaeus has finished his speech. We are left in the dark about what Hermocrates would have said, but, as noted above (on *Timaeus* 20A), his two speeches in book VI of Thucydides' *The Peloponnesian War* throw some light on the praise of contemporary Athens that might have come as a sequel to Critias' speech and are given below **(I 3)**.

SOCRATES: The festival of speeches that will entertain me in return for mine strikes me as a brilliant arrangement with nothing wanting. It is now your task, as it seems, Timaeus, to follow this introduction and give your speech, after you have followed custom and called upon the gods.

2. The *Critias*

Timaeus concludes the speech that he had agreed to give on the occasion of the Panathenaia.

TIMAEUS: **(106A)** What a pleasure it is, Socrates, to have completed the long march of my argument.[40] I feel the relief of the traveler who can rest after a long journey. Now I offer my prayer to that god who had existed in fact long before in reality, but who has now been created in my words. **(106B)** My prayer is that he grant the preservation of all that has been spoken properly; but that he will impose the proper penalty if we have, despite our best intentions, spoken any discordant note. For the musician who strikes the wrong note the proper penalty is to bring him back into harmony. To assure, then, that in the future we will speak as we should concerning the origin of the gods we pray that he will grant the best and most perfect remedy—understanding. And, now that we have offered our prayer, we will keep our agreement and hand over to Critias the speech that is to follow ours in its proper sequence.

CRITIAS: Very well, Timaeus, I will accept the task, but I will make the same plea as you made at the beginning of your speech, **(106C)** when you asked for our sympathy and understanding on account of the magnitude of the argument you were undertaking. **(107A)** I make this same entreaty now too, but I ask to be granted even greater understanding for what I am going to say. And I must admit that I realize that what I am pleading for is self-serving and a less polite request than it should be. But I must make it nevertheless. Now, who in his senses would undertake to maintain that your speech was not an excellent speech? As for the speech you are about to hear, I must somehow bring home to you the fact that it requires greater indulgence, given the difficulty of my subject. **(107B)** It is easier, Timaeus, for someone to give the impression that he is a successful speaker when he speaks of gods to an audience of mortals. The audience's lack of experience and

---

[40] Timaeus is referring to the long, unbroken speech he has just completed, on the origin of the world and humans (*Timaeus* 27C-92C).

sheer ignorance concerning a subject they can never know for certain supply the would-be speaker with great eloquence. We know how we stand when it comes to our knowledge of the gods. To make my meaning plainer, let me ask you to follow me in this illustration.

It is inevitable, I suppose, that everything we all have said[41] is a kind of representation and attempted likeness. Let us consider the graphic art of the painter that has as its object the bodies of both gods and men and the relative ease and difficulty involved in the painter convincing his viewers that he has adequately represented the objects of his art. **(107C)** We will observe first that we are satisfied if an artist is able to represent—even to some small extent—the earth and mountains and rivers and forests and all of heaven and the bodies that exist and move within it, and render their likeness; and next that, since we have no precise knowledge of such things, we do not examine these paintings too closely or find fault with them, **(107D)** but we are content to accept an art of suggestion and illusion for such things, as vague and deceptive as this art is. But, when a painter attempts to create a likeness of our bodies, we are quick to spot any defect, and, because of our familiarity and life-long knowledge, we prove harsh critics of the painter who does not fully reproduce every detail. We must view the case of speeches as precisely the same. We embrace what is said about the heavens and things divine with enthusiasm, even when what is said is quite implausible; but we are nice critics of what is said of things mortal and human.

Now, with these reflections in mind, which I have offered for the present occasion, **(107E)** if we are unable to speak fully and fittingly in representing our theme, we deserve your sympathy. You must realize that human life is no easy subject for representation, but rather one of great difficulty, if we are to satisfy people's opinions. **(108A)** I have reminded you of all this, Socrates, and spoken at this length, because I want to make a plea not for less but for greater sympathy and understanding for what I am about to say. If you find that I made a just claim on this favor, grant it with good will.

SOCRATES: Why, Critias, would we hesitate to grant it? Let this favor of ours

---

[41] By this, Critias might mean Socrates' speech on the occasion of the Panathenaia the day before (as reported at the beginning of the *Timaeus*) but he is certainly thinking of Timaeus' speech just completed.

be granted to Hermocrates as well who will follow you as the third to speak. It is clear that a little later, when it comes his turn to speak he will make the same entreaty as have you and Timaeus.[42] **(108B)** So to make it possible for him to invent another preamble and not compel him to repeat what Timaeus and Critias have said, let him speak when his turn comes, knowing that he has our sympathy. But now, my dear Critias, I must caution you about the attitude of your audience in this theater: the first of the poets to compete in it put on such a glorious performance that you will need a great measure of sympathy if you are going to be able to compete after him.

HERMOCRATES: The injunction you made to Critias here applies to me, Socrates, as well. **(108C)** But, even so, Critias, the fainthearted have never yet set up a victory monument. You must march bravely forward to encounter your speech, and, as you invoke Paion[43] and the Muses, display in your hymn of praise the bravery of your ancient citizens.

CRITIAS: Dear Hermocrates, you stand last in rank, but, since there is someone standing in front of you, you are still confident. That courage is needed, you will discover yourself, when you take my place. But I must pay attention to your exhortation and encouragement, **(108D)** and, in addition to the gods you just named, invoke the other gods and make a special prayer to Mnemosyne, the goddess of memory.[44] The success or failure of nearly everything that is most important in our speech lies in the lap of this goddess. If we can sufficiently recall and relate what was said long ago by the priests and brought here to Athens by Solon, you the audience in our theater will find, I am confident, that we have put on a worthy performance and acquitted ourselves of our task. So much said. Now we must act. Let us delay no more.

(108E) We should recall at the very beginning that, in very rough terms, it was some 9,000 years since the time when a war is recorded as having broken out between the peoples dwelling out-

---

[42] Critias has asked for understanding from his companions; at the beginning of his speech (*Timaeus* 27C-D) Timaeus had invoked the gods and goddesses.

[43] Apollo the healer. Hermocrates is also suggesting the paean (*paion* in Attic dialect) sung by a victorious army after a battle.

[44] The function of the Muses and their mother, Mnemosyne, was to inspire humans with a knowledge of the past that would be unavailable to them otherwise. In the *Iliad*, Homer invokes the Muses of Olympus before entering into the catalogue of ships: "You are goddesses, you are present and know everything, but we [mortals] hear only the report and know nothing" (*Iliad* II 485-486).

side the Pillars of Heracles and all those dwelling within.[45] This war I must now describe. Now they said that this city of Athens was the ruler of the [Mediterranean] peoples and fought for the duration of the entire war. They said, too, that the kings of the island of Atlantis were the rulers of the other peoples [of the Atlantic]. And we said that this island w̃ᵃˢ ᵃt one time greater than both Libya and Asia combined.[46] But now because of earthquakes it has subsided into the great Ocean and has produced a vast sea of mud that blocks the passage of mariners who would sail into the great Ocean from Greek waters **(109A)** and for this reason it is no longer navigable.[47]

In its progress, our tale will describe, as if it were unrolled, the many barbarian nations and all the different Greek peoples of that time, encountering them as they emerge from place to place. It is first necessary at the beginning of this tale to describe the condition of the Athenians of that age and the adversaries with whom they waged war: their respective power and their respective constitutions. But of these themes, pride of place must go to the condition of Athens before this war.

(109B) At one time, the gods received their due portions over the entire earth region by region—and without strife.[48] To claim that gods did not recognize what was proper to each would not be fitting, nor would it be right to say that, although they recognized what belonged by just title to others, some would attempt

---

[45] Critias repeats this same figure in *Critias* 111A (below). To be more precise, the war occurred some 9,000 years before Solon heard the Egyptian priest's account of it in the early sixth century; cf. *Timaeus* 23E.

[46] That is, two of the three massive divisions of the known world. Asia is defined by the Nile and Hellespont and Libya encloses the entire coast of Saharan Africa west of the Nile. The extent and history of the island of Atlantis is first mentioned in *Timaeus* 24E-25D (above). A map of this "O-T" world (see Introduction, §7) is given in Figures 5 and 6.

[47] The mud blocking navigation in the Atlantic might be recognized by Herodotus' account of the Persian Sataspes' attempt to circumnavigate Africa (then known as Libya) in the reign of Xerxes (485-464 BC), entering the Atlantic from the Straits of Gibraltar (IV 43.6); but it is first mentioned by Scylax in the fourth century who reports mud and sea-weed. His *Periplous* is probably to be dated between 361 and 357; see O. A. W. Dilke, *Greek and Roman Maps* (Ithaca, New York 1985) 133.

[48] The "strife" refers particularly to the Athenian tradition (commemorated on the west pediment of the Parthenon) of the struggle between Poseidon and Athena for possession of Attica. In Socrates' treatment of theological poetry in *Republic* II 378B-E such stories are to be banned from his new state. For the tradition of the strife between Poseidon and Athena, there is Pausanias' account in his *Description of Greece* I 24.5. Pausanias records a like contest between Poseidon and Athena for Argos, II 15.5.

to take possession of this for themselves—in open strife. But, as they received what was naturally theirs in the allotment of justice, they began to settle their lands. Once they had settled them, they began to raise us as their own chattel and livestock, as shepherds their sheep. **(109C)** But they did not compel us by exerting bodily force on our bodies, as do shepherds who drive their flocks to pasture by blows, but rather, by what makes a creature turn course most easily: as they pursued their own plans, they directed us from the stern, as if they were applying to the soul the rudder of Persuasion. And in this manner they directed everything mortal as do helmsmen their ships.

Now, as the gods received their various regions lot by lot, they began to improve their possessions. But, in the case of Hephaestus and Athena, they possessed a common nature, both because she was his sister of the same father and because they had entered the same pursuits in their love of wisdom and the arts. For this reason, they both received this land as their portion in a single lot, because it was congenial to their character and was naturally suited to them in its excellence and intelligence. **(109D)** And they fashioned in it good men sprung from the land itself[49] and gave them a conception of how to govern their society. The names of these first inhabitants have been preserved, but their deeds have perished on account of the catastrophes that befell those who succeeded them and the long passage of time intervening.

Those of their race who survived these successive destructions were, as I have said before,[50] left as an illiterate mountain people who had only heard the tradition of the names of the rulers of their territory and beyond these, only little of their deeds. Now, they were pleased to give their descendants the names of these rulers, **(109E)** even though they were unaware of their ancestors' virtues and institutions—except for some dim legends concerning each of them. Then, for many generations, these survivors and their children lived in distress for their survival and gave thought to their needs; they spoke only of supplying these needs, **(110A)** and had no interest in the events of the distant past. For it is in the train of Leisure that Mythology and Inquiry into the Past arrive in cities, once they have observed that for some peoples the necessities of life had been secured, but not before.

---

49   *Autochthones*, like the Atlanteans (*Critias* 113C-D). In Greek the word *chthon* means earth. Two of these inhabitants mentioned below in *Critias* 110A, Erichthonios and Erysichthon, have names revealing their chthonic origin.
50   Referring to the history of the Egyptian priest in *Timaeus* 22C.

This is why the names of the ancients have been preserved but not their deeds. I make this claim and cite as my evidence the statement of Solon who said that, in their account of the war of that time, the Egyptian priests gave for the most part names such as Cecrops and Erechtheus, and Erichthonios, and Erysichthon, **(110B)** and the names of most of the others which have come down in tradition before the generation of Theseus. And the same is true of the names of the women. Consider too the attributes of the goddess Athena and her statue. At that time the military training of women and men was common; for this reason the people of that age fashioned the statue of the goddess as armed to reflect that ancient custom—an indication that all the female and male creatures that live together in a flock can very well pursue in common **(110C)** and as much as is possible the special talents that are suited to each species.[51]

Now, at that time the other classes of citizens who dwelt in our city were engaged in manufacture and producing food from the earth, but the warrior class that had originally been separated from them by god-like men lived apart. They had all that was appropriate to their training and education. **(110D)** And none of them had any private possession, but they thought of all they had as the common property of all, and they asked to receive nothing from the other citizens beyond what they needed to live. Their activities were all of the activities that were spoken of yesterday, when the guardians proposed by our theory were discussed.[52]

Prehistoric Athens described

The report of the Egyptian priests concerning our territory was plausible and true. First of all, at that time its boundaries extended to the Isthmus of Corinth, and, on the rest of the mainland to the north, they extended to the summits of Kithairon and Parnes. **(110E)** And, descending to the east, the boundaries extended down to the region of Oropos to the north and they were defined by the Asopos river down to the sea. In its great fertility our land far surpassed every other, for it was then capable of supporting a great army of men who did not work the land. There is impressive evidence for this excellence. What has now survived of this land can rival any other in the variety and quality of its crops

---

[51]   Critias recalls the first of Socrates' political paradoxes in *Republic* V 451B-457C, also recalled in *Timaeus* 18C.

[52]   *Republic* V 461E-465D, recalled in *Timaeus* 17C-18C.

and the pasture it offers all species of animals. **(111A)** But at that time, our land produced all this not only of high quality but in great abundance. You might ask how this is credible and how our present land could possibly be called a vestige of our earlier land. From the interior this entire land extends a great distance into the sea as if it jutted out as a promontory. It so happens that the entire basin of the sea that surrounds it falls off precipitously. Many and great were the floods that occurred in the space of 9,000 years—for this is the number of years between that time and the present— **(111B)** and during this succession of natural disasters the soil was washed down from the high places. It did not form any considerable alluvial deposits, as in other regions, but it disappeared into the deep as in flood after flood it was continuously washed into the sea from all sides. What actually remains is like our small and barren islands, and, compared to the land it was once, Attica of today is like a skeleton revealed by a wasting disease, once all the rich topsoil has been eroded and only the thin body of the land remains. But in that age our land was undiminished and had high hills with soil upon them, **(111C)** and what we now call the Rocky Barrens were covered with deep rich soil. And on the mountains there were dense forests of which there still survives clear evidence. Some of our mountains can now grow just barely enough for bees, but it was not so long ago that [lofty trees grew there].[53] There can still be found intact rafters cut from trees that were felled and brought down to be used for the greatest building projects. And there were many trees that were cultivated for their fruit and they provided limitless fodder for flocks of sheep and goats.

Every year there was a harvest of Zeus-sent rain. **(111D)** It was not lost, as it is now, as it flows off the hard surface of the ground into the sea, but the deep soil absorbed the rain and it stored it away as it created a reservoir with a covering of clay soil above it; and, as it distributed the water it had absorbed from the high places into its hollows, it produced an abundant flow of water to feed springs and rivers throughout every region of the country. There are even today some sacred monuments at these ancient springs that are evidence of the truth of what we are now saying about our country.[54]

---

[53] There is a lacuna of a few words here in the manuscripts.

[54] Plato must have in mind the fountain house at the Ilissos first called Kallirhoe and then Enneakrounos by ancient sources. It is located in the area south of the acropolis excavated by John Travlos. Thucydides locates many monuments of great antiquity in this area, II 15.4-5; Travlos (1971) 289-298.

(111E) This was the nature of the countryside, and the land was cultivated with great skill, as we can reasonably conjecture, by farmers who were farmers in the true sense of the word and who devoted themselves to this single occupation—but farmers who had an eye for beauty and were of a truly noble nature, and who in addition possessed a most fertile land and water in abundance, and above this land, a climate and seasons that were most temperate.

As for the city itself, it was laid out at that time in a plan that I will now describe. First of all, the acropolis was very different then than it is now. **(112A)** A single night of torrential rain stripped the acropolis of its soil and reduced it to bare limestone in a storm that was accompanied by earthquakes. Before the destructive flood of Deucalion, this was the third such cataclysmic storm. In the past, the acropolis extended to the Eridanos and Ilissos, and held within its circuit the Pnyx and Mount Lykabettos facing the Pnyx, and it was entirely covered by soil and, except for some small outcroppings, level on top. **(112B)** Outside the acropolis and under its slopes there lived the class of artisans and those of the farmers who worked the neighboring land. But on the heights the class of warriors lived in isolation around the sanctuary of Athena and Hephaestus, as if they belonged to a single household, which they had enclosed by a single garden wall. On the far northern edge of the acropolis they inhabited common dwellings and ate together in common messes in buildings they had constructed for their winter quarters. And they had a supply of all that was needful for their communal institutions—**(112C)** both in buildings for themselves and for the priests. They made no use of gold or silver—possessions they never had any need of. But, in pursuing a mean between ostentation and servility, they built for themselves tasteful houses and they grew old in them in the company of their children and grand-children; for generation after generation they passed these dwellings down to descendants who were like themselves.[55] As for the south of the acropolis, when they left their orchards, gymnasia, and common messes, as they would for the summer season, they converted it to these uses.

There was a single spring in the location of the present acropolis, **(112D)** but it has been choked by the debris of the earthquakes [of that night] and its waters now flow only in a trickle about the

---

[55] Critias' description of the stability of the guardian class of prehistoric Athens echoes Socrates' idyllic description of the class of farmers, artisans, and merchants that make up his first city in *Republic* II 372A-C.

circuit wall.[56] But it provided the men of that age with an abundant supply of water, since it was situated in a location that made it neither too cold in the winter nor too hot in the summer.

This was the manner of their life: they were the guardians of their own citizens and the leaders of the rest of the Greek world, which followed them willingly. They kept their population stable as far as they could—both of men and women—for generation after generation, maintaining the population of those who had reached military age or were still of military age at close to 20,000 at most.

(112E) Such, to conclude, was the character of this people and such was their life generation after generation as they directed the life of their city and of Greece with justice. Their fame for the beauty of their bodies and for the variety and range of their mental and spiritual qualities spread through all of Asia and all of Europe. And the consideration in which they were held and their renown was the greatest of all the nations of that age.

Introduction to the history of the island of Atlantis

As for the state of those who went to war against them and the origins of that state, we will now freely reveal its history to you, our friends, as the common property of friends, if we have not lost the memory of what we heard when we were still boys. (113A) I must explain one small point before I enter into my history so that you will not be astonished as you hear Greek names frequently used for people who are not Greek. You will now learn the origins of these names. Solon, when he was contemplating his own poetic version of this legend and inquired into the meaning of these names, discovered that his Egyptian sources had been the first to record them, once they had translated their meaning into their own language. He, in his turn, recovered the meaning of each of these names and recorded it as he translated them into Greek. (113B) These very manuscripts were in the possession of my grandfather and they now remain in my possession. When I was a boy, I studied them carefully. Consequently, do not be astonished if you hear names that sound like Greek names; you now know their explanation.

How the god Poseidon fathered the race of the kings of Atlantis and created a precinct of concentric islands

---

[56] Probably the spring called Klepsydra which was in use in Mycenean times. There is another Mycenean spring on the north slope of the acropolis deep in the cave of Aglauros, see Travlos (1971) 73-75; 323-331.

What follows, approximately, was the introduction to the long account I heard then. As I said before concerning the distribution of territories among the gods, in some regions they divided the entire earth into greater apportionments and in others into lesser apportionments, **(113C)** as they established sanctuaries and sacrifices for themselves. So it was that Poseidon received as one of his domains the island of Atlantis, and he established dwelling places for the children he had fathered of a mortal woman in a place on the island that I shall describe.

Now seaward, but running along the middle of the entire island, was a plain which is said to have been the loveliest of all plains and quite fertile. Near this plain in the middle of the island and at about fifty stades distance was a uniformly low and flat hill.[57] Now, there lived on this hill one of the people of this island who had originally sprung up from the earth. **(113D)** His name was Evenor and he dwelt there with his wife Leucippe. They had an only child, a daughter by the name of Kleito. When this girl grew to marriageable age, both her mother and her father died. It was then that Poseidon conceived a desire for her and slept with her. To make the hill on which she lived a strong enclosure he broke it to form a circle and he created alternating rings of sea and land around it. Some he made wider and some he made narrower. He made two rings of land and three of sea as round as if he had laid them out with compass and lathe. **(113E)** They were perfectly equidistant from one another. And so the hill became inaccessible to humans. For at that time ships and the art of navigation had not yet come into existence.

And the god himself greatly beautified the island he had created in the middle to make it a dwelling suitable for a god. Because he was a god, he did this with little effort. He drew up two subterranean streams into springs. One gushed out in a warm fountain and the other in a cold fountain. And from the earth he produced all varieties of crops that were sufficient to his island. He sired five pairs of twin sons and he raised them to manhood. He divided the entire island of Atlantis into ten districts: to the first born of the first set of twins he gave as his portion the dwelling of his mother and the circular island, **(114A)** since it was the largest

Pythagoras

---

[57] There are three units of measure in Critias' description of the island of Atlantis and its divine and human improvements: the foot, the plethron (about 100 feet), and the stade (or *stadion*, about 600 feet). I have not converted these units of measure to allow the reader to calculate the proportions involved in the Greek.

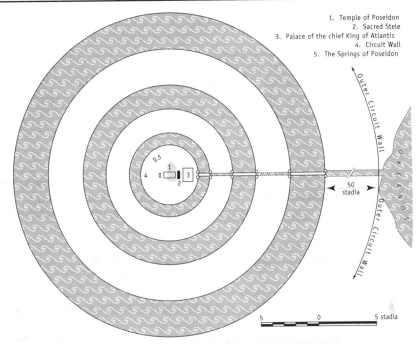

Figure 14 The capital of Atlantis, the works of Poseidon. Thomas Elliott, after Paul Friedländer.

and the best. And he made him king over the others. The other sons he made rulers (*archontes*) and to each of these he gave the rule over many men and a great extent of land.[58]

And he gave each of his sons names. To the son who was oldest and king he gave the name from which the entire island and its surrounding sea derive their names, because he was the first of the kings of that time. His name was Atlas; the island is called Atlantis and the sea Atlantic after him. **(114B)** The twin born after him received as his portion the cape of the island facing the Pillars of Heracles opposite what is now called the territory of Gadeira after this region. To him he gave the name that translates into Greek as Eumelos, but in the language of Atlantis, it is Gadeiros. It would seem that he gave his name to the region of Cadiz. The two brothers of the second set of twins he called

---

[58] Plato's choice of word for the rule of these kings is telling, for it points to an association between Atlantis and Athens of the fifth century. The nine kings appointed as *archontes* by the principal king of Atlantis correspond to the nine archons of Athens. See the discussion in Introduction §6.

Ampheres and the Euaimon. To the third set he gave the name Mneseas to the firstborn and Autochthon to the second born. **(114C)** Of the fourth set Elasippos was the firstborn, Mestor, the second. For the fifth set he gave the name Azaes to the firstborn and the name Diaprepes to the second.[59] Now all of these sons inhabited the island, as did their sons and descendants for many generations. They were the rulers of many other islands in the Atlantic and, as I have said,[60] they even extended their rule into the Mediterranean as near to us as Etruria and Egypt.

The island of Atlantis described, as are its flora, fauna, and rich mineral sources

(114D) The race of Atlas increased greatly and became greatly honored. And they maintained their kingdom through many generations, as the oldest king would hand his kingship on to his oldest son. They amassed more wealth than had ever been amassed before in the reign of any previous kings or could easily be amassed after them. And they provided for everything that was needed, both in the city and in the rest of the island. For their empire brought them many imports from outside, **(114E)** but the island itself provided most of what was needed for their livelihood. First, there were the mines that produced both hard and fusible ore. And in many regions of the island they exploited that metal which is now only a name to us, but which was then more than a name—oreichalkos.[61] In that age it was valued only less than gold. And the island provided all varieties of trees to be hewn and worked by builders and this in great abundance. It also produced abundant animal life, both domestic and wild. In addition to these there was a great population of elephants. There was pasture land for the other animals who graze in marshlands and along lakes and rivers and on mountainsides and plains, **(115A)** and this was plenty for them and as well as for the elephants, the greatest of all animals, which consume the most fodder.

The island produced all the aromatic plants the earth produces now—sweet smelling roots and greens, herbs, trees, and gums

---

[59] In Greek the meaning of these names is: Atlas, he who bears; Eumelos, he of many flocks; Ampheres, with oars on both sides; Euaimon, of noble blood; Mnaseas, he who remembers; Autochthon, earthborn; Elasippos, driver of horses; Mestor, adviser; the meaning of the name Azaes is uncertain, but it might be connected with the word Zeus or the Arcadian proper name, Azen; Diaprepes, outstanding.

[60] *Timaeus* 25A-B.

[61] Meaning "mountain copper" or yellow copper ore.

from flowers and fruits as well, and they flourished there. The island also produced the domesticated crop of grains on which we live and all the other crops on which we depend for our food. It also produced the kinds of crops we call "pulse" and **(115B)** the trees that give us our drink, food, and oils—and the crop that sprung up for the sake of our entertainment and pleasure, is hard to preserve, and comes from tree tops; it produced the side dishes we offer the weary guest as a relief after he has eaten his fill and that refresh him after dinner. All of these did that sacred island once bear in that age under a fostering sun—products lovely, marvelous, and of abundant bounty. And they took all these products from the earth, and from their proceeds they constructed their sanctuaries and their palaces, **(115C)** their harbors and their ship-sheds, and they improved the rest of their land according to the plan I will now describe.

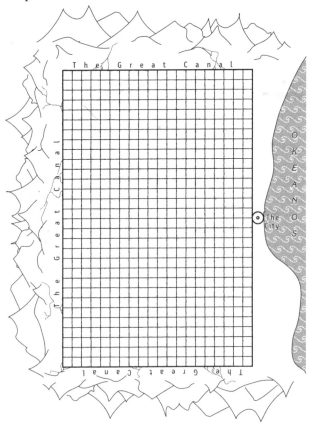

Figure 15 The main plain of the capital, the works of the kings of Atlantis. Thomas Elliott, after Paul Friedländer

How the succession of kings of Atlantis improved their metropolis

First, they constructed bridges spanning the rings of sea that sur-rounded the ancient metropolis, making a road out from the pal-ace and in to the palace. Their first project was to build a palace in the dwelling of the god and of their ancestors. One king inher-ited the project from his predecessor, and, **(115D)** as he improved on the beauty of what had already been improved, he would sur-pass to the extent of his resources what his predecessor had been able to achieve. They continued this progress until they had cre-ated for themselves a dwelling astonishing in its size and in its manifold beauty. Starting at the sea they excavated a canal three plethra in width, 100 feet in depth, and fifty stades in length up to the outermost sea ring. They then made the passage from the sea into the interior possible by opening a channel into the sea ring that was wide enough for the largest ships to sail into it as if it were a harbor. And, as for the land rings that separated the rings of sea, **(115E)** they pierced them at the point of the bridges, and thus joined them by water. The resulting canal was wide enough for a single trireme to sail through as it passed into a ring of water. They constructed a roof over the channel to protect the passage of ships, for the walls of the canal through the land rings were high enough from the sea to the bridge above to allow ships to pass under. The largest of the water rings into which the pas-sage from the sea had been excavated was three stades in width and the next land ring was equal to it. Of the next rings of water and land, the ring of water was two stades wide and, as in the first case, the land ring was equal to it as well. And, finally, the ring of water running around the island in the middle was a stade wide.[62]

(116A) The island where the palace was located had a diameter of five stades. They threw up an unbroken stone circuit wall around this island, and they also walled the land rings, and the bridge, which was a plethron wide. They built towers and gates at the point where the bridges crossed over the rings of water. They quarried stone from under the circular island that formed the center ring and from under the inner and outer land rings as well. There were three colors of stone: white, black, and red. As they quarried this stone, they fashioned ship-sheds for two ships in the rock roofed by the stone of the quarry itself.

---

[62] See Figure 14.

(116B) Some of their buildings they constructed of stones of uniform color. But to delight themselves they made of others a tapestry of stones of different colors, variegating the colors to bring out their natural charm. And they invested the entire circuit wall of the outermost land ring with bronze, as if the bronze revetment were a bright dye. The interior of the land wall they invested with tin. And the wall surrounding the acropolis itself they invested with oreichalkos, **(116C)** which glittered like darting fire.

The capital and works of Atlantis described

I will now describe the palace buildings erected within the acropolis. At its center was the shrine of Kleito and Poseidon. It was kept consecrated and no one was permitted to enter it. It was surrounded by a wall of gold. It was here that Poseidon and Kleito first begot and produced the race of the ten kings. It was to this shrine that each of the ten divisions came to offer their first fruits to each of the original kings in a yearly festival. There was the temple of Poseidon in this area one stade long, three plethra wide, **(116D)** and of a height that appeared to be proportional to its length and width, but it had something barbaric about its appearance.[63] They invested the entire exterior of the temple with silver, except for the acroteria, which they gilded with gold. The interior presented a roof of solid ivory inlaid with gold, silver, and oreichalkos; and they plated all the other areas of the temple with this same metal—the cella walls, the interior columns, and the floors. They placed gold statues within the temple: a statue of Poseidon standing in a chariot with a team of six winged horses. **(116E)** This statue was so tall that his head touched the rafter of the temple roof. There were 100 Nereids riding dolphins and arranged in a circle [about Poseidon]—men of that age thought that the Nereids were 100 in number.[64] There were many other statues inside which were the offerings of private individuals.

Outside and surrounding the temple there stood gold statues of all the descendants of the ten kings and their wives and many other offerings of great size made by the kings and private individuals who came from the city of Atlantis itself and from the subject peoples elsewhere. There was an altar on the same scale

---

[63] This would make for a proportion of 2:1—a proportion characteristic of the Doric architecture of the sixth century. The controlling ratio of the Parthenon is 4:9.

[64] The "ancient" belief that the daughters of Nereus (Nereids) were 100 in number is based on the virtuoso passages in Homer and Hesiod that name respectively thirty-four Nereids (including Thetis, in *Iliad* XVIII 35-51) and fifty (*Theogony* 240-264). Plato corrects both Homer and Hesiod.

as the temple **(117A)** and its workmanship was equally lavish. The palace was magnificent in its monumental architecture and it was worthy of the greatness of their empire and the adornment of the temple and shrines [of the precinct].

They drew their water from two springs—a spring of cold water and a spring of hot water.[65] Both had an abundant flow and in the amazing natural freshness and quality of its waters each had its own use. They built fountain houses around them and plantations of trees suitable to the temperature of the waters. **(117B)** And they also built reservoirs around the springs; some they left open, but to the north they covered the reservoirs to convert them to warm baths. The reservoirs of the kings were separate from those of the rest of the population. Some reservoirs were reserved for the use of women, others for watering horses and other draft animals, and each they fashioned appropriately to its use. The overflow they channeled into the grove of Poseidon, where, thanks to the fertility of the soil, there grew all varieties of trees of extraordinary beauty and height. They also irrigated the outer land rings by means of canals that crossed over along the bridges joining them.

(117C) Here there were constructed numerous shrines to numerous gods and the land was laid out for many orchards and gymnasia. There were gymnasia for men on each of the two ring islands and tracks for horses were set apart as well. And, remarkably, through the middle of the greatest of the islands they laid out a separate race course for horses, one stade wide, and it extended in a circle around the entire island. Located on each side of the central race course were quarters for the palace guard.[66] **(117D)** The garrison of the more reliable soldiers was established on the smaller of the ring islands, the island situated nearest to the acropolis. And quarters were built on the acropolis for the most reliable soldiers of all, surrounding the palaces of the kings themselves. The ship-sheds were filled with triremes and all the fittings needed for triremes, and all were in good working order. Such, then, were the buildings they constructed around the [dwelling of the] kings themselves.

---

[65] Both the importance of Poseidon to the royal family of Atlantis and the two springs of the central island are meant to recall the two springs of the "utopian" island of Scherie described in *Odyssey* VII 54-66 and 113-132. The contrasting rivers of the in the territory of Theopompos' Meropes are described in **V 3** below.

[66] Socrates distinguishes palace guards (*doryphoroi*) from the guardian class of Kallipolis (*phylakes*) in his description of the tyrant (*Republic* IX 567D and 575B).

Now, once you had crossed over the outer rings of water, which
• are three in number, you would come to a circuit wall that began
at the sea **(117E)** and surrounded the greatest of the land rings on
all sides at a uniform distance of fifty stades from the greatest
land ring and its harbor. It began at the point where the channel
had been dug through to the sea.[67] The entire area within the wall
was settled by a dense population whose houses were crowded
close together. And the waterway into the interior and the greatest harbor were teeming with ships and crowds of merchants who
had arrived from all over the world and whose voices and bustle
produced a commotion and hubbub that could be heard day and
night.

I have recalled this description of the capital and the ancient dwelling of the kings pretty much as it was told [to Solon] at that time.
(118A) But now I must attempt to recall the nature of the rest of
the country and the manner in which it was improved. To begin
with, the priest said that the entire country was very high and
that it rose sheer from the sea. The entire plain that surrounded
the capital was itself surrounded by a ring of mountains that
sloped down as far as the sea. The plain was smooth and level
and entirely rectangular. On its long sides it extended for 3,000
stades and, as measured from the sea, it was over 2,000 stades
across. **(118B)** The orientation of the island was to the south and
it was protected from the northerly winds. The mountains surrounding the plain were legendary for their number and size and
beauty. None of the mountain ranges that exist today can compare with them. They contained on their slopes and in their val-
leys many populous and wealthy villages. They contained rivers
and lakes and meadows that supplied enough to feed all the animals there, both domesticated and wild. In their abundance and
variety, the shrubs and trees were plentiful for all kinds of con-
structions and uses.

(118C) I will now relate how this plain had been developed by
nature and by many kings and over a long period of time. For the
most part, the plain was naturally rectangular, regular, and ob-
long. Where it was not perfectly straight and even they evened it
out by excavating a Great Canal around it. As described, its depth
and width and length provoke disbelief, since it was the work of

---

[67] This circuit wall makes the seventh and outermost of the system of seven concentric circles that inscribe the city plan of Atlantis. For the conception and the
contrast with the rectilinear plane, which is the work of the kings of Atlantis,
compare Figures 14 and 15.

human hands and so vast when compared to the other building projects. Nevertheless, I must repeat precisely what we heard then. The Great Canal was excavated to the depth of a plethron, it measured a stade wide along its entire length, **(118D)** and as it framed the entire plain it came to a total length of 10,000 stades. As it received the flow of water that came off the mountains, and as this water circulated and reached the city on two sides, the trench allowed the water to flow out to the sea. Towards the interior, canals were cut in straight lines from the city over the plain a hundred feet broad at most and these emptied their waters into the Great Canal facing the sea. These were spaced at an interval of 100 stades. They also cut horizontal connecting channels linking one canal with another and with the city, **(118E)** and it is by these canals that they transported timber and the other products of the land on barges from the mountains to the city.[68]

They harvested their crops twice a year. In the winter season they relied on the water of Zeus-sent rains, and in the summer season they used the waters stored in the earth drawing it into their canal system to irrigate the crops.

The military organization of the island of Atlantis detailed

Now, as for the numbers of the men of the plain who were fit to serve in the army: each military district was assigned to contribute one commander. **(119A)** The area of each district was as much as 100 stades. Of all these districts there was a total of 60,000. And as far as the population of the mountainous regions and the rest of the country goes, it was said to be too large to calculate. But, counted by regions and villages, all men fit for military service were assigned to one of the 60,000 military districts and they served under the commander of each district. In times of war each commander was assigned to have in readiness a sixth part of the complement of a war chariot as a contribution to a force of 10,000 chariots; **(119B)** and in addition, two horses and two riders, a pair of horses without a chariot, with its complement of two riders, a runner, a rider who could fight on foot armed with a small shield, and as a charioteer a rider who could mount either horse, two hoplites, two archers, and two sling men; three light-armed soldiers with stones and three with javelins. He also had to contribute four sailors to the crews manning 12,000 ships. These were the principles for raising an army in the royal city. The formulas varied in the nine other cities, and it would take a long time to describe them.

---

[68] See Figure 15.

The political organization of Atlantis detailed

(119C) The original ordering of powers and honors in Atlantis was as follows. Within his own patrimony and in his own city,
• each of the ten kings held power over the inhabitants and over most of the laws, and he could punish or put to death whomever he wished. But, as for their common empire and federation, the
• kings were regulated by the laws of Poseidon as these had been passed down by tradition and according to an inscription which the first kings had cut on a stele of oreichalkos. (119D) This inscription was placed in the middle of the island in the sanctuary of Poseidon. Here in every fifth or sixth year and in alternating sequence it was their custom to gather. To both the even and to the odd years they accorded an equal share. Once they had assembled, they deliberated on matters of common concern and held an assize to determine if anyone of them had broken the law, and they gave judgment. Whenever they were about to declare judgment, they first offered one another pledges in this manner: as all ten kings were alone in the sanctuary of Poseidon, where bulls had been allowed to run free, they joined in prayer to ask the god to be allowed to capture the bull that would be the most acceptable offering to him. (119E) They pursued the bulls with staffs and nooses—but with no iron weapon, and they led the bull they had captured to the stele. There they slaughtered it on the crest of the stele and let its blood spill down over the inscription. In addition to the laws written on the stele there was an oath inscribed calling terrible curses down upon those who broke them. And, when they had then sacrificed the bull following this ritual, (120A) they would burn all the limbs of the bull and, mixing his blood in a krater, they would pour a clot of his blood over the head of each of them, and, once they had scrubbed the stele clean, they would bring the remaining blood over to the fire.[69]

After this, they would draw the blood from the krater in gold pouring vessels. Pouring the blood over the fire, they would take an oath to render justice according to the laws inscribed on the stele and to punish anyone who had violated these laws since last they met. They swore that in the future they would not will-

---

[69] The ritual of pouring the blood of the sacrificial bull over the heads of the kings of Atlantis is clearly a rite of periodic purification. It recalls Heraclitus' invective against the practice of cleaning the stain of blood with blood, DK 22 B 5. The closest religious parallel comes from a Babylonian text called "Evil Demons of Illness"; this is reproduced in Burkert (1992) 58. On the Greek practice of purification of murderers by pig's blood see Parker (1983) 370-374.

ingly violate any of the provisions of the inscription and that they would neither govern nor obey a governor if either they or he did not issue commands **(120B)** that were in conformity with the laws of their father. When each of the kings had made this oath and engaged both himself and his descendants, they drank and dedicated their cup in the sanctuary of the god. And, once they had finished with their dinner and everything else they had to do and night had fallen and the fire about the sacrificial offerings had subsided, they all put on deep blue robes of the most splendid appearance and, sitting on the ground next to the embers of the sacrificial victim, at night, they put out the fire still flickering in the sanctuary **(120C)** and judged anyone accused of violating any of their laws and were judged themselves. Once they had passed judgment, when day dawned, they recorded their judgments on a gold tablet which they dedicated as a memorial offering along with their robes.

There were many other particular laws concerning the prerogatives of each of the kings, but the most important of these were those forbidding them to bear arms against one another and commanding them to help one another should anyone in any of their cities make an attempt to overturn the divine family; that they should deliberate together, as had generations before them, **(120D)** their decisions concerning war and their other actions; but that they should cede leadership to the royal family of Atlantis; and finally that the king should have power to put none of his kinsmen to death, if he could not obtain the approval of the majority of the ten kings.

How the decline of the kings of Atlantis prompts Zeus to call an assembly of the gods to punish their arrogance, in which, addressing the gods he said . . .

This was the power, so great and so extraordinary that existed in that distant region at that time. This was the power the god[70] mustered and brought against these [Mediterranean] lands. It was said that his pretense was something like what I shall describe. **(120E)** For many generations and as long as enough of their divine nature survived, they were obedient unto their laws and they were well disposed to the divinity they were kin to. They possessed conceptions that were true and entirely lofty. And in their

---

70   Zeus; cf. 121B. This scene is modelled on the assembly called by Zeus on Olympus at the opening of the *Odyssey* (I 26-43) and reproduces the scene on Olympus described by Aristophanes in Plato's *Symposium*. Here too Zeus calls an assembly of the gods to consider how to chastise offending mortals (*Symposium* 190B-D).

attitude to the disasters and chance events which constantly be-
fall men and in their relations with one another they exhibited a
combination of mildness and prudence, because, except for virtue, they held all else in disdain and thought their present good
fortune of no consequence. They bore their vast wealth of gold
and other possessions without difficulty, treating it as if it were a
•   burden. **(121A)** They did not become intoxicated with the luxury
of the life their wealth made possible; nor did they lose their self-
control and slip into decline. But in their sober judgment they
could see distinctly that even their very wealth increased with
their amity and its companion, virtue. But they saw that both
wealth and concord decline as possessions become pursued and
•   honored. And virtue perishes with them as well.

Now, because these were their thoughts and because of the divine nature that survived in them, they prospered greatly, as we
have already related. But when the divine portion in them began
to grow faint as it was often blended with great draughts of mortality **(121B)** and as their human nature gradually gained ascen-
dancy, at that moment, in their inability to bear their great good
fortune, they became disordered. To whomever had eyes to see
they appeared hideous, since they were losing the finest of what
were once their most treasured possessions. But to those who were
blind to the true way of life oriented to happiness it was at this
time that they gave the semblance of being supremely beauteous
and blessed. Yet inwardly they were filled with an unjust lust for
possessions and power. But as Zeus, god of the gods,[71] reigning
as king according to law, could clearly see this state of affairs, he
observed this noble race lying in this abject state and resolved to
punish them **(121C)** and to make them more careful and harmo-
nious as a result of their chastisement. To this end he called all
the gods to their most honored abode, which stands at the middle
of the universe and looks down upon all that has a share in generation.[72] And, when he had gathered them together, he said. . .

---

[71] In scene from the *Odyssey*, Zeus is called "father of men and gods" (I 28). Here,
he is called "god of the gods," a phrase that recalls Timaeus' description of the
gods created by the Demiurge—"gods of gods" (*Timaeus* 41A).

[72] To this point, Critias has made no reference to generation. But at the end of the
Critias, the beginning of the *Timaeus* is recalled. As he begins his speech, Timaeus
distinguishes between what is perpetually coming into being and what exists
forever (*Timaeus* 27D).

3. What Hermocrates Said

Hermocrates is best known from the pages of Thucydides, which include two speeches he gave in Sicily to prepare Syracuse and then the neighboring city of Kamerina for war with Athens. Both come from book VI of *The Peloponnesian War*. The first Hermocrates delivers before the assembly of Syracusans in the summer of 415; the second he delivers in Kamerina in winter of 414. In the first he is opposed by a speaker named Athenagoras; in the second, by an orator named Euphemos. The reader who wants the fuller context of these two speeches should begin with Thucydides' description of the magnificent departure of the Athenian fleet from the Peiraeus in the spring of 415 (in VI 31-32) and his grim conclusion describing the fate of the expedition and of Nicias, who was in charge of the Athenian expedition, in 413 (in VII 86-87). We know from Plutarch's *Nicias* that Hermocrates pleaded for the life of Nicias (*Life of Nicias* 28). Plato's close familiarity with Thucydides is demonstrated by the use he makes of Pericles' funeral oration (Thucydides II 34-36) in the *Menexenus*.

A. THUCYDIDES, VI 32.3-34: SUMMER OF 415, HERMOCRATES' SPEECH IN SYRACUSE

(32.3) Reports from all over began to reach Syracuse concerning the invasion, but for a long time none were credited. An assembly was held and two groups of speakers addressed it, as I shall describe. Some were convinced that the Athenians had launched an expedition; others that it had not; Hermocrates, son of Hermon,[73] addressed the assembly, thinking that he had some clear knowledge of the situation. This was his speech and these were his recommendations:

(33.1) "It could well be that I, like certain other speakers, give you the impression that I am making incredible statements concerning the reality of the expedition. And I realize that those who speak of or report on matters that do not appear to be true not only fail to convince their hearers; they seem to be fools as well. Even so, I am not daunted, but will hold my course at this moment of danger to the city. I have persuaded myself, if no one else, that I speak with better knowledge than another speaker.

• (33.2) What I know is that the Athenians are on the move to attack you—the prospect you find so astounding—with a large force, both of sailors and of infantry. Their pretext is their alliance

---

[73] Thucydides does not introduce Hermocrates at length, but he does give his estimate of his abilities in VI 72.2. Thucydides is the first author to mention Hermocrates; he is mentioned by Xenophon in his *Hellenika* (I.1.16; 18; and 27); Plato, as we have seen, in his *Timaeus/Critias*; Diodorus Siculus (XIII 18-19; 34; 38); and Plutarch, in his *Life of Nicias* (26; 27).

with Segesta and their colony of Leontini.[74] But their real motive is that they covet Sicily, and our city most of all. They calculate that, if they can control Syracuse, all Sicily will fall to them. (33.3) Since they will soon be at hand, take thought of how you can defend yourselves against them with the resources available to you. Do not, in your disdain for the Athenians, be taken with no defenses. Nor, in your credulity, let yourselves neglect your all. (33.4) And if anyone should find what I say believable, let him not be overwhelmed by the Athenians' audacity and power. For they cannot inflict greater harm upon you than can you upon them. Nor does the fear that they are coming against us with a large force mean that they can do us harm. So far as the rest of Sicily is concerned, this force represents an advantage to us: for in their fear and confusion the cities of Sicily will more readily join us as allies. If then, we either destroy them or thwart their ambitions and repel them—and I have no fear that they will not attain their object—an outcome of great nobility will be ours, that I do not doubt.

(33.5) Few great expeditions, either of Greeks or of barbarians, have sailed far from their own land and met with success. Invaders cannot come against us in numbers greater than the city dwellers of the island and its rural population, who are all driven by their fear to unite. If, because they lack provisions and supplies, they are defeated in a foreign country, they abandon glory to those they have threatened, even though their victims have made many mistakes concerning their own interests. Such was exactly the case of the Athenians themselves, when against reasonable expectations, the Persian expedition had failed in many theaters. (33.6) The Athenians won glory, because it was against Athens that the Persian attack was directed. In our case, it is not too much to hope that the conclusion will be similar.

(34.1) Let us take courage and make our preparations here in Syracuse. Let us send delegations to the other cities of Sicily in order to confirm our alliances with some and attempt to come to terms of friendship and alliance with others, if we can. Let us send missions to the other cities of Sicily to demonstrate that we all share in this threat. And to Italy as well, either to persuade the cities there to become our allies or to refuse to receive the Athenians. (34.2) I think that it would also be a wise plan to send a mission to Carthage. Such an embassy is nothing they have not foreseen.

---

[74] For the location of Syracuse and Carthage, see Figure I.

They live in constant fear that the Athenians will attack their city and, as a consequence, they will think that, if they neglect this threat, they would find themselves in real difficulties and would be willing to help protect us, either covertly or openly—or in some manner. They are now the greatest power, if they want to exert their power. They possess more gold and silver than any other state and these fuel war and other undertakings. **(34.3)** Let us also send a mission to Sparta and Corinth with two requests: send help as soon as possible and stir up war in Greece.

(34.4) Now I will speak of what I believe is our greatest opportunity. You will be very slow to believe me, because of your tolerance and indolence. Nevertheless, I will tell you what it is. If all of us in Sicily—or if not all at least most—were to launch all our available ships with two months of provisions and meet the Athenians at Tarentum and the Cape of Iapygia and make it clear to them that they will not contend for Sicily before they cross the Ionian Sea, we could by this plan throw them into confusion. And we will drive home to them the realization that we set out to meet them as defenders of a friendly country—for Tarentum will give us a base of operations—and that they must cross the open sea with their entire fleet; that because of the length of the crossing it is difficult for the fleet to stay in formation as it gradually makes its way. **(34.5)** But, then, if they were to lighten their cargoes and attack us with a massed formation of swift sailing ships, there are two possibilities: if they use their oars, we would attack exhausted sailors; but if they decide against this, we would withdraw to Tarentum. They would then find themselves in a difficult situation sailing along an uninhabited coast, because they made the crossing with scant supplies looking for a naval engagement. If this force were to remain on the coast, they could be hemmed in. If they were to make the attempt to sail along the coast and leave the rest of the fleet behind with no certainty that any city would receive them, they would become discouraged.[75]

(34.6) Therefore, I think that they will be cornered by these calculations and not as much as set sail from Kerkyra. Either they will take counsel and send out a scouting party to determine our numbers and position and be delayed to the onset of winter, or they will be unnerved by this unexpected development and disband

---

[75] Hermocrates uses the word *athymeo* in his second brief speech in *Critias* 108C (where I translate "the fainthearted"). He insists on this same word in VI 80.1 in encouraging the assembly of Kamerina to side with Syracuse against Athens.

the fleet. This is quite likely in view of the reports I have heard concerning the most experienced of their commanders.[76] He has accepted this command against his will and would gladly seize on a pretext, if we were to supply him with a suitable excuse. **(34.7)** I am certain that our numbers will be reported to be greater than they are. Men's minds are alert to rumor, and they fear those who seize the initiative or those who make it clear to those that do that they will defend themselves, reckoning that they are equally dangerous. **(34.8)** This would be the reaction of the Athenians now. They are attacking us because they think that we will not defend ourselves. They came to this conclusion because we did not join Sparta to destroy them. But, should they see unexpected daring on our part, they would be unnerved more by what they do not expect than our actual power.

(34.9) This is the course I urge on you most emphatically. If you will not follow my plan, then I urge you to make preparations for war. Each of you should remember to show his contempt for the invaders in the defense of taking action. And each of you should think that those preparations made in a state of fear are most secure. For action undertaken in a time of danger has the best results. The Athenians are coming; they are under sail, I am certain; they are already here!"

B. THUCYDIDES, VI 76-80: WINTER 414, HERMOCRATES SPEAKS BEFORE THE ASSEMBLY OF KAMERINA IN OPPOSITION TO A PRO-ATHENIAN ORATOR BY THE NAME OF EUPHEMOS

(76.1) "Citizens of Kamerina, we have been sent to urge you not to be unnerved by fear as you confront the might of the Athenians who have now reached Sicily, and even more by the fear of their speeches. Do not let what they say persuade you. **(76.2)** They have come to Sicily, and you are aware of their excuse for coming. But their real intention we all understand. In my view, they do not seem to want to establish a colony in Leontini but rather to overthrow your city. It is hardly likely that they would unsettle the cities of Greece, but settle cities in Sicily, or that they would feel kinship for the people of Leontini, who are related to the city of Chalcis. But, in truth, they hold in thrall the Chalcideans of Euboea, whose colony is Leontini in Sicily. **(76.3)** They are attempting to impress the shape of Greece on Sicily. History will

---

[76]   Nicias. Thucydides had described his lack of enthusiasm for the expedition in VI 8 and Nicias himself expresses his reservations in his speech before the Athenian assembly in VI 9-14.

show this: once they had become the leaders of willing followers in Ionia and the states which were once their colonies for the purpose of punishing the Medes, they subjugated their allies, some for abandoning the alliance and others for fighting with one another. In each case they offered a reason that seemed plausible. (76.4) Thus, the Athenians did not take their stand against the Mede for the sake of the freedom of the Greeks nor the Greeks for the sake of their own liberty. The Athenians stood for the enslavement of the Greeks—not against the Mede, but for themselves—and the Greeks stood to see the exchange of one despot for another. This master was not less intelligent than the first, but more evilly intelligent.

(77.1) But we have not come to display to you how many wrongs the city of Athens, which is open to so many charges, has committed. You know yourselves. We have come rather to find fault with you. We are holding up before your eyes examples of how the Greeks of Greece have been enslaved, because they failed to defend themselves. And we hold up to you the same specious arguments: they are kindred people to the colony of Leontini; they have come to the aid of their allies in Segesta. But with these examples before us, we are unwilling to unite and to demonstrate with force that Sicily is not Ionia nor are we cities on the Hellespont or islanders. These peoples are always enslaved and exchange one master for another—either the Mede or another. (77.2) We are free Dorians, who inhabit Sicily and come from the independent Peloponnesus. Shall we wait and do nothing until we are all taken, city by city, although we know that we can be taken in this way alone? As we observe the Athenians adopting this tactic, shall we allow them to divide some of us by their speeches, turn others to make war on other Sicilian cities in hopes of becoming Athenian allies, and harm us by flattering each city they address? Or do we fancy that, as a distant fellow colony is being destroyed before we are destroyed, the danger is to individual cities and that the city that is taken suffers this disaster in isolation?

(78.1) If one of you thinks that Syracuse and not he himself is an enemy of Athens and considers it a dangerous course to put himself at risk for my country, let him reflect that, fighting in the territory of Syracuse, he is fighting not so much for my city as for his own. He is safe as long as Syracuse has not first been destroyed. He will have me as an ally and he will not struggle alone. Let him recall that Athens does not want to punish the hostility of Syracuse as much as she wants to use Syracuse as a pretense to gain your friendship. **(78.2)** If one of you resents us or is afraid of us—and envy and fear are strong emotions—and is prompted by these feelings to want Syracuse to be harmed to teach us a lesson yet still survive to guarantee his own safety, he is entertaining a hope that, for mere mortals, cannot be fulfilled. For no single human can be the dispenser of the objects of his desire and chance alike. **(78.3)** But if he is mistaken in his calculations, it is very possible that, once he has lamented over his own misfortunes, the time will come when he will envy my good fortune. But it will not come, if he rejects our alliance and is unwilling to share our common danger, which does not call for words; it calls for action. One could well say that he has preserved our power, but in fact he has assured his own survival.

(78.4) Citizens of Kamerina, you share a boundary with us and in your turn you have come to face the threat of Athens. It behooved you to foresee these developments and not to be the luke-warm allies you are now. You should rather have approached us and made exactly the request for aid you would have, if the Athenians had reached Kamerina first, and to have openly urged us not to give an inch to the Athenians, just as we are urging you. But, at present, neither you nor the other Sicilians are yet prepared to make this move.

(79.1) But perhaps it is your cowardice that makes you so punctilious about fairness both to us and to the invaders, and invoke your alliance with the Athenians. You made this alliance not with your friends in mind but in case one of your enemies should attack you. You agreed to help the Athenians when injured by others, not, as is now the case, when they themselves are attacking your neighbors. **(79.2)** Not even the people of Rhegion, who are immigrants from Chalcis, are willing to restore the people of Leontini, who are Chalcidean. It would be passing strange if the people of Rhegion, in their respect for the weight of the claims of fairness, should be foolishly prudent, while you in your plausible excuses want to give aid to those who are your national enemies, but are willing to utterly ruin those who are even more naturally kindred to you, by joining with your worst enemies. **(79.3)** This is not fairness: fairness is defending yourselves and rejecting fear of their might. If we all stand together as one, they are nothing to be dreaded. But, if we fall into their designs and stand divided, we have reason to dread. When the Athenians attacked Syracuse and Syracuse alone and were victorious, they did not achieve their aim, but quickly departed. **(80.1)** So, if we do not stand together, we have reason to lose heart. But courage will inspire us, if we join in alliance, especially since help is on its way from the Peloponnesus, and the Spartans are superior in every way to these Athenians when it comes to warfare. For precisely these reasons none of you should think that this prudent policy of yours, of being allies to both sides but helping neither, is just to us or a safe course for yourselves. **(80.2)** This course is not, in fact, fair; it only pleads fairness. You have not joined either side. But if one side suffers and is defeated and the other emerges victorious, what will this mean? It means that because of your defection you did not defend and protect the vanquished and you did not stop the victor from his evil course. Yet it is the generous course of action to throw your lot in with those who are wronged and are your kin, and to secure the common good of Sicily and refuse to aid the Athenians, who are your 'friends' in their mistaken course.

(80.3) We of Syracuse have joined you in this assembly to say that there is no point in tutoring you or the allies in facts you know as well as we do. But we have this request and this representation: know that if we fail to persuade you, we are the victims of Ionians, who are our eternal enemies; we, who are Dorians, are betrayed by you, who are Dorians. **(80.4)** If the Athenians destroy us, they will be victorious because the decision you make in Kamerina; but the glory they receive will belong to them alone. And as the prize of victory they will take none other than the city that gave them their victory. If, on the other hand, it is we who are victorious, you yourself will be subject to reprisals for being responsible for the dangers we face. Reflect now and make your choice: you can either be slaves and for the present moment face no danger, or you can join us and, if we are victorious, you can avoid the disgrace of having Athenians as your masters, and escape our hatred of you that would not soon pass."

II. Euhemeros of Messene's *Sacred Inscription* or Panchaia

The *Sacred Inscription* of Euhemeros of Messene (in the southwestern Peloponnesus) does not survive intact. It is preserved only in the paraphrase of the Greek historian Diodorus Siculus (of Sicily, who was writing in Rome in the reigns of Caesar and Augustus) in books III and VI of his world history, *Library of History* (*Bibliotheke*). Book VI of his *Library* (or *Histories* as it was known to Eusebius) is itself lost, and we depend on Eusebius of Caesarea (*Praeparatio Evangelica* II 2.59B-61A) for our knowledge of Fragment 1.

Little is known of Euhemeros except what he said about himself and his eastern mission in the *Sacred Inscription*. He served the Macedonian Cassander (358-297 B.C.), who had gained control of mainland Greece after the death of Alexander of Macedon (in 323). Euhemeros seems to have been in his service from 311 to 298. His *Sacred Inscription*, which was well known (if not notorious) in antiquity, was not the only book he wrote. Diodorus mentions a separate monograph on the traditions concerning the "earthly gods" (VI 1.3, Winiarczyk T 8, **II A.3** below). Like Iamboulos' Islands of the Sun and Lucian's *True History*, the *Sacred Inscription* is a first person narration and to all appearances autobiographical. According to Eusebius, Euhemeros was on a mission for Cassander to the East when he reached an archipelago on the Indian Ocean containing the island Panchaia, which, in the Doric dialect, means "the Good Island."

We translate the Greek text of Marcus Winiarczyk, *Euhemerus Messenius Reliquiae*, Stuttgart and Leipzig 1991.

A. Fragment 1, from Eusebius of Caesarea (*Praeparatio Evangelica* II 2.59B-61A = Diodorus Siculus VI 1)

> **(1)** This is Diodorus' account of theology in the third book of his *Histories*. This same author confirms the same theology,[1] in his sixth book, taking his argument from Euhemeros of Messene. I quote his actual words: **(2)** "Now men of ancient times handed down to later ages a two-fold conception of the gods. Some gods, they say, are eternal and indestructible. The sun and moon and the other stars of heaven are examples of these, as are the winds

---

[1] That of the islanders of Atlantis, set out by Diodorus III 56-61.

and other gods of a similar nature. The reason for this is that each of these has an eternal source for its existence and an eternal duration. The other gods, they say, came into existence upon the earth, but, on account of their benefactions to humankind, they have attained to immortal honors and fame as have Heracles, Dionysus, Aristaios, and others like them.[2] **(3)** Many and complicated are the traditions concerning the earthly gods handed down by historians and students of myth. Among the historians, Euhemeros, the author of the *Sacred Inscription*, wrote a monograph on this question. Of the mythographers, Homer, Hesiod, Orpheus, and their successors invented a monstrous set of tales concerning the gods. For our part, we will attempt to preserve some balance in our attempt to give a cursory summary of these different kinds of history.

(4) The historian Euhemeros was a friend of King Cassander.[3] It was on Cassander's account that he carried out some missions for the king and went on long voyages. He says that he travelled as far as the ocean to the south.[4] According to his account, he set sail from Arabia Felix,[5] into the Ocean for a voyage of many days and sighted islands off the main. One of these was the island called Panchaia. Here he observed the Panchaians—a nation of exceptional piety, who honored the gods with the most sumptuous sacrifices and magnificent offerings in silver and gold. **(5)** The isle, he relates, is sacred to the gods. We have entered into the historical record the details of its quite amazing antiquity and the masterpieces of its architecture in the earlier books.[6] **(6)** There is on this island on the summit of a towering mountain a sanctuary of

---

2 Heracles is Euhemeros' first and most obvious example. The son of Zeus and Alcmena, he was a *heros* or *hemitheos*—half mortal and half god. In this ambiguous status he was worshipped both as a god and a hero (cf. Herodotus II 44.5). Dionysus was, in the Greek tradition, the son of Zeus and the mortal Semele of Thebes and in a widespread tradition he was represented as being put to death by the Titans. His gifts to mankind were well documented and greatly appreciated. Aristaios is an especially interesting case for Euhemeros' argument. He was the son of Apollo and the "nymph" Cyrene, a minor hero in Greek cult and the protector of cattle. We know nothing of his death.

3 This puts Euhemeros into the context of the enormous expansion of the Greek world with the eastern campaign of Alexander of Macedon. Cassander was the son of Antipater of Macedon. He gained control of much of the Greek world, but also had ambitions and crucial military contacts in Asia and the East.

4 For any Greek navigator to reach the East, he would have to sail south, either through the Red Sea or the Persian Gulf.

5 "Prosperous Arabia," on the southeastern coast of the Red Sea (now Saudi Arabia).

6 Diodorus V 41.4-46.7, translated in B below.

Triphylian Zeus established by Zeus himself at the time when he was king of the inhabited world and still dwelt among men. **(7)** Within this sanctuary there is a gold stele on which are inscribed in the characters of Panchaia[7] a summary account of the deeds of Ouranos, Kronos, and Zeus.

(8) Euhemeros goes on to say that Ouranos was the first king. He was an impressive man and did much good; he also understood the movements of the stars and he was the first to honor with sacrifices the gods of heaven (*ouranioi theoi*). For this reason he too was called Heaven (*Ouranos*). **(9)** His wife Hestia bore him two sons: Titan and Kronos, and two daughters: Rhea and Demeter. Kronos succeeded Ouranos as king. He married Rhea and begat Zeus and Hera and Poseidon. Zeus succeeded him to the kingship and married Hera and Demeter and Themis. From Hera he had the Kouretes as sons; from Demeter he had Persephone; and from Themis, Athena. **(10)** Now when he traveled to Babylon he was hospitably entertained by Belos,[8] and afterward he arrived at Panchaia, an island near the Ocean, and established an altar for his grandfather, Ouranos. From Panchaia he travelled through Syria to meet Kasios, who was then ruler of Syria and who gave his name to Mt. Kasios. And travelling to Cilicia he met Kilix the ruler of this land in battle and conquered him. He travelled to numerous other nations as well and among all he was shown honors and addressed as a god.

(11) To this account concerning the gods which he viewed as mortal men Euhemeros added similar details in his history. We will rest content with this account of Euhemeros, the author of the *Sacred Inscription*. Now we shall attempt a cursory and brief account of Greek legends of the gods following Hesiod and Homer and Orpheus."[9]

B. DIODORUS SICULUS V 41.4-46.7

(41.4) A number of islands lie to the East of the extremity of Arabia Felix that is bound by the Ocean. Three of these deserve to be recorded by history. One of these is the island called Sacred. There it is not permitted to bury the dead. The other island is its neigh-

---

7   That is, hieroglyphics; cf. V 46.7, below.
8   Bel, or Baal, the Semitic word for "lord" or "king."
9   That this is the language of Diodorus himself is suggested by Diodorus' concluding words at V 46.7: "We will rest content with this account . . . ".

bor and is at a distance of not quite a mile.[10]

Now the Sacred Isle bears no crop except for frankincense, and it bears enough frankincense to provide a sufficient supply for honoring the gods to the entire inhabited world. It also produces more myrrh than any other country and a great variety of other kinds of incense. Their fragrance is quite powerful. **(5)** I will describe the frankincense bush and its exploitation. It is a small tree and in appearance it resembles the white *Acacia* of Egypt. Its leaves resemble the species of tree called the willow and it flowers in a golden bloom. **(6)** The gum of frankincense oozes out of the tree as if it were a tear. The myrrh tree resembles our mastic, but its leaf is narrower and thicker. When the soil around its roots has been tilled its roots discharge the gum and the trees that grow in fertile terrain can be tapped twice a year, in the spring and summer. In the spring the sap is reddish because of the dew; in the summer it is white. They also gather the fruit of the buckthorn (spina-Christi) and they use it in their food and drink and as a medicine for diarrhea.

(42.1) The land of the island is divided into districts and the king has the best of these as his possession. And he receives the tenth part of the crops harvested in the island. They say that the width of the island is about twenty-three miles.[11] **(2)** The inhabitants of the island are called Panchaians,[12] and they export frankincense and myrrh to the mainland and sell it to Arab merchants; other traders buy these cargoes and transport them to Phoenicia and to Hollow Syria and to Egypt as well. And in a final stage traders from these countries transship [these cargoes] to the entire inhabited world. **(3)** There is another large island some three miles or so distant from the Sacred Isle to the eastern extent of the Ocean and it is of considerable length. They say that from the promontory that extends to the east, India is visible and seems covered with mist on account of the great distance.[13]

---

[10]   Seven stades or 4,200 feet. It is to this island that the Panchaians evidently transport the bodies of the dead when they make their request to bury them. The third island is described in 42.3. Atlantis is called "sacred,"*Critias* 115 B.

[11]   200 stades or 120,000 feet.

[12]   *Panchaioi*, a compound whose meaning seems to be: "completely" (*pan*) "genuine, good, or true." (LSJ s.v. *chaïos*) Significantly, the word *chaïos* is Doric, the dialect spoken in most of the Peloponnesus and in Crete, the mother country of the Panchaian colony in the Indian Ocean, according to the legend reported in 46.3.

[13]   This third island, Ceylon (Sri Lanka), is the Taprobane of the Greek explorers of the Hellenistic Age. See *OCD*[3] s.v. Taprobane and Figures 2 and 3.

(4) Of itself, Panchaia has many features worthy of the historical record. The people who inhabit it, the Panchaians, are autochthonous, whereas the Oceanitai, Indians, Scythians, and Cretans come from elsewhere. (5) On it there is a remarkable city by the name of Panara.[14] It is exceptionally prosperous. The inhabitants of this city are called "the Suppliants of Triphylian Zeus."[15] These are the only inhabitants of Panchaia who are independent and not ruled by the king. Every year they appoint three archons. They do not have power of life or death, but they make all other decisions; the most weighty of these decisions they voluntarily refer to the priests. (6) About nine miles[16] from this city is the sanctuary of Triphylian Zeus. It is located on a great plain and is a wonder for its great antiquity, the craftsmanship of its construction, and the fertility of its soil.

(43.1) The plain surrounding the sanctuary is sheltered by a lattice of all varieties of trees—not only trees that bear fruits and nuts but other varieties that can enchant the eye of the spectator. The plain abounds in exquisite cypress of great height, with plane, laurel, and myrtle, since natural springs well up throughout the plain. (2) And near the sacred enclosure a sweet water spring gushes up in a stream that flows in such abundance that it feeds a navigable river. This river is divided into many tributaries and these are channelled to irrigate the plain and throughout this region there are dense and continuous growths of tall trees in which great crowds of the islanders spend the hot months of summer. The trees are also the homes of a great profusion of birds of every color and of melodious calls that delight. Manifold are the gardens and plantations. There are many meadows that produce a variety of greenery and flowers. All this divine magnificence makes the plain the mirror of the gods of the country. (3) There were palm trees of great trunks,[17] and the dates were unlike those of palm trees elsewhere, and the numerous nut-bearing trees pro-

---

[14] Evidently a compound formed from *Pan* ("all") and either *ara* ("prayer") or the *ar* of *aristos* ("best").

[15] Zeus "of the three tribes." These tribes are later identified as the Panchaians, the Oceanitai, and Doians (Diodorus V 44.6, quoted below). This is another Dorian feature of Panchaia. The three tribes of the Dorians were the Hylleis, the Dymanes, and the Pamphyloi; cf. Homer *Odyssey* XIX 177; Hesiod frag. 191. A similar division of a settlement into three tribes is attested for the colony, Cyrene, which the Dorian island of Thera established on the coast of North Africa (Herodotus IV 161).

[16] 600 stades.

[17] The tense indicates that in Euhemeros' narrative the astonishing fertility of the Sacred Isle was represented as a thing of the past.

vided the islanders with abundant delicacies. And these apart, there were dense growths of many kinds of grape vines that climbed on tall arbors, and these were plaited in intricate patterns to offer pleasure to the eye and cool relief in the hot season. **(44.1)** The temple was a remarkable work of architecture. Its length was 200 feet and its width was proportional to its length. It was supported by tall and thick columns and articulated into friezes of fine workmanship. It contained statues of the gods that deserve notice: their skill was exceptional and they were executed on a massive scale. **(2)** The priests who were devoted to the cult of the gods and who were in charge of the sanctuary lived in houses surrounding the temple. Before the temple a great esplanade was constructed of a length of half a mile and a breadth of 100 feet. Flanking the esplanade on each side were monumental bronze statues with rectangular plinths. **(3)** The river we have described is at the border of the esplanade and it pours out in abundant swift flowing streams. Its waters are translucent and of great purity and it contributes greatly to the health of those who drink from it. This river is called "The Water of the Sun." **(4)** On each side, this entire spring is enclosed by a bank made of exquisite masonry. It extends for a half a mile. This area up to the water's edge cannot be entered by anyone except the priests. **(5)** The plain lying under the temple for some twenty-six miles is sacred to the gods and they use its produce for sacrifices.

Beyond the plain we have described there is a high mountain which is sacred to the gods and called "The Throne of Ouranos" and "Triphylian Olympos." **(6)** Legend is that in ancient times, when Ouranos was king of the inhabited world, he took great pleasure in this mountain and spent his time there. From its height he observed the heaven and its array of stars. Later it was called "Triphylian Olympos" because the islanders were divided into three tribes. These were called the Panchaians, the Oceanites, and the Doians.[18] They say that in a later age Ammon[19] expelled the Doians **(7)** and that he not only drove this people into exile but that he utterly destroyed their cities, reducing to rubble the cities of Doia and Asterousia.[20] Every year the priests offer a sacrifice

---

[18] For the name, Panchaians (= Panchaioi), see note on 42.2 above. The Oceanitai are the people of the Ocean to the east; the Doians might be intended as an aboriginal form of Dorians.

[19] Also known as Amana and Amun—the name of the Egyptian god worshipped at the Siwah oasis and later assimilated to the Greek Zeus.

[20] "Star City."

on this mountain with great ritual propriety.

(45.1) Beyond this mountain and in the rest of the territory of Panchaia, they say that there exist a great number of animals of many species. There are to be found many elephants and leopards and gazelle and many other species unusual in their appearance and of astonishing ferocity. **(2)** The island also contains three important cities, Hyracia, Dalis, and Oceanis. The entire island is fertile especially in many varieties of grape. **(3)** The men of the island are warlike and in their battles they employ chariots in the manner of the ancients.

Their class structure is threefold. They are divided first into the class of priests, and on these the artisans depend.[21] The second division is that of farmers and the third, that of warriors. And to these is added the profession of shepherds and herders. **(4)** The priests served as the ruling class and they acted as arbiters in disputes and they exercised authority over all other questions of concern to the state. The farmers who cultivate the soil contribute their crops to the community, and whichever farmer in the group seems to have been most successful receives a prize of great value in the distribution of the crops. The priests choose the farmer for the first prize and the second and so on down to the tenth. These awards are made in order to spur on the others. **(5)** And in a similar system the herders surrender animals for sacrifice and other livestock to the state stores, some by number and some by weight, with great exactness. As a general principle there is no private property except one's house and garden, but all products and all produce are taken over by the priests who fairly distribute to each according to his need.

(6) Because they have sheep which produce exceptionally soft wool, their garments are finespun and soft. Men as well as the women wear gold jewelry around their necks. They wear collars of twisted gold, gold bracelets on their wrists, and gold earrings that hang from their ears in Persian fashion. Both men and women wear the same kind of shoes and they are unusual for their variety of colors.

---

[21]   The clear implication is that in contrast to the class structure of Plato's *Republic* the artisans of Panchaia are not a part of the polity but are the virtual slaves of the priestly class. In Plato's *Republic* both artisans and farmers make up the first and lowest social class. Diodorus gives a confused account of his source here, since it is clear from the sequel that herdsmen are also assigned to the priestly class. For the connections with Plato, see Introduction §8.

(46.1) The warriors receive contributions which are a proportion of the state revenues. They guard the territory in garrisons established in forts or outposts.[22] The reason is that a part of this country is subject to the depredations of bold outlaws who ambush the farmers and make attacks on them. **(2)** The priests for their part live a highly civilized life—both in the cleanliness of their daily life and in its elegance. They wear linen robes that are exceptionally fine and soft and occasionally they wear garments woven of the softest wool. In addition, they wear caps interwoven with gold thread. For footwear they have sandals of intricate patterns and workmanship. Except for earrings they wear the same gold ornaments as do the women. They are in charge of the worship of the gods and their anthems and praise. In their songs they relate the deeds of the gods and their benefactions to humankind.[23] **(3)** The traditional account which the priestly class gives of their origin is that they came from Crete to Panchaia in a voyage of colonization led by Zeus at a time when he lived among mortals and was king of the inhabited world.[24] They adduce their dialect as an indication of this and point to the many Cretan names that survive in their language. They also point to the ties of kinship and the good will they have inherited from their ancestors as this tradition has been passed down from generation to generation. And they used to point to records preserved by their ancestors, which they say Zeus made up in the time when he was still dwelling among men and constructed the sacred precinct.

(4) The land possesses extensive veins of gold, silver, bronze, tin, and iron. They allow none of these metals to be exported from the island. The priests too are absolutely forbidden from setting foot outside the land dedicated to the gods. Whoever finds a priest outside these lands is permitted to kill him. **(5)** With its passage, time has piled up the number of offerings dedicated to the gods,

---

[22] A feature that seems more suitable for a country with inland borders (like Attica and Messene) than an island.

[23] The poetry of Plato's *Republic* is restricted to "the praise of men and hymns to the gods" (X 607A). By the theory that the gods of the present were once great human beings who made great contributions to human civilization—now known as "Euhemerism"—the past Greek distinction between hymns (to the gods) and encomia (to men) is blurred.

[24] By this account, the class of priests on Panchaia are immigrants from Crete; cf. 42.4. By one Greek tradition, Zeus was born on Crete.

and many and monumental are the dedications deposited for the gods. **(6)** The doors of the temple are fabulous works of art and made of silver, gold, and ivory with panels of citron wood.[25] The couch of the god,[26] six cubits long and four in width, is of solid gold and the skill of the goldsmith is refined down to the smallest detail. **(7)** And of very much the same material dimensions and exquisite workmanship is the table of the god that stands near his couch. At the middle of the couch there stands a tall stele, inscribed with letters known in Egypt as hieroglyphs.[27] These represented the deeds of Ouranos and Zeus. And after these inscriptions Hermes added a sequel recording the deeds of Artemis and Apollo.

We will rest content with this account of the Oceanic islands opposite Arabia.

---

[25] This type of wood (*thua*) is thought to be the same type of wood (*thuon*) that is found on the *Odyssey*'s island of Ogygie, where Calypso lived (*Odyssey* V 60).

[26] Zeus, represented as reclining at a banquet, except for one detail: instead of a statue of the god there is an inscribed stele on the bed.

[27] The name and conception of such a sacred inscription goes back to Plato *Timaeus* 23A and E, and 27B.

III. Iamboulos' Island of the Sun, with an Appendix on Lucian's Marvels of the Moon

Iamboulos is named only twice in Greek literature. He is first cited by Diodorus Siculus, who gives a summary of Iamboulos' first person narrative of his life and his travels to Arabia, Ethiopia, the Islands of the Sun, India, and his return by land to Greece. He seems to have given his trip to India a separate treatment (cf. Diodorus II 60.3). He is mentioned too by Lucian of Samosata in the second century AD as an example of an author of a lying tale. But Lucian admired his art: "Iamboulos too wrote of many wonders in the Great Sea [the Indian Ocean], and he created a fiction that was recognized as such by everyone; but his art in narrating this tale is not without its delights" (*True History* I 3). Like Euhemeros' *Sacred Inscription*, Iamboulos' Island of the Sun belongs to the Hellenistic age and the opening of the *oikoumene* to the East with the conquests of Alexander of Macedon.

Diodorus Siculus II 55-60

(55.1) We will now attempt a brief and cursory account of the island which has been discovered to the south in the Ocean and the amazing things that are said about it. First we will set out precisely the history of its discovery. (2) Iamboulos was an avid scholar from his boyhood. His father was a merchant and after his father's death he turned to the same career. Now, he made a trip into the interior of Arabia and its spice country, and there he and his fellow travellers were captured by bandits. At first he and one of his fellow captives were put in charge of a herd of goats, but later both were captured by some Ethiopians and brought across [the Red Sea] to the coast of Ethiopia.[1] (3) The Ethiopians took them as captives in order to purify their land, since they were of a different race.

Such was the ancient and ancestral custom of the Ethiopians living in this region. It was a tradition, confirmed by oracles, extending over a period of twenty generations or 600 years, count-

---

[1] Homer has Poseidon visiting the Ethiopians, who live at the edges of the known world (*Odyssey* I 22-25). For the Greek traditions concerning the Ethiopians see **V 3** and Introduction §3.

ing thirty years as a generation. Now, when the period for their purification arrived,[2] they constructed a ship big enough to hold two passengers and strong enough to weather storms at sea but capable of being managed by a crew of two. They stowed in this ship provisions for two men that would last for six months. They put the captives on board and ordered them to put out to sea as the oracle had commanded. And they enjoined them to sail to the south. (4) For if they sailed in that direction they would reach a fertile and populated island and discover a virtuous people inhabiting it and live a life of bliss with them. Just so, they said, their own people would enjoy peace and a life blessed in every respect over a period of 600 years, if the captives they sent away were to reach the island safely. But if, said they, they were daunted by the vastness of the open sea and turned their ship back, they would suffer the greatest punishment because they would be godless men and polluters of the entire race.

(5) They say that the Ethiopians celebrated a great festival on the seashore and, once they had performed magnificent sacrifices, they placed garlands on the heads of the men who were to set out for the island and effect the purification of their race and they sent them off on their voyage. They sailed on the great Ocean and were tossed by storms and in a voyage of four months they were driven to the island the Ethiopians had spoken of. It was a round island and its circumference measured some 5,000 stades.[3]

(56.1) As they were approaching the island some of the inhabitants came out to meet them and towed their boat to shore. Others ran down to shore from all parts of the island in amazement that they had made the sea voyage. But the islanders treated the strangers kindly and offered them some of their provisions. (2) These islanders are in their body and in their customs far different from men in our part of the inhabited world. They resemble one another very closely in the configuration of their bodies; in height they reach four cubits and more.[4] Their bones can be bent to an extent and then returned to their normal position as if they were muscles. (3) Their bodies are extremely soft but stronger and more agile than ours. If they grasp anything in their hands no one can

---

2   Evidently at the end of a period of 600 years.
3   Or approximately 568 miles. The shape of the island is appropriate for the Island of the Sun; its circumference might represent a calculation of the circumference of the sun. That it is the principle island of an archipelago of seven islands is significant. The sun was part of a system of seven planets.
4   A cubit is the measure from elbow to wrist; the inhabitants were therefore at least four feet tall.

wrest it from their grip. They have no hair anywhere on their bodies except on their heads, eyebrows, and eyelids, and also on their chins. But the other parts of their bodies are so extremely smooth that not even the finest down can be sighted on them. **(4)** They are creatures of great beauty and elegant and well proportioned in the shape of their bodies. The openings of their ears are much broader than ours and flaps grow from them which serve as valves to close them. **(5)** Their tongues have an unusual feature: in part it is a product of nature, but in part it has been elaborated by human artifice. Their tongues divide into two lobes to a certain length, but they divide them further to double the tongue to its root. **(6)** Because of this they can articulate a great variety of sounds and they can imitate not only every human and articulate form of speech but the range of bird songs and every variety of sound. The most wonderful thing about them is this: they can speak with a company of two simultaneously and both answer their companions' questions and speak to the point of any subject of conversation. They conduct these conversations by using one lobe of their tongues to speak to one of their interlocutors and the other to speak to the other with equal fluency.

(7) The climate of this island is extremely temperate, as if they were living on the equator,[5] and they suffer neither from heat nor from cold. Their crops and trees ripen throughout the entire year, just as Homer says,[6]

> Pear ripens upon pear, apple upon apple,
> And grape upon grape too, and fig upon fig.

Here day is forever the same length as night and here no shadow is cast at midday, for the sun is straight overhead.

(57.1) These people live in groups based on kinship and no more than 400 kin are gathered into any one group. They spend their lives in meadows and the land supplies their sustenance abundantly. For on account of the excellence of their soil and the mildness of their climate, the products that the land produces spontaneously are more than enough to feed them. **(2)** A reed with a thick stock grows there and it produces a fruit in plenty which resembles our bitter white vetch. They gather the fruits of this plant and steep them in warm water until they rise to the size of

---

[5] The middle of the globe where days and nights are of equal length.

[6] Of the Phaeacians, in *Odyssey* VII 120-121. Cf. Hesiod *Works and Days* 118-119, 172-173 and *Odyssey* XIX 109-114 and **V 1** for similar descriptions of the god-sent fertility of the Age of Gold, of the heroes on the Islands of the Blest, and in the land of the good king.

a pigeon's egg. They then crack the fruit, grind it, and with their hands they expertly shape loaves which they bake for their food. These are very sweet to taste. **(3)** On the island there are abundant springs. Some of these are hot springs and are excellent for bathing and relaxation after work. Others are of cold and excellent sweet water and they contribute to the good health of the islanders. The islanders pursue every form of learning and are particularly interested in astronomy. **(4)** They have an alphabet of twenty-eight symbols, which represent the sounds of their language, but it is made up of only seven characters, each of which can be turned into four different positions. They do not write from left to right, as do the Greeks, but from top to bottom in parallel columns. These islanders live far longer than do men elsewhere. They live to about 150 years of age and their lives are for the most part free of disease. **(5)** Any person who is maimed or whose body has suffered some loss of function they compel to remove himself from life in accordance with a law that recognizes no exceptions. Their laws permit them to live for a fixed span of years. At the end of this period of years they do away with themselves willingly by an extraordinary means. There grows on this island a unique species of plant. If a person lies down upon it, he imperceptibly falls into a peaceful slumber and dies in his sleep.

(58.1) The islanders do not marry but they have their women in common. They raise the children born of their unions in common and cherish them equally. When these children are still infants, the wet nurses will exchange the children they are nursing so that not even their actual mothers can recognize their own children. Thanks to this institution no rivalry arises among them and they live their lives free of internal discord, setting the greatest value on social harmony.[7]

(2) There also exists on this island a unique species of animal. These creatures are small, but they have wonderful bodies and a wonderful potency to their blood. They are round and closely resemble our turtles. On their backs there are two diagonal stripes of yellow color in the form of an X. At the end of each of these stripes they have an eye and a mouth. **(3)** And so, even though they see with four eyes and take their food into as many mouths which lead into a single gullet, they swallow their food through this single gullet and all their food passes into a single stomach. And likewise they have only one set of intestines and internal

---

[7]   Comparable and the evident source for Iamboulos are the arrangements in Plato *Republic* IV 423D, V 449 C, 457D-461C, and *Timaeus* 18C-19A.

organs. They are supported by numerous feet that extend around the circumference of their bodies and with these they can move in any direction they like. **(4)** The blood of this creature has a fantastic property: it can re-attach any living member that has been severed, even if this member is a hand that has been amputated or another member. This is true of all other members of the body which are not vital organs on which life depends.

(5) Now each of these groups raises a large species of bird the likes of which are not found elsewhere. They employ this bird to test their children when they are still infants and to determine their character and disposition. They lift their children onto the backs of these creatures and the birds take to flight. Those of the babes who can endure this flight through the air they raise, but those who become nauseous and terrified they dispose of, reckoning that they will not live long and are not worth raising because of the weakness of their character.[8]

Figure 16 Children of the Island of the Sun. Drawing by Joanne Lorah.

---

8   This provision for testing infants is evidently inspired by the proposals of Socrates in *Republic* III 413D-E; cf. V 467E.

(6) In each of the island communities the oldest man has uninterrupted authority, as if he were a king, and all members of his community are obedient unto him. And, when the oldest man has fulfilled his allotted time of 150 years and removed himself from life according to their law, the person who is nearest to him in age takes over his rule.

(7) There are strong currents in the sea surrounding this island and it is subject to extremes of high and low tide. The sea is of sweet water. The Big Dipper and Little Dipper and many of the stars of our hemisphere are not visible there at all. In this archipelago there are seven islands. All are very similar in size and they stand at equal distances from one another. The islanders all follow the same customs and the same laws.

(59.1) Although the inhabitants of these islands have an abundance of produce to supply their every need without cultivating the soil, they do not enjoy these without restraint, but they maintain a simple diet and eat only as much as they need. They cook their meat by roasting it or boiling it in water, but they are entirely innocent of any notion of the sauces of our gourmet chefs or the variety of condiments these use in their cooking.

(2) They worship as divinities the firmament that encompasses all things and the sun and the heavenly bodies in general. They are ingenious fishermen and catch fish of many kinds as well as a number of species of birds. **(3)** Many kinds of nut trees flourish on this island without cultivation, and olive trees grow there as do vines. From these they press great quantities of oil and wine. Giant snakes are found there, but they do not harm the inhabitants. Their meat is edible and exceedingly sweet.

(4) They manufacture their clothing from certain reeds that contain a soft and bright down inside their stalks. They tease this down into strands and mix these with crushed sea shells to produce gowns of a wonderful purple hue. There are also animals on this island unlike those found elsewhere which are so strange as to be unbelievable.

(5) There is a fixed system to the diet of the islanders. They do not eat every variety of food at the same time. Rather, according to a fixed sequence, they eat fish on some days and fowl on others. There are days when they eat only land animals and days when they eat only olives and appetizers. **(6)** And they take turns in being of service to their community: some devote themselves to fishing and others to manufacture; others are occupied with the other necessities of life, and others contribute to the needs of the community according to a fixed calendar.[9] The only exception is in the case of persons of advanced age. **(7)** During their religious festivals and feast days, the islanders recite and sing hymns to the gods and speeches of praise and especially in honor of the Sun (Helios), who has given his name to both the islands and their inhabitants.[10]

(8) Their dead they bury by digging a trench in the sand of the sea shore exposed at low tide so that with the high tide the grave will be covered over with sand. They say that the stalks of the plants whose fruit they use to make their bread increases in size to the thickness of a span when the moon is waxing and shrinks in size in proportion to the size of the moon as it wanes. **(9)** The water from their hot springs is sweet and salubrious and it retains its heat and does not cool except when cold water or wine is mixed with it.

(60.1) Iamboulos writes that, after he and his companions[11] had remained on the island for seven years, they were expelled against their will since the islanders regarded them as wicked men and men raised in vicious ways. When they had refitted their small ship and stored provisions for the voyage in it, they were forced to make their departure together. They sailed for more than seven months. They were shipwrecked on a sandy and marshy stretch of the coast of India. **(2)** Iamboulos' companion was drowned in the surf, but Iamboulos himself was brought by the natives to their village and from there to their king at the city of Palibothra.[12]

---

9   It would seem that this last group is devoted to supplying the needs for the religious festivals of the island. In this system of a cycle in which the islanders engage in different occupations Iamboulos is describing a society unlike that of Plato's Kallipolis in its most basic principle. For Plato, a just society depended on each individual performing the function for which he or she was naturally suited; on Iamboulos' Island of the Sun, each individual would work at a number of different occupations in a fixed sequence.

10   Presumably in Greek, the names of the islands and islanders would be: *Helionesoi* and *Helionesiotai*. It is not clear from Diodorus' hurried and disjointed account whether some of the islanders receive the honor of encomia, as is the case of the citizens who have distinguished themselves for their bravery in Plato's Kallipolis (cf. *Republic* X 607A) or whether there is a strain of Euhemerism in the assignment of both hymns and encomia to the gods.

11   The plural is something of a mystery, since Iamboulos made it clear in the beginning of his narrative that he was put to sea in a boat with only one other companion and in the immediate sequel he speaks of only one other companion.

12   Pataliputra (modern Patna). This reference seems to establish the event as narrated in the third century BC (280-200), since the Seleucid kings of Asia Minor had ambassadors there; cf. Strabo II 70 and XV 702; Pliny *Natural History* VI 63; Ptolemy *Geography* I 1219; Tarn (1951) 121-33; and Altheim (1948) 155-162.

Palibothra is many days journey from the coast. **(3)** The king, who was a philhellene and had a passion for learning, treated Iamboulos to a magnificent reception. After some time he was granted safe passage and he first reached the territory of Persia and finally arrived safely in Greece.

Iamboulos, who regarded this history as worth recording, also wrote a considerable account of India and included a number of details unknown to other writers. But we will conclude this present book at this point, since we have now completed the project announced at its beginning.

Appendix:
Lucian's Marvels of the Moon

Other than Diodorus Siculus, Lucian is the only ancient writer to mention Iamboulos (in *True History* I 3), expressing his admiration for him (as quoted above in the introduction to Iamboulos) before beginning his own story. In his *True History*, Lucian might well be imitating Iamboulos' first person narrative of his travels. (He names himself as Loukianos for the only time in his works in *True History* II 28.) Lucian relates his own experiences, not on an island in the Indian Ocean, but on a planet which had first seemed an island, the moon. This excerpt comes from *True History* I 22-26. Our traveller relates all the wonders he had observed while he was in the palace of King Endymion during the seven-day period between the king's decision that he and his companions must leave the moon and their actual departure. It is significant that both Lucian and Iamboulos are expelled from their marvelous islands.

LUCIAN *True History* I 22-26

(I 22) I want to tell of the strange and extraordinary things I observed on the moon in the time before my departure. The very first thing to report is that the inhabitants of the moon are not born of women but of males. The Selenitai mate with males and are completely innocent of the word "woman." Up until the age of twenty-five they are brides but afterwards they are husbands. They do not conceive in a womb but in the soft back of the knee. When the embryo begins to develop, the knee begins to swell and with the passage of time they make an incision and draw the fetus out dead. But they revive the fetus by exposing it to the wind with its mouth open. Now I think that this must be the derivation of the Greek medical term "*gastroknemia*."[13] It is in the back of the knee and not the stomach that the fetus of the Selenitai develops.

I can top this with another report. On the moon there is a species of humans, the species of the so-called Dendritai or Tree People. They come about in this manner. They cut off the right testicle of

---

[13] Literally, the "stomach of the shin" (i.e., the calf of the leg).

a person and plant it in the ground. A towering tree springs up from it. It is fleshy and somewhat like a phallos and it has branches and leaves. It bears nuts which are about a yard across. When these ripen, they press them like grapes and human beings hatch out from them. These Dendritai have prosthetic genitals. Some have ivory genitals, but the poor have wood peckers. These are the organs with which they mount their partners and have sex.

(23) When a Selenites grows old, he does not die but dissolves into thin air, like smoke. They all have the same diet. They build a wood fire and once the fire subsides, they roast frogs over the coals. Let me tell you—there are many frogs flying through the air on the moon. As the frogs are roasting, the Selenitai sit around the fire, as if at table and breathe in the smoke as it wafts upward and enjoy the smoky feast. This is their food. Their drink is air which has been condensed and poured into a drinking vessel and which sublimates as a dewy moisture. They do not urinate or relieve themselves, as do we. They have no body apertures like ours. Nor do the young men offer their buttocks to their lovers. They have an opening in the thigh above the back of the knee.

On the moon beauty is regarded as baldness and hairlessness. They loath men with long hair. But the opposite is true on the maned stars called "comets."[14] There people with long hair are considered good looking. I know this from some visitors from the comets who spoke of their admiration for long hair. Another thing is that the Selenitai grow beards just above their knees. They have no toes on their feet, but they all have only a single toe for a foot. Just above their buttocks sprouts a head of cabbage. This is quite long and a kind of tail. It is always in leaf and it will not break even when they fall on their backsides.

(24) The mucus from their noses is extremely tart honey. When they work hard or exercise, a film of milk covers their entire bodies like sweat. They make cheese of this and pour some drops of "miel du nez" on it. They press oil from onions. It is thick, bright, and as fragrant as frankincense. They have many vines whose grapes yield water. The seeds of these grapes are like hailstones and it was my impression that, when a gust of wind buffets these vines, the grapes burst open and hail falls down to earth.

They use their stomachs as pouches and they put everything they need inside of them. They can open their stomachs up and close them tight. There are no entrails visible. All you can see inside is

---

[14]   Literally, "having heads of hair," referring to the trailing tail of the comet.

a thick fur lining. Their newborn babes slip into these pouches when they are cold.

(25) The well-to-do among them wear garments of the supplest glass; the poor, clothes of woven bronze. Their country is rich in copper deposits and they work their bronze by sprinkling it with water as if it were wool. Now I am reluctant to say anything about their eyes. My reader might think that I am telling lies, because what I have to report is so incredible. Even so, I will tell about their eyes. They can take their eyes out. Whoever wants to, can remove his eyes and store them away until he needs to see. And, once he puts them back, presto! he can see. Many of the Selenitai misplace their own eyes and have to borrow their neighbor's eyes. There are those too who have a large collection of eyes. These are the wealthy. Their ears very much resemble the broad leaves of plane trees. The exception is the case of the Dendritai,[15] who come from the nuts I have described. These and these alone have wooden ears.

(26) I observed still another wonder of the moon in the palace of King Endymion. There is an enormous mirror positioned over a well of no great depth. Now, if you were to go down into this well, you can hear everything that is being said on earth below. And, if you look up to the mirror, you can see in it all the cities and peoples of the world, just as if you were actually standing right there. When I looked up, I could see my friends and relatives and all of my native land. But I cannot say for certain if they could see me too. If anyone does not believe what I say, he will know that what I am saying is true—if ever he travels to these regions himself!

---

[15] The "Tree People."

FRANCISCI

DE VERULAMIO,
Summi Angliæ
CANCELARII,
Instauratio
magna.

Sim: Pass: sculp:

Multi pertransibunt & augebitur scientia.

Anno

LONDINI
Apud Joannem Billium
Typographum
Regium.

1620.

Figure 17 A Carvel heads out into the Atlantic, beyond the pillars of Heracles. Frontispiece to *the Instauratio Magna* (1620). University of Minnesota Library.

IV. Francis Bacon's New Atlantis

Francis Bacon's *New Atlantis* is the only work included in this collection devoted to utopian literature which can be described as "utopian" in the unexamined sense of this word. He is, in fact, attached to an ideal. His ideal is that of a society governed by the pursuit of science and its benefits for mankind. Like many utopian works in the tradition of Euhemeros and Iamboulos, *New Atlantis* is a first-person narrative. We never learn, however, who its narrator is. With *New Atlantis*, the project of Plato's Atlantis has moved 180 degrees around the globe—from the vast lost island of Atlantis in the Ocean named after it and from the mid-fourth century BC to the middle of the South Sea (or Pacific) in the third decade of the seventeenth century. The remote island civilization discovered there by English sailors is dedicated to science or what Bacon knew of as "natural philosophy" or "history." Bacon was as fervently committed to the project of the House of Salomon and the College of Six Days' Works as was Raphael Hythlodaeus to the society he discovered in his voyage to Utopia.

Bacon makes his debt to Plato abundantly clear in the history of the island that its governor relates to the narrator of *New Atlantis* and his companions. The governor speaks of "the narration and description which is made by a great man with you" (§ 26). But he corrects Plato on one point; Atlantis was not plunged to the bottom of the Atlantic by an earthquake; it was overwhelmed by a deluge (§ 28). Bacon did not believe that Atlantis had completely vanished; he identifies his "great Atlantis" with America. Bacon imitates Plato's *Critias* in leaving his narrative a fragment. But unlike Plato, whose dramatic art he cannot match, Bacon ends with a complete sentence.

New Atlantis was published the year after Bacon's death in 1627. It was printed by Bacon's chaplain William Rawley at the end of his *Sylva Sylvarum: Or A Natural History* in an edition of Bacon's posthumous works. It is thought to have been written in the 1620s, after his disgrace and dismissal as Lord Chancellor of England in 1621.

Our text is that of James Spedding, R. L. Ellis, and D. D. Heath, *The Works of Francis Bacon* (London 1857-1859). We have retained the spelling but have added headings and paragraphs to break down the long runs of text in the edition of Rawley. We have modified the punctuation only rarely to accommodate these divisions. The Introduction to *New Atlantis* reproduced below is that of Bacon's Rawley, who also translated *New Atlantis* into Latin.

We have also profited greatly from the text and annotations of *The Oxford Authors, Francis Bacon*, ed. Brian Vickers (Oxford 1996) 457-488.

New Atlantis

A Work Unfinished

written by

The Right Honourable
Francis Lord Verulam,
Viscount St. Alban

[1624]

To the Reader

This fable my Lord devised, to the end that he might exhibit therein a model or description of a college instituted for the interpreting of nature and the producing of great and marvellous works for the benefit of men, under the name of Salomon's House, or the College of the Six Days' Works. And even so far his Lordship hath proceeded, as to finish that part. Certainly the model is more vast and high than can possibly be imitated in all things; notwithstanding most things therein are within men's power to effect. His Lordship thought also in this present fable to have composed a frame of Laws, or of the best state or mould of a commonwealth; but foreseeing it would be a long work, his desire of collecting the Natural History diverted him, which he preferred many degrees before it.

This work of the New Atlantis (as much as concerneth the English edition) his Lordship designed for this place; in regard it hath so near affinity (in one part of it) with the preceding Natural History.

New Atlantis

Our narrator describes how, in a trip to China and Japan from Peru he and fifty of his companions were blown off course to the north and came upon the island of Ben Salem in the middle of the Pacific.

§ 1   We sailed from Peru, (where we had continued by the space of one whole year,) for China and Japan, by the South Sea;[1] taking with us victuals for twelve months; and had good winds from the east, though soft and weak, for five months' space and more. But then the wind came about, and settled in the west for many days, so as we could make little or no way, and were sometimes in purpose to turn back. But then again there arose strong and great winds from the south, with a point east; which carried us

---

[1]   The Pacific Ocean.

up (for all that we could do) towards the north; by which time our victuals failed us, though we made good spare of them. So that finding ourselves in the midst of the greatest wilderness of waters in the world, without victual, we gave ourselves for lost men, and prepared for death. Yet we did lift up our hearts and voices to God above, who "showeth his wonders in the deep";[2] beseeching him of his mercy, that as in the beginning he discovered the face of the deep,[3] and brought forth dry land, so he would now discover land to us, that we might not perish.

§ 2 And it came to pass that the next day about evening, we saw within a kenning before us, towards the north, as it were thick clouds, which did put us in some hope of land; knowing how that part of the South Sea was utterly unknown; and might have islands or continents, that hitherto were not come to light. Wherefore we bent our course thither, where we saw the appearance of land, all that night; and in the dawning of the next day, we might plainly discern that it was a land; flat to our sight, and full of boscage; which made it shew the more dark. And after an hour and a half's sailing, we entered into a good haven, being the port of a fair city; not great indeed, but well built, and that gave a pleasant view from the sea: and we thinking every minute long till we were on land, came close to the shore, and offered to land.

§ 3 But straightways we saw divers of the people, with bastons in their hands, as it were forbidding us to land; yet without any cries or fierceness, but only as warning us off by signs that they made. Whereupon being not a little discomforted, we were advising with ourselves what we should do. During which time there made forth to us a small boat, with about eight persons in it; whereof one of them had in his hand a tipstaff of a yellow cane, tipped at both ends with blue, who came aboard our ship, without any show of distrust at all. And when he saw one of our number present himself somewhat afore the rest, he drew forth a little scroll of parchment, (somewhat yellower than our parchment, and shining like the leaves of writing tables, but otherwise soft and flexible,) and delivered it to our foremost man. In which scroll were written in ancient Hebrew, and in ancient Greek, and in good Latin of the School, and in Spanish, these words; "Land ye not, none of you; and provide to be gone from this coast within sixteen days, except you have further time given you. Meanwhile, if you want fresh water, or victual, or help for your sick, or that

---

[2] Psalms 107: 23-24.
[3] Genesis 1: 9.

your ship needeth repair, write down your wants, and you shall have that which belongeth to mercy." This scroll was signed with a stamp of cherubins' wings, not spread but hanging downwards, and by them a cross. This being delivered, the officer returned, and left only a servant with us to receive our answer.

§ 4   Consulting hereupon amongst ourselves, we were much perplexed. The denial of landing and hasty warning us away troubled us much; on the other side, to find that the people had languages and were so full of humanity, did comfort us not a little. And above all, the sign of the cross to that instrument was to us a great rejoicing, and as it were a certain presage of good. Our answer was in the Spanish tongue; "That for our ship it was well; for we had rather met with calms and contrary winds than any tempests. For our sick, they were many, and in very ill case; so that if they were not permitted to land, they ran danger of their lives." Our other wants we set down in particular; adding "that we had some little store of merchandise, which if it pleased them to deal for, it might supply our wants without being chargeable unto them." We offered some reward in pistolets[4] unto the servant, and a piece of crimson velvet to be presented to the officer; but the servant took them not, nor would scarce look upon them; and so left us, and went back in another little boat which was sent for him.

§ 5   About three hours after we had dispatched our answer, there came towards us a person (as it seemed) of place. He had on him a gown with wide sleeves, of a kind of water chamolet, of an excellent azure colour, far more glossy than ours; his under apparel was green; and so was his hat, being in the form of a turban, daintily made, and not so huge as the Turkish turbans; and the locks of his hair came down below the brims of it. A reverend man was he to behold. He came in a boat, gilt in some part of it, with four persons more only in that boat; and was followed by another boat, wherein were some twenty. When he was come within a flight-shot of our ship, signs were made to us that we should send forth some to meet him upon the water; which we presently did in our ship-boat, sending the principal man amongst us save one, and four of our number with him. When we were come within six yards of their boat, they called us to stay, and not to approach further; which we did. And thereupon the man whom I before described stood up, and with a loud voice in Spanish, asked, "Are

---

⁴   Gold coins issued by Spain. The aversion of the inhabitants of New Atlantis to gold is a deliberate reference to both Plato's *Republic* and More's *Utopia*.

ye Christians?" We answered, "We were"; fearing the less, because of the cross we had seen in the subscription. At which answer the said person lifted up his right hand towards heaven, and drew it softly to his mouth, (which is the gesture they use when they thank God,) and then said: "If ye will swear (all of you) by the merits of the Saviour that ye are no pirates, nor have shed blood lawfully nor unlawfully within forty days past, you may have licence to come on land." We said, "We were all ready to take that oath." Whereupon one of those that were with him, being (as it seemed) a notary, made an entry of this act. Which done, another of the attendants of the great person, which was with him in the same boat, after his lord had spoken a little to him, said aloud; "My lord would have you know, that it is not of pride or greatness that he cometh not aboard your ship; but for that in your answer you declare that you have many sick amongst you, he was warned by the Conservator of Health of the city that he should keep a distance."

§ 6   We bowed ourselves towards him, and answered, "We were his humble servants; and accounted for great honour and singular humanity towards us that which was already done; but hoped well that the nature of the sickness of our men was not infectious." So he returned; and a while after came the notary to us aboard our ship; holding in his hand a fruit of that country, like an orange, but of colour between orange-tawney and scarlet, which cast a most excellent odour. He used it (as it seemeth) for a preservative against infection. He gave us our oath; "By the name of Jesus and his merits": and after told us that the next day by six of the clock in the morning we should be sent to, and brought to the Strangers' House, (so he called it,) where we should be accommodated of things both for our whole and for our sick. So he left us; and when we offered him some pistolets, he smiling said: "He must not be twice paid for one labour": meaning (as I take it) that he had salary sufficient of the state for his service. For (as I after learned) they call an officer that taketh rewards, *twice paid.*

The crew, arrived from Peru to the harbor of Bensalem, are brought ashore and lodged in the Stranger's House, where those of the crew who had fallen ill are taken care of.

§ 7   The next morning early, there came to us the same officer that came to us at first with his cane, and told us, "He came to conduct us to the Strangers' House; and that he had prevented the hour, because we might have the whole day before us for our business. "For," he said, "if you will follow my advice, there shall first go with me some few of you, and see the place, and how it may be made convenient for you; and then you may send for your sick, and the rest of your number which ye will bring on land." We thanked him, and said, "That this care which he took of desolate strangers God would reward." And so six of us went on land with him: and when we were on land, he went before us, and turned to us, and said, "He was but our servant and our guide." He led us through three fair streets; and all the way we went there were gathered some people on both sides standing in a row; but in so civil a fashion, as if it had been not to wonder at us but to welcome us; and divers of them, as we passed by them, put their arms a little abroad; which is their gesture when they bid any welcome.

§ 8   The Strangers' House is a fair and spacious house, built of brick, of somewhat a bluer colour than our brick; and with handsome windows, some of glass, some of a kind of cambric oiled. He brought us first into a fair parlour above stairs, and then asked us, "What number of persons we were? And how many sick?" We answered, "We were in all (sick and whole) one and fifty persons, whereof our sick were seventeen." He desired us to have patience a little, and to stay till he came back to us; which was about an hour after; and then he led us to see the chambers which were provided for us, being in number nineteen; they having cast it (as it seemeth) that four of those chambers, which were better than the rest, might receive four of the principal men of our company, and lodge them alone by themselves; and the other fifteen chambers were to lodge us two and two together. The chambers were handsome and cheerful chambers, and furnished civilly. Then he led us to a long gallery, like a dorture,[5] which he showed us all along the one side (for the other side was but wall and window) seventeen cells, very neat ones, having partitions of cedar wood. Which gallery and cells, being in all forty, (many more than we needed,) were instituted as an infirmary for sick persons. And he told us withal, that as any of our sick waxed well, he might be removed from his cell to a chamber; for which purpose there were set forth ten spare chambers, besides the number we spake of before.

§ 9   This done, he brought us back to the parlour, and lifting up his cane a little, (as they do when they give any charge or command,) said to us, "Ye are to know that the custom of the land requireth,

---

5   Dormitory.

that after this day and tomorrow, (which we give you for removing your people from the ship,) you are to keep within doors for three days. But let it not trouble you, nor do not think yourselves restrained, but rather left to your rest and ease. You shall want nothing, and there are six of our people appointed to attend you, for any business you may have abroad." We gave him thanks with all affection and respect, and said, "God surely is manifest in this land." We offered him also twenty pistolets; but he smiled, and only said; "What? twice paid!" And so he left us.

§ 10   Soon after our dinner was served in; which was right good viands, both for bread and meat; better than any collegiate diet that I have known in Europe. We had also drink of three sorts, all wholesome and good; wine of the grape; a drink of grain, such as is with us our ale, but more clear; and a kind of cider made of a fruit of that country; a wonderful pleasing and refreshing drink. Besides, there were brought in to us great store of those scarlet oranges for our sick; which (they said) were an assured remedy for sickness taken at sea. There was given us also a box of small grey or whitish pills, which they wished our sick should take, one of the pills every night before sleep; which (they said) would hasten their recovery.

§ 11   The next day, after that our trouble of carriage and removing of our men and goods out of our ship was somewhat settled and quiet, I thought good to call our company together; and when they were assembled said unto them: "My dear friends, let us know ourselves, and how it standeth with us. We are men cast on land, as Jonas was out of the whale's belly, when we were as buried in the deep; and now we are on land, we are but between death and life; for we are beyond both the old world and the new; and whether ever we shall see Europe, God only knoweth. It is a kind of miracle hath brought us hither: and it must be little less that shall bring us hence. Therefore in regard of our deliverance past, and our danger present and to come, let us look up to God, and every man reform his own ways. Besides we are come here amongst a Christian people, full of piety and humanity: let us not bring that confusion of face upon ourselves, as to show our vices or unworthiness before them. Yet there is more. For they have by commandment (though in form of courtesy) cloistered us within these walls for three days: who knoweth whether it be not to take some taste of our manners and conditions? and if they find them bad, to banish us straightways; if good, to give us further time. For these men that they have given us for attendance may withal have an eye upon us. Therefore for God's love, and as we love the weal of our souls and bodies, let us so behave ourselves as we may be at peace with God, and may find grace in the eyes of this people." Our company with one voice thanked me for my good admonition, and promised me to live soberly and civilly, and without giving any the least occasion of offence. So we spent our three days joyfully and without care, in expectation what would be done with us when they were expired. During which time, we had every hour joy of the amendment of our sick; who thought themselves cast into some divine pool of healing,[6] they mended so kindly and so fast.

The strangers are greeted by the Governor of the House of Strangers, a Christian priest, who informs them of the conditions of their sojourn on the island.

§ 12　The morrow after our three days were past, there came to us a new man that we had not seen before, clothed in blue as the former was, save that his turban was white, with a small red cross on the top. He had also a tippet of fine linen. At his coming in, he did bend to us a little, and put his arms abroad. We of our parts saluted him in a very lowly and submissive manner; as looking that from him we should receive sentence of life or death. He desired to speak with some few of us: whereupon six of us only stayed, and the rest avoided the room. He said, "I am by office governor of this House of Strangers, and by vocation I am a Christian priest; and therefore am come to you to offer you my service, both as strangers and chiefly as Christians. Some things I may tell you, which I think you will not be unwilling to hear. The state hath given you licence to stay on land for the space of six weeks; and let it not trouble you if your occasions ask further time, for the law in this point is not precise; and I do not doubt but myself shall be able to obtain for you such further time as may be convenient.

§ 13　Ye shall also understand, that the Strangers' House is at this time rich, and much aforehand; for it hath laid up revenue these thirty-seven years; for so long it is since any stranger arrived in this part: and therefore take ye no care; the state will defray you all the time you stay; neither shall you stay one day the less for that. As for any merchandise ye have brought, ye shall be well used, and have your return either in merchandise or in gold and silver: for to us it is all one. And if you have any other request to make, hide it not. For ye shall find we will not make your countenance

---

[6]　A reference to the pool of Bethesda, John 5: 1-17.

to fall by the answer ye shall receive. Only this I must tell you, that none of you must go above a *karan*" (that is with them a mile and an half) "from the walls of the city, without especial leave."

§ 14   We answered, after we had looked awhile one upon another admiring this gracious and parentlike usage; "That we could not tell what to say: for we wanted words to express our thanks; and his noble free offers left us nothing to ask. It seemed to us that we had before us a picture of our salvation in heaven; for we that were awhile since in the jaws of death, were now brought into a place where we found nothing but consolations. For the commandment laid upon us, we would not fail to obey it, though it was impossible but our hearts should be inflamed to tread further upon this happy and holy ground." We added; "That our tongues should first cleave to the roofs of our mouths, ere we should forget either his reverend person or this whole nation in our prayers." We also most humbly besought him to accept of us as his true servants, by as just a right as ever men on earth were bounden; laying and presenting both our persons and all we had at his feet. He said; "He was a priest, and looked for a priest's reward: which was our brotherly love and the good of our souls and bodies." So he went from us, not without tears of tenderness in his eyes; and left us also confused with joy and kindness, saying amongst ourselves, "That we were come into a land of angels, which did appear to us daily and prevent us with comforts, which we thought not of, much less expected."

The ship's company is visited once again by the Governor of the House of Strangers.

§ 15   The next day, about ten of the clock, the governor came to us again, and after salutations said familiarly, "That he was come to visit us:" and called for a chair, and sat him down: and we, being some ten of us, (the rest were of the meaner sort, or else gone abroad,) sat down with him. And when we were set, he began thus: "We of this island of Bensalem,[7]" (for so they call it in their language,) "have this; that by means of our solitary situation, and of the laws of secrecy which we have for our travellers, and our rare admission of strangers, we know well most part of the habitable world, and are ourselves unknown. Therefore because he that knoweth least is fittest to ask questions, it is more reason, for the entertainment of the time, that ye ask me questions, than that I ask you."

---

[7]   In Hebrew, "the son of peace."

§ 16 We answered; "That we humbly thanked him that he would give us leave so to do: and that we conceived by the taste we had already, that there was no worldly thing on earth more worthy to be known than the state of that happy land. But above all," (we said,) "since that we were met from the several ends of the world, and hoped assuredly that we should meet one day in the kingdom of heaven, (for that we were both parts Christians,) we desired to know (in respect that land was so remote, and so divided by vast and unknown seas, from the land where our Saviour walked on earth,) who was the apostle of that nation, and how it was converted to the faith?" It appeared in his face that he took great contentment in this our question: he said, "Ye knit my heart to you, by asking this question in the first place; for it sheweth that you "first seek the kingdom of heaven";[8] and I shall gladly and briefly satisfy your demand.

The Governor of House of Strangers relates to ten of his guests how it was that the word of Christ came to the island of Bensalem.

§ 17 "About twenty years after the ascension of our Saviour, it came to pass that there was seen by the people of Renfusa, (a city upon the eastern coast of our island,) within night, (the night was cloudy and calm,) as it might be some mile into the sea, a great pillar of light; not sharp, but in form of a column or cylinder, rising from the sea a great way up towards heaven: and on the top of it was seen a large cross of light, more bright and resplendent than the body of the pillar.[9] Upon which so strange a spectacle, the people of the city gathered apace together upon the sands, to wonder; and so after put themselves into a number of small boats, to go nearer to this marvellous sight. But when the boats were come within about sixty yards of the pillar, they found themselves all bound, and could go no further; yet so as they might move to go about, but might not approach nearer: so as the boats stood all as in a theatre, beholding this light as an heavenly sign. It so fell out, that there was in one of the boats one of the wise men of the society of Salomon's House; which house or college (my good brethren) is the very eye of this kingdom; who having awhile attentively and devoutly viewed and contemplated this pillar and cross, fell down upon his face; and then raised himself upon his knees, and lifting up his hands to heaven, made his prayers in this manner:

---

8 From the Sermon on the Mount, Matthew 6: 33; Luke 12: 31.
9 A reference to the pillar of cloud and fire that God created to lead the people of Israel out of Egypt, Exodus 13: 21-22.

§ 18   "'Lord God of heaven and earth, thou hast vouchsafed of thy grace to those of our order, to know thy works of creation, and the secrets of them; and to discern (as far as appertaineth to the generations of men) between divine miracles, works of nature, works of art, and impostures and illusions of all sorts. I do here acknowledge and testify before this people, that the thing which we now see before our eyes is thy Finger and a true Miracle; and forasmuch as we learn in our books that thou never workest miracles but to a divine and excellent end, (for the laws of nature are thine own laws, and thou exceedest them not but upon great cause,) we most humbly beseech thee to prosper this great sign, and to give us the interpretation and use of it in mercy; which thou dost in some part secretly promise by sending it unto us.'

§ 19   "When he had made his prayer, he presently found the boat he was in moveable and unbound; whereas all the rest remained still fast; and taking that for an assurance of leave to approach, he caused the boat to be softly and with silence rowed towards the pillar. But ere he came near it, the pillar and cross of light brake up, and cast itself abroad, as it were, into a firmament of many stars; which also vanished soon after, and there was nothing left to be seen but a small ark or chest of cedar, dry, and not wet at all with water, though it swam. And in the fore-end of it, which was towards him, grew a small green branch of palm; and when the wise man had taken it with all reverence into his boat, it opened of itself, and there were found in it a Book and a Letter; both written in fine parchment, and wrapped in sindons[10] of linen. The Book contained all the canonical books of the Old and New Testament, according as you have them, (for we know well what the Churches with you receive); and the Apocalypse itself, and some other books of the New Testament which were not at that time written, were nevertheless in the Book. And for the Letter, it was in these words: "'I Bartholomew, a servant of the Highest, and Apostle of Jesus Christ, was warned by an angel that appeared to me in a vision of glory, that I should commit this ark to the floods of the sea. Therefore I do testify and declare unto that people where God shall ordain this ark to come to land, that in the same day is come unto them salvation and peace and good-will, from the Father, and from the Lord Jesus.'

§ 20   "There was also in both these writings, as well the Book as the Letter, wrought a great miracle, conform to that of the Apostles

---

[10] Bands.

in the original Gift of Tongues. For there being at that time in this land Hebrews, Persians, and Indians, besides the natives, every one read upon the Book and Letter, as if they had been written in his own language. And thus was this land saved from infidelity (as the remain of the old world was from water) by an ark, through the apostolical and miraculous evangelism of St. Bartholomew."[11] And here he paused, and a messenger came, and called him from us. So this was all that passed in that conference.

The Governor of the House of Strangers visits on the morrow and is questioned by his guests touching the Bensalemites' knowledge of the outside world.

§ 21   The next day, the same governor came again to us immediately after dinner, and excused himself, saying, "That the day before he was called from us somewhat abruptly, but now he would make us amends, and spend time with us, if we held his company and conference agreeable." We answered, "That we held it so agreeable and pleasing to us, as we forgot both dangers past and fears to come, for the time we heard him speak; and that we thought an hour spent with him, was worth years of our former life." He bowed himself a little to us, and after we were set again, he said; "Well, the questions are on your part." One of our number said, after a little pause; "That there was a matter we were no less desirous to know, than fearful to ask, lest we might presume too far. But encouraged by his rare humanity towards us, (that could scarce think ourselves strangers, being his vowed and professed servants,) we would take the hardiness to propound it: humbly beseeching him, if he thought it not fit to be answered, that he would pardon it, though he rejected it."

The guests of the House of Strangers make bold to ask how it passes that the inhabitants of the island of Bensalem know of other parts of the world but are unknown elsewhere.

§ 22   We said; "We well observed those his words, which he formerly spake, that this happy island where we now stood was known to few, and yet knew most of the nations of the world; which we found to be true, considering they had the languages of Europe, and knew much of our state and business; and yet we in Europe (notwithstanding all the remote discoveries and navigations of this last age,) never heard any of the least inkling or glimpse of this island. This we found wonderful strange; for that all nations have inter-knowledge one of another either by voyage into for-

---

[11]   According to Eusebius, *Ecclesiastical History* V 10, the apostle Bartholomew spread the gospel as far as India.

eign parts, or by strangers that come to them: and though the traveller into a foreign country doth commonly know more by the eye, than he that stayeth at home can by relation of the traveller; yet both ways suffice to make a mutual knowledge, in some degree, on both parts. But for this island, we never heard tell of any ship of theirs that had been seen to arrive upon any shore of Europe; no, nor of either the East or West Indies; nor yet of any ship of any other part of the world that had made return from them. And yet the marvel rested not in this. For the situation of it (as his lordship said) in the secret conclave of such a vast sea might cause it. But then that they should have knowledge of the languages, books, affairs, of those that lie such a distance from them, it was a thing we could not tell what to make of; for that it seemed to us a condition and propriety of divine powers and beings, to be hidden and unseen to others, and yet to have others open and as in a light to them."

§ 23 At this speech the governor gave a gracious smile, and said; "That we did well to ask pardon for this question we now asked; for that it imported as if we thought this land a land of magicians, that sent forth spirits of the air into all parts, to bring them news and intelligence of other countries." It was answered by us all, in all possible humbleness, but yet with a countenance taking knowledge that we knew that he spake it but merrily, "That we were apt enough to think there was somewhat supernatural in this island; but yet rather as angelical than magical. But to let his lordship know truly what it was that made us tender and doubtful to ask this question, it was not any such conceit, but because we remembered he had given a touch in his former speech, that this land had laws of secrecy touching strangers." To this he said; "You remember it aright; and therefore in that I shall say to you I must reserve some particulars, which it is not lawful for me to reveal; but there will be enough left to give you satisfaction.

The sea commerce of three thousand years past is described and the causes of its cessation explained and the fate of the empire of Atlantis described.

§ 24 "You shall understand (that which perhaps you will scarce think credible) that about three thousand years ago, or somewhat more, the navigation of the world, (specially for remote voyages,) was greater than at this day. Do not think with yourselves that I know not how much it is increased with you within these six-score years: I know it well: and yet I say greater then than now; whether it was, that the example of the ark, that saved the remnant of men from the universal deluge, gave men confidence to adventure upon the waters; or what it was; but such is the truth. The Phoenicians, and especially the Tyrians, had great fleets. So had the Carthaginians, their colony, which is yet further west. Toward the east, the shipping of Egypt and of Palestina was likewise great. China also, and the great Atlantis (that you call America), which have now but junks and canoes, abounded then in tall ships. This island (as appeareth by faithful registers of those times) had then fifteen hundred strong ships, of great content. Of all this there is with you sparing memory, or none; but we have large knowledge thereof.

§ 25   "At that time, this land was known and frequented by the ships and vessels of all the nations before named. And (as it cometh to pass) they had many times men of other countries, that were no sailors, that came with them; as Persians, Chaldeans, Arabians; so as almost all nations of might and fame resorted hither; of whom we have some stirps and little tribes with us at this day. And for our own ships, they went sundry voyages, as well to your Straits, which you call the Pillars of Hercules, as to other parts in the Atlantic and Mediterrane Seas; as to Paguim[12] (which is the same with Cambaline[13]) and Quinzy, upon the Oriental Seas, as far as the boarders of the East Tartary.

§ 26   "At the same time, and an age after, or more, the inhabitants of the great Atlantis did flourish. For though the narration and description which is made by a great man with you,[14] that the descendants of Neptune planted there; and of the magnificent temple, palace, city, and hill; and the manifold streams of goodly navigable rivers, (which, as so many chains, environed the same site and temple);[15] and the several degrees of ascent whereby men did climb up to the same, as if it had been a *scala coeli*;[16] be all poetical and fabulous: yet so much is true, that the said country of Atlantis, as well that of Peru, then called Coya, as that of Mexico, then named Tyrambel, were mighty and proud kingdoms in arms, shipping, and riches: so mighty, as at one time (or at least within the space of ten years) they both made two great expeditions;

---

[12]   Peking.
[13]   As Ellis notes, Cambalu is the reading of the common text of Marco Polo; the word is properly Khambalik. It is the Tartar name for Peking.
[14]   Plato in I *Timaeus/Critias*.
[15]   See Figures 14-15 to I *Timaeus/Critias*.
[16]   Evidently Bacon reads the description of the rings with which Poseidon invested the sanctuary of Cleito in I 2, *Critias* 113C-E as an emblem or Platonic allegory of an ascent to heaven. This reading of Plato's text was probably influenced by the tradition of Jacob's ladder in Genesis 28: 16.

they of Tyrambel through the Atlantic to the Mediterrane Sea; and they of Coya through the South Sea upon this our island.

The tradition of the destruction of great Atlantis described and corrected

§ 27 And for the former of these, which was into Europe, the same author amongst you (as it seemeth) had some relation from the Egyptian priest whom he citeth.[17] For assuredly such a thing there was. But whether it were the ancient Athenians that had the glory of the repulse and resistance of those forces, I can say nothing: but certain it is, there never came back either ship or man from that voyage. Neither had the other voyage of those of Coya upon us had better fortune, if they had not met with enemies of greater clemency. For the king of this island (by name Altabin) a wise man and a great warrior, knowing well both his own strength and that of his enemies, handled the matter so, as he cut off their land-forces from their ships; and entoiled both their navy and their camp with a greater power than theirs, both by sea and land; and compelled them to render themselves without striking stroke: and after they were at his mercy, contenting himself only with their oath that they should no more bear arms against him, dismissed them all in safety.

§ 28 But the Divine Revenge[18] overtook not long after those proud enterprises. For within less than the space of one hundred years, the great Atlantis was utterly lost and destroyed: not by a great earthquake, as your man saith,[19] (for that whole tract is little subject to earthquakes,) but by a particular deluge or inundation; those countries having, at this day, far greater rivers and far higher mountains to pour down waters, than any part of the old world. But it is true that the same inundation was not deep; not past forty foot, in most places, from the ground: so that although it destroyed man and beast generally, yet some few wild inhabitants of the wood escaped. Birds also were saved by flying to the high trees and woods. For as for men, although they had buildings in many places higher than the depth of the water, yet that inundation, though it were shallow, had a long continuance; whereby they of the vale that were not drowned, perished for

---

[17] Critias cites the tradition in **I** 1, *Timaeus* 22B.

[18] Bacon seems to recognize the end of **I** 2, Plato's *Critias*, where Zeus calls an assembly of the gods to deliberate on how to punish the kings of Atlantis (121B-C).

[19] **I** 1 *Timaeus* 25C-D; Bacon makes the same correction to the Platonic account in his essay "Of Vicissitudes of Things" (58), *Francis Bacon*, ed. Brian Vickers (Oxford 1996) 451.

want of food and other things necessary. So as marvel you not at the thin population of America, nor at the rudeness and ignorance of the people; for you must account your inhabitants of America as a young people; younger a thousand years, at the least, than the rest of the world; for that there was so much time between the universal flood and their particular inundation. For the poor remnant of human seed which remained in their mountains peopled the country again slowly, by little and little; and being simple and savage people, (not like Noah and his sons, which was the chief family of the earth,) they were not able to leave letters, arts, and civility to their posterity; and having likewise in their mountainous habitations been used (in respect of the extreme cold of those regions) to clothe themselves with the skins of tigers, bears, and great hairy goats, that they have in those parts; when after they came down into the valley, and found the intolerable heats which are there, and knew no means of lighter apparel, they were forced to begin the custom of going naked, which continueth at this day. Only they take great pride and delight in the feathers of birds, and this also they took from those their ancestors of the mountains, who were invited unto it by the infinite flights of birds that came up to the high grounds, while the waters stood below. So you see, by this main accident of time, we lost our traffic with the Americans, with whom of all others, in regard they lay nearest to us, we had most commerce.

§ 29   As for the other parts of the world, it is most manifest that in the ages following (whether it were in respect of wars, or by a natural revolution of time,) navigation did every where greatly decay; and specially far voyages (the rather by the use of galleys, and such vessels as could hardly brook the ocean,) were altogether left and omitted. So then, that part of intercourse which could be from other nations to sail to us, you see how it hath long since ceased; except it were by some rare accident, as this of yours. But now of the cessation of that other part of intercourse, which might be by our sailing to other nations, I must yield you some other cause. For I cannot say (if I shall say truly,) but our shipping, for number, strength, mariners, pilots, and all things that appertain to navigation, is as great as ever: and therefore why we should sit at home, I shall now give you an account by itself: and it will draw nearer to give you satisfaction to your principal question.

§ 30   "There reigned in this island, about nineteen hundred years ago, a King, whose memory of all others we most adore; not superstitiously, but as a divine instrument, though a mortal man; his name was Solamona: and we esteem him as the lawgiver of our nation. This king had a "large heart,"[20] inscrutable for good; and was wholly bent to make his kingdom and people happy. He therefore, taking into consideration how sufficient and substantive this land was to maintain itself without any aid at all of the foreigner; being five thousand six hundred miles in circuit, and of rare fertility of soil in the greatest part thereof; and finding also the shipping of this country might be plentifully set on work, both by fishing and by transportations from port to port, and likewise by sailing unto some small islands that are not far from us, and are under the crown and laws of this state; and recalling into his memory the happy and flourishing estate wherein this land then was, so as it might be a thousand ways altered to the worse, but scarce any one way to the better; thought nothing wanted to his noble and heroical intentions, but only (as far as human foresight might reach) to give perpetuity to that which was in his time so happily established. Therefore amongst his other fundamental laws of this kingdom, he did ordain the interdicts and prohibitions which we have touching entrance of strangers; which at that time (though it was after the calamity of America) was frequent; doubting novelties, and commixture of manners. It is true, the like law against the admission of strangers without licence is an ancient law in the kingdom of China, and yet continued in use. But there it is a poor thing; and hath made them a curious, ignorant, fearful, foolish nation. But our lawgiver made his law of another temper. For first, he hath preserved all points of humanity, in taking order and making provision for the relief of strangers distressed; whereof you have tasted."

§ 31 At which speech (as reason was) we all rose up, and bowed ourselves. He went on. "That king also, still desiring to join humanity and policy together; and thinking it against humanity to detain strangers here against their wills, and against policy that they should return and discover their knowledge of this estate, he took this course: he did ordain that of the strangers that should be permitted to land, as many (at all times) might depart as would; but as many as would stay should have very good conditions and means to live from the state. Wherein he saw so far, that now in so many ages since the prohibition, we have memory not of one ship that ever returned; and but of thirteen persons only, at several times, that chose to return in our bottoms. What those few that returned may have reported abroad I know not. But you

---

[20] I Kings 4: 29-34.

must think, whatsoever they have said could be taken where they came but for a dream. Now for our travelling from hence into parts abroad, our Lawgiver thought fit altogether to restrain it. So is it not in China. For the Chinese sail where they will or can; which sheweth that their law of keeping out strangers is a law of pusillanimity and fear. But this restraint of ours hath one only exception, which is admirable; preserving the good which cometh by communicating with strangers, and avoiding the hurt; and I will now open it to you.[21]

The Governor now relates how the House of Salomona was founded.

§ 32 And here I shall seem a little to digress, but you will by and by find it pertinent. Ye shall understand (my dear friends) that amongst the excellent acts of that king, one above all hath the preeminence. It was the erection and institution of an Order or Society which we call Salomon's House; the noblest foundation (as we think) that ever was upon the earth; and the lanthorn of this kingdom. It is dedicated to the study of the Works and Creatures of God. Some think it beareth the founder's name a little corrupted, as if it should be Solamona's House. But the records write it as it is spoken. So as I take it to be denominate of the King of the Hebrews, which is famous with you, and no stranger to us. For we have some parts of his works which with you are lost; namely, that Natural History which he wrote, of all plants, from the "cedar of Libanus" to the "moss that groweth out of the wall," and of "all things that have life and motion."[22] This maketh me think that our king, finding himself to symbolize in many things with that king of the Hebrews (which lived many years before him), honoured him with the title of this foundation. And I am the rather induced to be of this opinion, for that I find in ancient records this Order or Society is sometimes called Salomon's House, and sometimes the College of the Six Days Works; whereby I am satisfied that our excellent king had learned from the Hebrews that God had created the world and all that therein is within six days; and therefore he instituting that House for the finding out of the true nature of all things, (whereby God might have the more glory in the workmanship of them, and men the more fruit in the use of them,) did give it also that second name.

---

[21] It is possible that this provision owes something to the Nocturnal Council of Plato's *Laws*. As in the case of the fellows of the College of Six Days' Works, some of the members of the Nocturnal Council are required to bring back word of the world outside of Crete, *Laws* XII 962A.

[22] I Kings 4: 3.

§ 33 But now to come to our present purpose. When the king had forbidden to all his people navigation into any part that was not under his crown, he made nevertheless this ordinance; That every twelve years there should be set forth out of this kingdom two ships, appointed to several voyages; That in either of these ships there should be a mission of three of the Fellows or Brethren of Salomon's House; whose errand was only to give us knowledge of the affairs and state of those countries to which they were designed, and especially of the sciences, arts, manufactures, and inventions of all the world; and withal to bring unto us books, instruments, and patterns in every kind; That the ships, after they had landed the brethren, should return; and that the brethren should stay abroad till the new mission.[23] These ships are not otherwise fraught, than with store of victuals, and good quantity of treasure to remain with the brethren, for the buying of such things and rewarding of such persons as they should think fit. Now for me to tell you how the vulgar sort of mariners are contained from being discovered at land; and how they that must be put on shore for any time, colour themselves under the names of other nations; and to what places these voyages have been designed; and what places of *rendez-vous* are appointed for the new missions; and the like circumstances of the practique; I may not do it: neither is it much to your desire. But thus you see we maintain a trade, not for gold, silver, or jewels; nor for silks; nor for spices; nor any other commodity of matter; but only for God's first creature, which was Light: to have light (I say) of the growth of all parts of the world."[24]

§ 34 And when he had said this, he was silent; and so were we all. For indeed we were all astonished to hear so strange things so probably told. And he, perceiving that we were willing to say somewhat but had it not ready, in great courtesy took us off, and descended to ask us questions of our voyage and fortunes; and in the end concluded, that we might do well to think with ourselves what time of stay we would demand of the state; and bade us not to scant ourselves; for he would procure such time as we desired.

---

[23] The occupation of these fellows is briefly described again at the conclusion of the speech of one of the Fathers of Salomon's house. He refers to them as the Merchants of Light, §87.

[24] Referring to Genesis 1: 3 and God's command "Let there be light." Bacon's prepared for this conception of the enlightenment of the College of Six Days' Works in his essay "On Truth": "The first creature of God, in the works of the days, was the light of the sense; the last was the light of reason; and his sabbath work ever since, is the illumination of his Spirit," in Vickers (1996) 342.

Whereupon we all rose up, and presented ourselves to kiss the skirt of his tippet; but he would not suffer us; and so took his leave. But when it came once amongst our people that the state used to offer conditions to strangers that would stay, we had work enough to get any of our men to look to our ship, and to keep them from going presently to the governor to crave conditions. But with much ado we refrained them, till we might agree what course to take.

The guests from Europe are given freedom to visit the capital city of Bensalem.

§ 35 We took ourselves now for free men, seeing there was no danger of our utter perdition; and lived most joyfully, going abroad and seeing what was to be seen in the city and places adjacent within our tedder;[25] and obtaining acquaintance with many of the city, not of the meanest quality; at whose hands we found such humanity, and such a freedom and desire to take strangers as it were into their bosom, as was enough to make us forget all that was dear to us in our own countries: and continually we met with many things right worthy of observation and relation; as indeed, if there be a mirror in the world worthy to hold men's eyes, it is that country.

Two of the Ship's Company attend the solemn Feast of the Family.

§ 36 One day there were two of our company bidden to a Feast of the Family, as they call it.[26] A most natural, pious, and reverend custom it is, shewing that nation to be compounded of all goodness. This is the manner of it. It is granted to any man that shall live to see thirty persons descended of his body alive together, and all above three years old, to make this feast; which is done at the cost of the state. The Father of the Family, whom they call the *Tirsan*, two days before the feast, taketh to him three of such friends as he liketh to choose; and is assisted also by the governor of the city or place where the feast is celebrated; and all the persons of the family, of both sexes, are summoned to attend him.

§ 37 These two days the Tirsan sitteth in consultation concerning the good estate of the family. There, if there be any discord or suits between any of the family, they are compounded and appeased. There, if any of the family be distressed or decayed, order is taken

---

25 Tether.
26 In describing this feast, Bacon might have had in mind the common meals of the Utopians and their Final Feasts at the end of each Utopian month, *Utopia* II 79-81 and 143/II **140**.17-**144**.26 and **232**.21-31.

for their relief and competent means to live. There, if any be subject to vice, or take ill courses, they are reproved and censured. So likewise direction is given touching marriages, and the courses of life which any of them should take, with divers other the like orders and advices. The governor assisteth, to the end to put in execution by his public authority the decrees and orders of the Tirsan, if they should be disobeyed; though that seldom needeth; such reverence and obedience they give to the order of nature.

§ 38   The Tirsan doth also then ever choose one man from amongst his sons, to live in house with him: who is called ever after the Son of the Vine. The reason will hereafter appear. On the feast-day, the Father or Tirsan cometh forth after divine service into a large room where the feast is celebrated; which room hath an half-pace[27] at the upper end. Against the wall, in the middle of the half-pace, is a chair placed for him, with a table and carpet before it. Over the chair is a state,[28] made round or oval, and it is of ivy; an ivy somewhat whiter than ours, like the leaf of a silver ash, but more shining; for it is green all winter. And the state is curiously wrought with silver and silk of divers colours, broiding or binding in the ivy; and is ever of the work of some of the daughters of the family; and veiled over at the top with a fine net of silk and silver. But the substance of it is true ivy; whereof, after it is taken down, the friends of the family are desirous to have some leaf or sprig to keep.

§ 39   The Tirsan cometh forth with all his generation or lineage, the males before him, and the females following him; and if there be a mother from whose body the whole lineage is descended, there is a traverse placed in a loft above on the right hand of the chair, with a privy door, and a carved window of glass, leaded with gold and blue; where she sitteth, but is not seen. When the Tirsan is come forth, he sitteth down in the chair; and all the lineage place themselves against the wall, both at his back and upon the return of the half-pace, in order of their years without difference of sex; and stand upon their feet. When he is set; the room being always full of company, but well kept and without disorder.

§ 40   After some pause there cometh in from the lower end of the room a *Taratan* (which is as much as an herald) and on either side of him two young lads; whereof one carrieth a scroll of their shining yellow parchment; and the other a cluster of grapes of gold,

---

27   A low platform.
28   A canopy of fabric or baldachin.

with a long foot or stalk. The herald and children are clothed with mantles of seawater green sattin; but the herald's mantle is streamed with gold, and hath a train. Then the herald with three curtesies, or rather inclinations, cometh up as far as the half-pace; and there first taketh into his hand the scroll. This scroll is the King's Charter, containing gift of revenew, and many privileges, exemptions, and points of honour, granted to the Father of the Family; and is ever styled and directed, "To such an one our well-beloved friend and creditor": which is a title proper only to this case. For they say the king is debtor to no man, but for propagation of his subjects. The seal set to the king's charter is the king's image, embossed or moulded in gold; and though such charters be expedited of course, and as of right, yet they are varied by discretion, according to the number and dignity of the family.

§ 41 This charter the herald readeth aloud; and while it is read, the father or Tirsan standeth up, supported by two of his sons, such as he chooseth. Then the herald mounteth the half-pace, and delivereth the charter into his hand: and with that there is an acclamation by all that are present in their language, which is thus much: "Happy are the people of Bensalem." Then the herald taketh into his hand from the other child the cluster of grapes, which is of gold, both the stalk and the grapes. But the grapes are daintily enamelled; and if the males of the family be the greater number, the grapes are enamelled purple, with a little sun set on the top; if the females, then they are enamelled into a greenish yellow, with a crescent on the top. The grapes are in number as many as there are descendants of the family. This golden cluster the herald delivereth also to the Tirsan; who presently delivereth it over to that son that he had formerly chosen to be in house with him: who beareth it before his father as an ensign of honour when he goeth in public, ever after; and is thereupon called the Son of the Vine.

§ 42 After this ceremony ended, the father or Tirsan retireth; and after some time cometh forth again to dinner, where he sitteth alone under the state, as before; and none of his descendants sit with him, of what degree or dignity soever, except he hap to be of Salomon's House. He is served only by his own children, such as are male; who perform unto him all service of the table upon the knee; and the women only stand about him, leaning against the wall.

§ 43 The room below the half-pace hath tables on the sides for the guests that are bidden; who are served with great and comely order; and towards the end of dinner (which in the greatest feasts with them lasteth never above an hour and an half) there is an hymn sung, varied according to the invention of him that composeth it, (for they have excellent poesy,) but the subject of it is (always) the praises of Adam and Noah and Abraham; whereof the former two peopled the world, and the last was the Father of the Faithful: concluding ever with a thanksgiving for the nativity of our Saviour, in whose birth the births of all are only blessed.

§ 44   Dinner being done, the Tirsan retireth again; and having withdrawn himself alone into a place where he maketh some private prayers, he cometh forth the third time, to give the blessing; with all his descendants, who stand about him as at the first. Then he calleth them forth by one and by one, by name, as he pleaseth, though seldom the order of age be inverted. The person that is called (the table being before removed) kneeleth down before the chair, and the father layeth his hand upon his head, or her head, and giveth the blessing in these words: "Son of Bensalem," (or Daughter of Bensalem,) "thy father saith it: the man by whom thou hast breath and life speaketh the word: The blessing of the everlasting Father, the Prince of Peace, and the Holy Dove be upon thee, and make the days of thy pilgrimage good and many." This he saith to every of them; and that done, if there be any of his sons of eminent merit and virtue, (so they be not above two,) he calleth for them again; and saith, laying his arm over their shoulders, they standing; "Sons, it is well ye are born, give God the praise, and persevere to the end." And withal delivereth to either of them a jewel, made in the figure of an ear of wheat, which they ever after wear in the front of their turban or hat. This done, they fall to music and dances, and other recreations, after their manner, for the rest of the day. This is the full order of that feast.

Our narrator relates his conversation with Joabin touching the customs of the Bensalemites, particularly their marriage customs.

§ 45   By that time six or seven days were spent, I was fallen into strait acquaintance with a merchant of that city, whose name was Joabin. He was Jew, and circumcised: for they have some few stirps of Jews yet remaining among them, whom they leave to their own religion. Which they may the better do, because they are of a far differing disposition from the Jews in other parts. For whereas they hate the name of Christ, and have a secret inbred rancour against the people amongst whom they live: these (contrariwise) give unto our Saviour many high attributes, and love the nation of Bensalem extremely. Surely this man of whom I speak would ever acknowledge that Christ was born of a Virgin, and that he was more than a man; and he would tell how God made him ruler of the Seraphims which guard his throne; and they call him also the Milken Way, and the Eliah of the Messiah;[29] and many other high names; which though they be inferior to his divine Majesty, yet they are far from the language of other Jews.

§ 46   And for the country of Bensalem, this man would make no end of commending it: being desirous, by tradition among the Jews there, to have it believed that the people thereof were of the generations of Abraham, by another son, whom they call Nachoran[30]; and that Moses by a secret cabala ordained the laws of Bensalem which they now use; and that when the Messiah should come, and sit in his throne at Hierusalem, the king of Bensalem should sit at his feet, whereas other kings should keep a great distance.

§ 47   But yet setting aside these Jewish dreams, the man was a wise man, and learned, and of great policy, and excellently seen in the laws and customs of that nation. Amongst other discourses, one day I told him I was much affected with the relation I had from some of the company, of their custom in holding the Feast of the Family; for that (methought) I had never heard of a solemnity wherein nature did so much preside. And because propagation of families proceedeth from the nuptial copulation, I desired to know of him what laws and customs they had concerning marriage; and whether they kept marriage well; and whether they were tied to one wife? For that where population is so much affected, and such as with them it seemed to be, there is commonly permission of plurality of wives.

Joabin discourseth on marriage in Bensalem.

§ 48   To this he said, "You have reason for to commend that excellent institution of the Feast of the Family. And indeed we have experience, that those families that are partakers of the blessing of that feast do flourish and prosper ever after in an extraordinary manner. But hear me now, and I will tell you what I know. You shall understand that there is not under the heavens so chaste a nation as this of Bensalem; nor so free from all pollution or foulness. It is the virgin of the world. I remember I have read in one of your European books, of an holy hermit amongst you that desired to

---

[29]   The prophet Elijah; called the prophet of Christ in Matthew 17: 10.
[30]   In the Old Testament, Nahor or Nachor is one of the brothers of Abraham. Nachor had many sons and Bacon gives one of these the name Nachoran. For Nachor, see Genesis 11: 22-26 and 22: 20-22; Luke 3: 34.

see the Spirit of Fornication; and there appeared to him a little foul ugly Æthiop.[31] But if he had desired to see the Spirit of Chastity of Bensalem, it would have appeared to him in the likeness of a fair beautiful Cherubin. For there is nothing amongst mortal men more fair and admirable, than the chaste minds of this people.

§ 49 Know therefore, that with them there are no stews, no dissolute houses, no courtesans, nor anything of that kind. Nay they wonder (with detestation) at you in Europe, which permit such things. They say ye have put marriage out of office: for marriage is ordained a remedy for unlawful concupiscence; and natural concupiscence seemeth as a spur to marriage. But when men have at hand a remedy more agreeable to their corrupt will, marriage is almost expulsed. And therefore there are with you seen infinite men that marry not, but chuse rather a libertine and impure single life, than to be yoked in marriage; and many that do marry, marry late, when the prime and strength of their years is past. And when they do marry, what is marriage to them but a very bargain; wherein is sought alliance, or portion, or reputation, with some desire (almost indifferent) of issue; and not the faithful nuptial union of man and wife, that was first instituted.

§ 50 Neither is it possible that those that have cast away so basely so much of their strength, should greatly esteem children, (being of the same matter,) as chaste men do. So likewise during marriage, is the case much amended, as it ought to be if those things were tolerated only for necessity? No, but they remain still as a very affront to marriage. The haunting of those dissolute places, or resort to courtesans, are no more punished in married men than in bachelors. And the depraved custom of change, and the delight in meretricious embracements, (where sin is turned into art,) maketh marriage a dull thing, and a kind of imposition or tax.

§ 51 They hear you defend these things, as done to avoid greater evils; as advoutries,[32] deflouring of virgins, unnatural lust, and the like. But they say this is a preposterous wisdom; and they call it "Lot's offer,"[33] who to save his guests from abusing, offered his daughters: nay they say farther that there is little gained in this; for that the same vices and appetites do still remain and abound; unlawful lust being like a furnace, that if you stop the flames altogether,

---

[31] Bacon describes this fable more fully in his Latin work *On the Wisdom of the Ancients* (*De Veterum Sapientia*), *Works* VI 737-739.
[32] Adulteries.
[33] Referring to Lot's offer of his two virgin daughters to the men of Sodom, Genesis 19:8.

it will quench; but if you give it any vent, it will rage. As for masculine love, they have no touch of it; and yet there are not so faithful and inviolate friendships in the world again as are there; and to speak generally, (as I said before,) I have not read of any such chastity in any people as theirs. And their usual saying is, "That whosoever is unchaste cannot reverence himself"; and they say, "That the reverence of a man's self is, next religion, the chiefest bridle of all vices."

§ 52   And when he had said this, the good Jew paused a little; whereupon I, far more willing to hear him speak on than to speak myself, yet thinking it decent that upon his pause of speech I should not be altogether silent, said only this; "That I would say to him, as the widow of Sarepta said to Elias; that he was come to bring to memory our sins; and that I confess the righteousness of Bensalem was greater than the righteousness of Europe."[34]

§ 53   At which speech he bowed his head, and went on in this manner: "They have also many wise and excellent laws touching marriage. They allow no polygamy. They have ordained that none do intermarry or contract, until a month be passed from their first interview. Marriage without consent of parents they do not make void, but they mulct[35] it in the inheritors: for the children of such marriages are not admitted to inherit above a third part of their parents' inheritance. I have read in a book of one of your men, of a Feigned Commonwealth, where the married couple are permitted, before they contract, to see one another naked.[36] This they dislike; for they think it a scorn to give a refusal after so familiar knowledge: but because of many hidden defects in men and women's bodies, they have a more civil way; for they have near every town a couple of pools, (which they call Adam and Eve's pools,) where it is permitted to one of the friends of the man, and another of the friends of the woman, to see them severally bathe naked."

This conversation ended, a messenger arrives to announce a matter of some importance to Joabin: A Father from Salomon's House is to arrive in a week's time.

§54   And as we were thus in conference, there came one that seemed to be a messenger, in a rich huke,[37] that spake with the Jew: where-

---

[34]   I Kings 17: 8-24.
[35]   Penalize.
[36]   The reference is to Thomas More, *Utopia* II 110/II **186.33-188**.27.
[37]   A hooded cloak. In Rawley's Latin it is described as an embroidered tunic with gilt thread.

upon he turned to me and said; "You will pardon me, for I am commanded away in haste." The next morning he came to me again, joyful as it seemed, and said, "There is word come to the governor of the city, that one of the Fathers of Salomon's House will be here this day sevennight: we have seen none of them this dozen years. His coming is in state; but the cause of his coming is secret. I will provide you and your fellows of a good standing to see his entry." I thanked him, and told him, "I was most glad of the news."

§ 55   The day being come, he made his entry. He was a man of middle stature and age, comely of person, and had an aspect as if he pitied men. He was clothed in a robe of fine black cloth, with wide sleeves and a cape. His under garment was of excellent white linen down to the foot, girt with a girdle of the same; and a sindon or tippet of the same about his neck. He had gloves that were curious, and set with stone; and shoes of peach-coloured velvet. His neck was bare to the shoulders. His hat was like a helmet, or Spanish Montera; and his locks curled below it decently: they were of colour brown. His beard was cut round, and of the same colour with his hair, somewhat lighter.

§ 56   He was carried in a rich chariot without wheels, litter-wise; with two horses at either end, richly trapped in blue velvet embroidered; and two footmen on each side in the like attire. The chariot was all of cedar, gilt, and adorned with crystal; save that the fore-end had pannels of sapphires, set in borders of gold, and the hinder-end the like of emeralds of the Peru colour. There was also a sun of gold, radiant, upon the top, in the midst; and on the top before, a small cherub of gold, with wings displayed. The chariot was covered with cloth of gold tissued upon blue. He had before him fifty attendants, young men all, in white sattin loose coats to the mid-leg; and stockings of white silk; and shoes of blue velvet; and hats of blue velvet; with fine plumes of divers colours, set round like hat-bands. Next before the chariot went two men, bare-headed, in linen garments down the foot, girt, and shoes of blue velvet; who carried the one a crosier,[38] the other a pastoral staff like a sheep-hook; neither of them of metal, but the crosier of balm-wood, the pastoral staff of cedar. Horsemen he had none, neither before nor behind his chariot: as it seemeth, to avoid all tumult and trouble. Behind his chariot went all the officers and principals of the Companies of the City. He sat alone,

---

[38]   A staff in the form of a cross.

upon cushions of a kind of excellent plush, blue; and under his foot curious carpets of silk of divers colours, like the Persian, but far finer. He held up his bare hand as he went, as blessing the people, but in silence.

§ 57   The street was wonderfully well kept: so that there was never any army had their men stand in better battle-array, than the people stood. The windows likewise were not crowded, but every one stood in them as if they had been placed. When the shew was past, the Jew said to me; "I shall not be able to attend you as I would, in regard of some charge the city hath laid upon me, for the entertaining of this great person." Three days after, the Jew came to me again, and said; "Ye are happy men; for the Father of Salomon's House taketh knowledge of your being here, and commanded me to tell you that he will admit all your company to his presence, and have private conference with one of you that ye shall choose: and for this hath appointed the next day after tomorrow. And because he meaneth to give you his blessing, he hath appointed it in the forenoon."

§ 58   We came at our day and hour, and I was chosen by my fellows for the private access. We found him in a fair chamber, richly hanged, and carpeted under foot, without any degrees to the state. He was set upon a low throne richly adorned, and a rich cloth of state over his head, of blue sattin embroidered. He was alone, save that he had two pages of honour, on either hand one, finely attired in white. His under-garments were the like that we saw him wear in the chariot; but instead of his gown, he had on him a mantle with a cape, of the same fine black, fastened about him.

The Father of Salomon's House greets the European guests and speaks to them of his College of Six Days' Works.

§ 59   When we came in, as we were taught, we bowed low at our first entrance; and when we were come near his chair, he stood up, holding forth his hand ungloved, and in posture of blessing; and we every one of us stooped down, and kissed the hem of his tippet. That done, the rest departed, and I remained. Then he warned the pages forth of the room, and caused me to sit down beside him, and spake to me thus in the Spanish tongue: "GOD bless thee, my son; I will give thee the greatest jewel I have. For I will impart unto thee, for the love of God and men, a relation of the true state of Salomon's House. Son, to make you know the true state of Salomon's House, I will keep this order.

§ 60   First, I will set forth unto you the end of our foundation. Secondly, the preparations and instruments we have for our works. Thirdly, the several employments and functions whereto our fellows are assigned. And fourthly, the ordinances and rites which we observe.

The end of the House of Solomon described

§ 61   "The End of our Foundation is the knowledge of Causes, and secret motions of things; and the enlarging of the bounds of Human Empire, to the effecting of all things possible.

How instruments are fashioned for the works of the House

§ 62   "The Preparations and Instruments are these. We have large and deep caves of several depths: the deepest are sunk six hundred fathom; and some of them are digged and made under great hills and mountains: so that if you reckon together the depth of the hill and the depth of the cave, they are (some of them) above three miles deep. For we find that the depth of a hill, and the depth of a cave from the flat, is the same thing both remote alike from the sun and heaven's beams, and from the open air. These caves we call the Lower Region. And we use them for all coagulations, indurations, refrigerations, and conservations of bodies. We use them likewise for the imitation of natural mines; and the producing also of new artificial metals, by compositions and materials which we use, and lay there for many years. We use them also sometimes, (which may seem strange,) for curing of some diseases, and for prolongation of life in some hermits that choose to live there, well accommodated of all things necessary; and indeed live very long; by whom also we learn many things.

§ 63   "We have burials in several earths, where we put divers cements, as the Chineses do their porcellain. But we have them in greater variety, and some of them more fine. We have also great variety of composts, and soils, for the making of the earth fruitful.

§ 64   "We have high towers; the highest about half a mile in height; and some of them likewise set upon high mountains; so that the vantage of the hill with the tower is in the highest of them three miles at least. And these places we call the Upper Region: accounting the air between the high places and the low, as a Middle Region. We use these towers, according to their several heights and situations, for insolation, refrigeration, conservation; and for the view of divers meteors; as winds, rain, snow, hail; and some of the fiery meteors also. And upon them, in some places, are dwellings of hermits, whom we visit sometimes, and instruct what to observe.

§ 65 "We have great lakes both salt and fresh, whereof we have use for the fish and fowl. We use them also for burials of some natural bodies: for we find a difference in things buried in earth or in air below the earth, and things buried in water. We have also pools, of which some do strain fresh water out of salt; and others by art do turn fresh water into salt. We have also some rocks in the midst of the sea, and some bays upon the shore, for some works wherein is required the air and vapour of the sea. We have likewise violent streams and cataracts, which serve us for many motions: and likewise engines for multiplying and enforcing of winds, to set also on going divers motions.

§ 66 "We have also a number of artificial wells and fountains, made in imitation of the natural sources and baths; as tincted upon vitriol, sulphur, steel, brass, lead, nitre, and other minerals. And again we have little wells for infusions of many things, where the waters take the virtue quicker and better than in vessels or basons. And amongst them we have a water which we call Water of Paradise, being, by that we do to it, made very sovereign for health, and prolongation of life.

§ 67 "We have also great and spacious houses, where we imitate and demonstrate meteors; as snow, hail, rain, some artificial rains of bodies and not of water, thunders, lightnings; also generations of bodies in air, as frogs, flies, and divers others.

§ 68 "We have also certain chambers, which we call Chambers of Health, where we qualify the air as we think good and proper for the cure of divers diseases, and preservation of health.

§ 69 "We have also fair and large baths, of several mixtures, for the cure of diseases, and the restoring of man's body from arefaction: and others for the confirming of it in strength of sinews, vital parts, and the very juice and substance of the body.

§ 70 "We have also large and various orchards and gardens, wherein we do not so much respect beauty, as variety of ground and soil, proper for divers trees and herbs: and some very spacious, where trees and berries are set whereof we make divers kinds of drinks, besides the vineyards. In these we practise likewise all conclusions of grafting and inoculating, as well of wild-trees as fruit-trees, which produceth many effects. And we make (by art) in the same orchards and gardens, trees and flowers to come earlier or later than their seasons; and to come up and bear more speedily than by their natural course they do. We make them also by art greater much than their nature; and their fruit greater and sweeter and of differing taste, smell, colour, and figure, from their nature. And many of them we so order, as they become of medicinal use.

§ 71 "We have also means to make divers plants rise by mixtures of earths without seeds; and likewise to make divers new plants, differing from the vulgar; and to make one tree or plant turn into another.

§ 72 "We have also parks and inclosures of all sorts of beasts and birds, which we use not only for view or rareness, but likewise for dissections and trials; that thereby we may take light what may be wrought upon the body of man. Wherein we find many strange effects; as continuing life in them, though divers parts, which you account vital, be perished and taken forth; resuscitating of some that seem dead in appearance; and the like. We try also all poisons and other medicines upon them, as well of chirurgery as physic. By art likewise, we make them greater or taller than their kind is; and contrariwise dwarf them, and stay their growth: we make them more fruitful and bearing than their kind is; and contrariwise barren and not generative. Also we make them differ in colour, shape, activity, many ways. We find means to make commixtures and copulations of different kinds; which have produced many new kinds, and them not barren, as the general opinion is. We make a number of kinds of serpents, worms, flies, fishes, of putrefaction; whereof some are advanced (in effect) to be perfect creatures, like beasts or birds; and have sexes, and do propagate. Neither do we this by chance, but we know beforehand of what matter and commixture what kind of those creatures will arise.

§ 73 "We have also particular pools, where we make trials upon fishes, as we have said before of beasts and birds.

§ 74 "We have also places for breed and generation of those kinds of worms and flies which are of special use; such as are with you your silk-worms and bees.

§ 75 "I will not hold you long with recounting of our brew-houses, bake-houses, and kitchens, where are made divers drinks, breads, and meats, rare and of special effects. Wines we have of grapes; and drinks of other juice of fruits, of grains, and of roots: and of mixtures with honey, sugar, manna, and fruits dried and decocted. Also of the tears or woundings of trees, and of the pulp of canes. And these drinks are of several ages, some to the age or last of forty years. We have drinks also brewed with several herbs, and roots, and spices; yea with several fleshes, and white meats;

whereof some of the drinks are such, as they are in effect meat and drink both: so that divers, especially in age, do desire to live with them, with little or no meat or bread. And above all, we strive to have drinks of extreme thin parts, to insinuate into the body, and yet without all biting, sharpness, or fretting; insomuch as some of them put upon the back of your hand will, with a little stay, pass through to the palm, and yet taste mild to the mouth. We have also waters which we ripen in that fashion, as they become nourishing; so that they are indeed excellent drink; and many will use no other. Breads we have of several grains, roots, and kernels: yea and some of flesh and fish dried; with divers kinds of leavenings and seasonings: so that some do extremely move appetites; some do nourish so, as divers do live of them, without any other meat; who live very long. So for meats, we have some of them so beaten and made tender and mortified, yet without all corrupting, as a weak heat of the stomach will turn them into good chylus, as well as a strong heat would meat otherwise prepared. We have some meats also and breads and drinks, which taken by men enable them to fast long after; and some other, that used make the very flesh of men's bodies sensibly more hard and tough, and their strength far greater than otherwise it would be.

§ 76 "We have dispensatories, or shops of medicines. Wherein you may easily think, if we have such variety of plants and living creatures more than you have in Europe, (for we know what you have,) the simples, drugs, and ingredients of medicines, must likewise be in so much the greater variety. We have them likewise of divers ages, and long fermentations. And for their preparations, we have not only all manner of exquisite distillations and separations, and especially by gentle heats and percolations through divers strainers, yea and substances; but also exact forms of composition, whereby they incorporate almost, as they were natural simples.

§ 77 "We have also divers mechanical arts, which you have not; and stuffs made by them; as papers, linen, silks, tissues; dainty works of feathers of wonderful lustre; excellent dyes, and many others; and shops likewise, as well for such as are not brought into vulgar use amongst us as for those that are. For you must know that of the things before recited, many of them are grown into use throughout the kingdom; but yet if they did flow from our invention, we have of them also for patterns and principals.

§ 78 "We have also furnaces of great diversities, and that keep great diversity of heats; fierce and quick; strong and constant; soft and mild; blown, quiet; dry, moist; and the like. But above all, we have heats in imitation of the sun's and heavenly bodies' heats, that pass divers inequalities and (as it were) orbs, progresses, and returns, whereby we produce admirable effects. Besides, we have heats of dungs, and of bellies and maws of living creatures, and of their bloods and bodies; and of hays and herbs laid up moist; of lime unquenched; and such like. Instruments also which generate heat only by motion. And farther, places for strong insolations; and again, places under the earth, which by nature or art yield heat. These divers heats we use, as the nature of the operation which we intend requireth.

§ 79   "We have also perspective-houses, where we make demonstrations of all lights and radiations; and of all colours; and out of things uncoloured and transparent, we can represent unto you all several colours; not in rain-bows, as it is in gems and prisms, but of themselves single. We represent also all multiplications of light, which we carry to great distance, and make so sharp as to discern small points and lines; also all colorations of light: all delusions and deceits of the sight, in figures, magnitudes, motions, colours: all demonstrations of shadows. We find also divers means, yet unknown to you, of producing of light originally from divers bodies. We procure means of seeing objects afar off; as in the heaven and remote places; and represent things near as afar off, and things afar off as near; making feigned distances. We have also helps for the sight, far above spectacles and glasses in use. We have also glasses and means to see small and minute bodies perfectly and distinctly; as the shapes and colours of small flies and worms, grains and flaws in gems, which cannot otherwise be seen; observations in urine and blood, not otherwise to be seen. We make artificial rain-bows, halos, and circles about light. We represent also all manner of reflexions, refractions, and multiplications of visual beams of objects.

§ 80   "We have also precious stones of all kinds, many of them of great beauty, and to you unknown; crystals likewise; and glasses of divers kinds; and amongst them some of metals vitrificated, and other materials besides those of which you make glass. Also a number of fossils, and imperfect minerals, which you have not. Likewise loadstones of prodigious virtue; and other rare stones, both natural and artificial.

§ 81   "We have also sound-houses, where we practise and demonstrate all sounds, and their generation. We have harmonies which you have not, of quarter-sounds, and lesser slides of sounds. Divers instruments of music likewise to you unknown, some sweeter than any you have; together with bells and rings that are dainty and sweet. We represent small sounds as great and deep; likewise great sounds extenuate and sharp; we make divers tremblings and warblings of sounds, which in their original are entire. We represent and imitate all articulate sounds and letters, and the voices and notes of beasts and birds. We have certain helps which set to the ear do further the hearing greatly. We have also divers strange and artificial echos, reflecting the voice many times, and as it were tossing it: and some that give back the voice louder than it came; some shriller, and some deeper; yea, some rendering the voice differing in the letters or articulate sound from that they receive. We have also means to convey sounds in trunks and pipes, in strange lines and distances.

§ 82   "We have also perfume-houses; wherewith we join also practices of taste. We multiply smells, which may seem strange. We imitate smells, making all smells to breathe out of other mixtures than those that give them. We make divers imitations of taste likewise, so that they will deceive any man's taste. And in this house we contain also a confiture-house; where we make all sweetmeats, dry and moist, and divers pleasant wines, milks, broths, and sallets, in far greater variety than you have.

§ 83   "We have also engine-houses, where are prepared engines and instruments for all sorts of motions. There we imitate and practise to make swifter motions than any you have, either out of your muskets or any engine that you have; and to make them and multiply them more easily, and with small force, by wheels and other means: and to make them stronger, and more violent than yours are; exceeding your greatest cannons and basilisks. We represent also ordnance and instruments of war, and engines of all kinds: and likewise new mixtures and compositions of gunpowder, wildfires burning in water, and unquenchable. Also fireworks of all variety both for pleasure and use. We imitate also flights of birds; we have some degrees of flying in the air; we have ships and boats for going under water, and brooking of seas; also swimming-girdles and supporters. We have divers curious clocks, and other like motions of return, and some perpetual motions. We imitate also motions of living creatures, by images of men, beasts, birds, fishes, and serpents. We have also a great number of other various motions, strange for equality, fineness, and subtilty.

§ 84 "We have also a mathematical house, where are represented all instruments, as well of geometry as astronomy, exquisitely made.

§ 85 "We have also houses of deceits of the senses; where we represent all manner of feats of juggling, false apparitions, impostures, and illusions; and their fallacies. And surely you will easily believe that we that have so many things truly natural which induce admiration, could in a world of particulars deceive the senses, if we would disguise those things and labour to make them seem more miraculous. But we do hate all impostures and lies: insomuch as we have severely forbidden it to all our fellows, under pain of ignominy and fines, that they do not shew any natural work or thing, adorned or swelling; but only pure as it is, and without all affectation of strangeness.

§ 86 "These are (my son) the riches of Salomon's House.

Of the divers employment of the Fellows of the House

§ 87 "For the several employments and offices of our fellows; we have twelve that sail into foreign countries, under the names of other nations, (for our own we conceal;) who bring us the books, and abstracts, and patterns of experiments of all other parts. These we call Merchants of Light.

§ 88 "We have three that collect the experiments which are in all books. These we call Depredators.[39]

§ 89 "We have three that collect the experiments of all mechanical arts; and also of liberal sciences; and also of practices which are not brought into arts. These we call Mystery-men.

§ 90 "We have three that try new experiments, such as themselves think good. These we call Pioners or Miners.

§ 91 "We have three that draw the experiments of the former four into titles and tables, to give the better light for the drawing of observations and axioms out of them. These we call Compilers.

§ 92 "We have three that bend themselves, looking into the experiments of their fellows, and cast about how to draw out of them things of use and practice for man's life, and knowledge as well for works as for plain demonstration of causes, means of natural divinations, and the easy and clear discovery of the virtues and parts of bodies. These we call Dowry-men or Benefactors.

§ 93 "Then after divers meetings and consults of our whole number, to consider of the former labours and collections, we have three

---

[39] Literally, "those that capture game" or those that cull from available data.

that take care, out of them, to direct new experiments, of a higher light, more penetrating into nature than the former. These we call Lamps.

§ 94   "We have three others that do execute the experiments so directed, and report them. These we call Inoculators.

§ 95   "Lastly, we have three that raise the former discoveries by experiments into greater observations, axioms, and aphorisms. These we call Interpreters of Nature.

§ 96   "We have also, as you must think, novices and apprentices, that the succession of the former employed men do not fail; besides a great number of servants and attendants, men and women. And this we do also: we have consultations, which of the inventions and experiences which we have discovered shall be published, and which not: and take all an oath of secrecy, for the concealing of those which we think fit to keep secret: though some of those we do reveal sometimes to the state, and some not.

The ordinances and rites of the House detailed

§ 97   "For our ordinances and rites: we have two very long and fair galleries: in one of these we place patterns and samples of all manner of the more rare and excellent inventions: in the other we place the statuas of all principal inventors. There we have the statua of your Columbus, that discovered the West Indies: also the inventor of ships: your monk that was the inventor of ordnance and of gunpowder: the inventor of music: the inventor of letters: the inventor of printing: the inventor of observations of astronomy: the inventor of works in metal: the inventor of glass: the inventor of silk of the worm: the inventor of wine: the inventor of corn and bread: the inventor of sugars: and all these by more certain tradition than you have. Then have we divers inventors of our own, of excellent works; which since you have not seen, it were too long to make descriptions of them; and besides, in the right understanding of those descriptions you might easily err. For upon every invention of value, we erect a statua to the inventor, and give him a liberal and honourable reward. These statuas are some of brass; some of marble and touch-stone; some of cedar and other special woods gilt and adorned: some of iron; some of silver; some of gold.

§ 98   "We have certain hymns and services, which we say daily, of laud and thanks to God for his marvellous works: and forms of prayers imploring his aid and blessing for the illumination of our labours, and the turning of them into good and holy uses.

§ 99 "Lastly, we have circuits or visits of divers principal cities of the kingdom; where, as it cometh to pass, we do publish such new profitable inventions as we think good. And we do also declare natural divinations of diseases, plagues, swarms of hurtful creatures, scarcity, tempest, earthquakes, great inundations, comets, temperature of the year, and divers other things; and we give counsel thereupon what the people shall do for the prevention and remedy of them."

§ 100 And when he had said this, he stood up; and I, as I had been taught, kneeled down; and he laid his right hand upon my head, and said; "God bless thee, my son, and God bless this relation which I have made. I give thee leave to publish it for the good of other nations; for we here are in God's bosom, a land unknown." And so he left me; having assigned a value of about two thousand ducats, for a bounty to me and my fellows. For they give great largesses where they come upon all occasions.[40]

[The Rest was not Perfected.]

---

[40] The unfinished state of *New Atlantis* is a studied imitation of Plato's *Critias*; but Bacon ends with a full sentence and thus fails to imitate the dramatic end of the *Critias*, which ends in mid-sentence **I** 1, 121C: **I** 2, 121C. Some comments on the significance of the unperfected state of *New Atlantis* will be found in the Introduction §10.

V. SUPPLEMENT: UTOPIAN PROTOTYPES, DEVELOPMENTS, AND VARIATIONS

1. The Elysian Field(s) and the Island(s) of the Blest

The Elysian fields are the prototype of several later utopias and appear first in Greek literature in Homer's *Odyssey* (A). They closely resemble the Island(s) of the Blest of Hesiod (B) and Pindar (D), and are considered one region of the island by Lucian (E). Both sites are reserved for the afterlife of those favored by the gods; Elysion, in fact, seems to derive from a word meaning "struck by lightening," and thus designates selection by Zeus.[1] This type of place is common to other Indo-European cultures (for example, the Sumerians and the Celts), is often (but not always) set in the distant west, and probably developed out of accounts much older than the Greek writings that have come down to us.[2] In Greek tradition, the afterlife paradise is reserved for the most righteous of humans and especially for heroes of both myth and history, as is evident from an anonymous drinking song about the so-called Athenian tyrant-slayer, Harmodius: "Most beloved Harmodius, you are not dead at all, but, they say, you exist on the Islands of the Blest, where swift-footed Achilles is and, they say, Diomedes son of Tydeus" (*PMG* 894). Ibycus and Simonides are reputed to have written about the Elysian field, or at least to have mentioned that Achilles married Medea there,[3] but of Simonides' extant works, the passage below (C = frag. 22 West) seems rather to portray the poet as narrator in a paradise after death, although the original context of the surviving words is unknown and what remains is quite fragmentary. Diskin Clay suggests that the elegy is connected to another fragment of Simonides, a hymn to Achilles followed by an account of the battle of Plataea (frag. 11 West): Simonides seems to hold up the blessed fate of Achilles and Patroclus as the model for the afterlife promised the Spartans and Athenians who died at Plataea and

---

[1]   Walter Burkert, "Elysion," *Glotta* 39 (1961) 208-213 (in German); summarized in Burkert (1985) 198; see also Nagy (1979) 190.
[2]   On the cross-cultural tradition, see Koenen (1994) 5 and n72; Konrad (1994) 108. On the variation in names and locations, see Introduction §3.
[3]   Scholium on Apollonius Rhodius IV 814-815a, p. 293, in C. Wendel, *Die Überlieferung der Scholien zu Apollonios von Rhodos* (Abh. Göttingen 3,1, 1932).

perhaps for his own destiny as a poet. These later heroes are referred to in Hesiodic terms as "the generation of heroes fated to a short life" (frag. 11 West, line 18). Scholars generally agree that the text of the fragment translated here (C) begins with the description of a voyage by sea.[4] The poet describes the beauty of the place he desires to reach. He will find there an island caressed by gentle breezes, with many trees. The last lines of the piece have been interpreted as an idyllic and highly charged erotic scene in which the speaker imagines himself stretched out on a meadow, with a garland on his head, delighting in the company of a young man named Echekratides, and reciting his poetry to his beloved—imitating, perhaps, Achilles and Patroclus.

Roughly contemporary with Simonides' elegy is Pindar's *Olympian* II (D), which evokes the fate not only of heroes such as Cadmus, Peleus, and Achilles, but also those who have led righteous lives. Pindar envisioned two different afterlife paradises, one in Hades, the other, for those who had proved themselves worthy after several reincarnations, on the Island of the Blest. He elsewhere wrote a very similar account of the abode of the pious in Hades (frag. 129, see Introduction §3).

Lucian's fuller description of the Islands of the Blest in his *True History* (E) reflects the themes we find in the earlier authors and probably other lost accounts as well. If the above interpretation of Simonides' fragment is correct, we rediscover its erotic scene in Lucian's Island, where disembodied souls enjoy poetry and the blessed heroes (including Achilles) make love to lovers of both sexes in the fragrant open air (E).[5]

A. HOMER *Odyssey* IV 561-569: THE SEA-GOD PROTEUS PROPHESIES TO MENELAOS:

> But it is not decreed that you, Zeus-cherished Menelaos,
> Will die and encounter your fate in horse-grazing Argos,
> But to the Elysian field and the edges of earth
> The immortals will send you, where sandy-haired
>   Rhadamanthys dwells,
> 175 At which place life is easiest for humans—
> There is no snowfall, nor is there much winter, nor ever any
>   rain,
> But continually Ocean sends forth
> Clear-toned breezes of blowing Zephyr to revive[6] humans—
> Because you have Helen and you are Zeus' son-in-law.

---

4   For a recent discussion with earlier bibliography see Mace (1996) 233-247.
5   *True History* II 15 (below) and 19, where Socrates has chosen for his young lovers Hyacinth and Narcissus.
6   On Ocean as a reviving force, see Nagy (1979) 196.

B. Hesiod *Works and Days* 167-173: In the fourth Age dwelled the "godlike generation of heroes who are called demigods," and who fought and died in the wars of Thebes and Troy.

> Granting to these a life and habitat separate from humans,
> Father Zeus, son of Kronos, settled them at the edges of earth,
> Far from the immortals; Kronos is king over them,
> 170 And they dwell with a carefree spirit
> On the Islands of the Blest alongside Ocean with its deep
>   currents,
> Fortunate heroes, for whom three times a year
>   the wheat-giving land bears honey-sweet fruit.

C. Simonides frag. 22 (West) seems to present a fantasy in which the poet enjoys rejuvenation (unparalleled elsewhere) and erotic love on an Island of the Blest.

> . . . of the sea
> . . . passageway;
> . . . reach there . . .
> . . .
> 5   . . . I would . . . path . . .
>   . . . glory of violet-crowned
>   . . . (I would)[7] come to the densely wooded abode . . .
> . . . island with fair br[eeze]s, delight of l[ife;]
> And [seeing with my eyes] fair-haired Echek[ratid]es
> 10 (I) would take his hand
> So as to take youthful bloom from his lovely skin
> And yearning [desire] would pour forth from (his) e[ye]s.
> And (I) [, with the bo]y, [would live luxuriously,] in
>   whi[te] flow(ers)
> Reclining, [having] re[moved] wrinkles,
> 15 Wea[ving for his] hair a lov[ely] newly-grown . . .
> . . . flourishing [garland;]
> . . . and the lovely clear-voiced . . .
> Guiding language of well-crafted [words] from my mouth
> . . .
> 20 . . . of the . . .
> Well-escorted[8] . . . .

---

7   Parentheses enclose words whose restoration by editors is reasonably certain; square brackets enclose words or parts of words that do not appear in the Greek text, but have been suggested by editors (I have tried to represent in the translation the percentage of the word still visible in the Greek text).

8   West's emendation; the papyrus has "loud- (or fair-)sound(ing)."

D. Pindar *Olympian* II 68-80: to Theron of Akragas on his victory in a chariot race (476 BC). Pindar conceives of the afterlife as a cycle of reincarnations after which the best humans reach the Islands of the Blest. In earlier cycles, souls are judged in the underworld and, if deemed worthy, are permitted to dwell without labor, in the company of gods, enjoying sunshine "in equal nights and equal days," while the evil suffer.

> As many as have dwelled three times
> In each place[9] and have endured to restrain
>
> 70 Their souls entirely from injustice, these complete Zeus' road
>   to the tower of Kronos; there
> Ocean breezes surround with their breath the Island of the
>   Blest; and golden flowers shine forth,
> Some, out of the ground, from brilliant trees, but water feeds
>   others,
> From which they entwine their hands with wreaths and (they
>   make) garlands
>
> 75 In the upright decrees of Rhadamanthys,
> Whom the great father[10] keeps ready, seated beside him,
> Husband of Rhea who holds the highest throne of all.
> Peleus and Cadmus are counted among these,
> And Achilles was brought here by his mother
>
> 80 When she had persuaded Zeus' heart with prayers . . .

E. Lucian *True History* II 4-6, 11-16: In the course of many adventures in their journey throughout the world (and after their journey to the Selenitai, III appendix above), Lucian and his companions arrive at the Island of the Blest.

> (4) At the prow appeared one flat and low-lying (island) no less than fifty stades away. (5) And now we were coming near and a certain wondrous breeze surrounded us with its breath, sweet and fragrant, such as the historian Herodotus says comes out of blessed Arabia. For such sweet pleasure assaulted our senses as comes from roses, narcissus, hyacinths, lilies, and violets, and further, from myrtle and laurel and the vine blossom. Delighting in the odor and looking forward to good things after our long toils, we gradually came closer to the island. At this very point we observed numerous harbors around the whole island, without waves and spacious, as well as transparent rivers flowing

---

9   That is, earth and Hades.
10 Kronos.

softly into the sea, and, in addition, meadows and woods and lyrical birds, some singing from the shores, but many others upon branches. Airy mist, light and fragrant, spread over the land, but certain breezes blowing sweetly and softly shook the forest trees so that from their stirred branches whistled a delightful and continuous tune, like snatches of music out of the blue from flanking woodwinds; and, in fact, a voice commingled from many into one was heard, not turbulent, but like the sound that arises in a symposium from the woodwind players and the reciters of praise as well as from those clapping to the woodwind or kithara.

(6) Enchanted by all this we landed and, after anchoring the ship, disembarked, leaving behind Skintharos and two companions on the ship. Advancing through the flowering meadow, we met up with the guards and watchmen, who bound us with rose garlands—for this is the strongest restraining device here—and led us to the chief magistrate. From these men we found out along the way that the island was called that of the Blest and that the Cretan Rhadamanthys ruled it. . . . *Lucian and his companions attend the court of Rhadamanthys, where they observe the trials of Homeric heroes and are then judged themselves; they are permitted to attend the feast of the Heroes before leaving the island, but will have to stand trial after death for being restless busy-bodies and not staying at home.*

(11) At this moment our garlands slipped off by themselves and we were freed and led to the city and symposium of the Blest. Now the city itself was entirely golden, and the surrounding wall, of smaragdos.[11] And there were seven gates, each a solid panel of cinnamon. The foundation of the city and the land within the wall, however, were of ivory. The temples of all the gods were constructed of beryl stone[12] and the altars within them were very large and entirely of amethyst, upon which they offer hecatombs. Around the city flows a river of the loveliest perfume, 100 royal cubits in width, 5 in depth, so that swimming is easy. And their bathtubs are huge crystal chambers, heated with cinnamon. But instead of water in the tub there is warm dew.

(12) For clothing they use delicate purple spider webs. They do not have bodies, however, but are intangible and without flesh, each being visible as a form and distinct visage, and although without body, they cohere as form and move, think, and emit a voice; in short, it seems that their naked soul walks around cov-

---

[11]   Emerald or other green gemstone; cf. **V 5 A**, Diodorus Siculus III 53.6 below.
[12]   A sea-green gem.

ered with the likeness of a body. At any rate, unless someone touched one of them, he would not dispute that it was a real body that he saw. For they are just like walking shadows, but not black. And no one ages, but remains at the time of life he was when he arrived.

Further, there is no night among them, nor very bright daylight, but the light that covers the earth is just like the faint gleam towards dawn when the sun has not yet risen. Moreover, they know one season of the year, for it is always spring for them and one wind, Zephyr, blows for them. **(13)** The land blooms with all kinds of flowers as well as all kinds of crops and shade-producing plants. In fact the vines bloom twelve times a year and every month each bears fruit; they said that pomegranates, apples, and other fruit bloom thirteen times a year. For within one month, the one they call Minoan,[13] they bear fruit twice. Instead of ears of wheat, bread grows from the tops of plants ready to eat, just like mushrooms. There are 365 springs of water around the city, and just as many of honey, 500 of perfume, these, however, being smaller, seven rivers of milk, and eight of wine.

(14) They held the symposium outside the city in the field called Elysion; this is a very beautiful meadow and around it are all sorts of densely growing trees which provide shade to those reclining. They lie on a tapestry of flowers, and the winds wait on them and serve them everything except that they do not pour wine; there is no need for this, since there are trees around the symposium, large crystal ones of the most transparent glass, and the fruits of these trees are wine glasses of all sorts of shapes and sizes. And so whenever someone arrives at the symposium, he plucks one or two of the drinking vessels and sets them on the table, and at once they become full of wine. Thus they drink; and instead of garlands, nightingales and other lyrical birds from the nearby meadows gather flowers in their beaks and shower them as they fly overhead with song. In addition, they perfume themselves in this way: thick clouds which have drawn in fragrance from the springs and the river settle over the symposium and rain down delicately like dew as the winds press them gently.

(15) At dinner they leisurely enjoy music and songs. The epics of Homer especially are sung to them; and he himself is present and feasts with them in the place just above Odysseus.[14] Now the cho-

---

13   Or "of Minos," legendary king of Crete and brother of Rhadamanthys.

14   Homer is significant as the most prominent of Greek poets as well as the earliest to mention the Elysian field (**V 1 A**).

ruses consist of boys and girls; Eunomos of Lokris, Arion of Lesbos,[15] Anacreon,[16] and Stesichorus lead off and sing together. The latter, in fact, I saw among them, when Helen had made peace with him.[17] Whenever these cease from their singing, a second . chorus of swans[18] and swallows and nightingales makes an entrance. And when these sing, too, the whole forest supplies woodwind accompaniment with the winds leading off.

(16) They also have another very great source of merriment: there are two springs beside the symposium, one of laughter, the other of pleasure; at the beginning of the feast everyone drinks from each of these and thus spends the rest of the festivities in pleasure and laughter.

2. The Hyperboreans

The Hyperboreans were familiar to the Greeks from the Archaic period onward as a distant exotic race. Most sources place them to the north of the Greek world, but there was no consensus on their specific location. Accounts of the Hyperboreans are related to Golden Age utopias. This particular race lives in an ideal climate, is just, peaceful, and above all, pious, and is exceptionally favored by Apollo. Their name was interpreted in antiquity to mean "those beyond the Boreas" (the North Wind), but by some modern scholars is thought to mean "those who bring (gifts) overland" in reference to the historical pilgrimages made by people from the north to the sanctuaries of Apollo at Delphi and Delos.[19] In myth, the Hyperboreans have the natural advantage of a climate beyond the reaches of winter, but they justify and attract the god's favor also by their pious way of life. Like the Panchaians, they are ruled by priests. Nearly all the testimonia on them concern their religious activities; they are a paradigm of piety and origin of cult beyond an ordinary human's reach, leading an idyllic life of peace, order, and joyful celebrations of the god. Implicit in the traditions is the

[15] Nothing survives of the works of Eunomos and Arion, although the latter was famed for his innovations in choral song and dance and is thus fitting in the immediate context concerning choruses.

[16] Anacreon is mentioned probably because his songs focused on the pleasures of the symposium, especially love and drinking.

[17] Lucian alludes to Stesichorus' "Palinode," his second poem about Helen in which he recanted his claim in an earlier poem that she had deserted her husband, Menelaos, and run off with Paris. Lucian may have used a now lost poem of Stesichorus as a source for his own account. The "Palinode" is linked to the White Island in Pausanias (III 19.11-13), and fragments of Stesichorus' poetry suggest that he wrote about the Islands of the Blest (Aristophanes Peace 775 ff. with scholia; Philodemus On Piety 1088 III p. 39 Gomperz).

[18] Cf. V 2 E, Hecataeus of Abdera below.

[19] See V 2 C, Herodotus IV 32-36; Farnell (1907) 99-112; Romm (1992) 60-67.

notion that benevolence to other peoples and continual focus on worship, to the exclusion of acquisitive and aggressive relations with one's fellow-citizens and with outsiders, result in a blessed and painless existence.

A. ALCAEUS (LATE SEVENTH-EARLY SIXTH CENTURY BC) FRAG. 307C, PARAPHRASED BY HIMERIUS *Orations* 48.10-11, WHO SAYS THAT ALCAEUS COMPOSED A PAEAN TO APOLLO CONTAINING THE FOLLOWING STORY.

When Apollo was born, Zeus, adorning him with a golden headband and giving him a lyre and, in addition, a chariot to drive—and the chariot was in the form of swans[20]—sent him to Delphi and the springs of Castalia in order to expound justice (*dike*) and law (*themis*[21]) to the Greeks. But he, stepping upon the chariot, incited the swans to fly to the Hyperboreans. Now the Delphians, when they perceived this, stood around the tripod, having composed a paean with song and choruses of youths, and they summoned the god to come from the Hyperboreans. And he, after declaring laws (*themisteusas*) among the people there for a whole year, bade the swans to fly away from the Hyperboreans, when he judged it time for the Delphian tripods also to echo forth. Now this was during the summer, and the very middle of summer when Alcaeus leads Apollo from the Hyperboreans. For which reason, with summer shining forth and Apollo present, the lyre as well is luxurious in its summer song about the god. . . .

B. PINDAR *Pythian* X 27-46: THE HYPERBOREANS ARE DESCRIBED FOLLOWING PINDAR'S DISCUSSION OF HUMAN LIMITATIONS: WHILE A GOD IS FREE OF PAIN, THE BEST A MAN CAN HOPE AND STRIVE FOR ARE VICTORY (IN ATHLETIC CONTESTS), THE RECOGNITION AND PRAISE THAT ACCOMPANY IT, AND SEEING ONE'S SON ACHIEVE SIMILAR VICTORIES.

27   Bronze heaven is never trodden by (*a man*).
      And with as much glory as we can grasp as mortals,
          he reaches the end
      Of the cruise. But travelling neither by ship nor on foot
          could you find

30   The amazing road to the arena of assembled Hyperboreans.
      With these people, Perseus, Leader of the Host, once
          feasted,

---

[20]   On the association of swans with Apollo and the Hyperboreans see **V 2 E**, Hecataeus of Abdera; Krappe (1942).

[21]   *Themis* contains the concepts "law"; "justice"; "right"; "oracle." The root of the word recurs as the name of the Hyperborean princess, Themistos ("oracular"; "permitted by law"; "righteous"), daughter of the king of the Hyperboreans, Zabios ("strong force"; "strong life"; or "strong bow"?); Themistos had a son by Apollo named Galeotes, whose descendants lived in Attica or as prophets in Sicily: Stephanus of Byzantium (sixth century AD), s.v. "Galeotai." In some ancient accounts, the goddess Themis preceded Apollo at the Delphic oracle (e.g. Aeschylus *Eumenides* 1 ff.).

Going to their homes,
Happening upon them as they offered illustrious hecatombs
Of donkeys to the god. Their continual festivities
And prayers of praise Apollo welcomes
35   Most, and laughs, perceiving
The high-pitched insolence of the beast.
The Muse is at home
With their way of life; and on all sides, choruses of
  maidens,
Crying of lyres, ringing of flutes vibrate.
40   Binding their hair with golden laurel they celebrate
  together merrily.
Neither illness nor destructive old age associates
With this sacred race. And without toil and battles
They dwell, immune from harsh-judging Nemesis. And
  inspired in his courageous heart,
45   Once the son of Danae went to the society of these blessed
  men,
And Athena led the way. He slew the Gorgon and went away
  . . . .

C. HERODOTUS (IV 13-36 PASSIM) REPORTS ON AN EARLIER POETIC ACCOUNT OF THE HYPERBOREANS AS WELL AS THEIR CONNECTION WITH DELOS, BUT REFRAINS FROM SPECULATING ABOUT THE CHARACTER OF THEIR LAND OR WAY OF LIFE.

(IV 13) Aristeas of Proconnesus, son of Caystrobius, composed hexameter verses saying that, seized with enthusiasm by Phoebus (*Apollo*), he reached the Issedones, and that beyond the Issedones dwell the Aramaspians, one-eyed men, and beyond these, gold-guarding griffins, and next, the Hyperboreans, whose land extends to the sea. He said that all of these, with the exception of the Hyperboreans, and beginning with the Arimaspians, continually attack their neighbors . . . . *Herodotus tells the tale of Aristeaus, and then describes these northern lands and peoples with their strange customs as reported by the Scythians, who got their information from the Issedones.*

(IV 32) Concerning the Hyperborean people, the Scythians and any others dwelling in the region say nothing worthwhile, except perhaps for the Issedones. But as I see it, these too say nothing worthwhile. For then the Scythians would speak (*the same as the Issedones*) as they do of the one-eyed men. But things have been said about the Hyperboreans by Hesiod and by Homer, in the *Epigonoi* (*Descendants*) if in fact Homer really composed these verses.[22]

(33) The Delians, however, have the most to say about them by far, reporting that sacred (*offerings*) covered in stalks of wheat and carried by the Hyperboreans reach Scythia, and from Scythia, each nearby land in turn receives them and brings them westward as far as the Adriatic . . . . *The offerings proceed in relay south to Dodona, east to Euboea, and then across the Aegean islands until they reach Delos. In IV 34-35 Herodotus describes the earliest journeys of the Hyperborean envoys to Delos; the five men and two maidens who carried the offerings did not return. The Delians worship the maidens as heroines, as well as two others who came earlier.*[23]

(36) This is my account of the Hyperboreans. For I do not tell the story of Abaris, said to be a Hyperborean, that he carried an arrow throughout the whole earth, eating nothing.[24] But if some people are Hyperboreans, others are Hypernotions (*Beyond the South Wind*). *Herodotus goes on to dispute the commonly accepted mapping of the world, contending that Europe, Asia, and Africa are not really symmetrical and equal in size, and that in some regions, the edges of these lands are unknown rather than definitively surrounded by Ocean.*[25]

D. DIODORUS SICULUS II 47, REPORTING HECATAEUS OF ABDERA (360-290 BC) AND OTHERS (*FGrHist* 264 F 7), COMBINES EARLIER TRADITIONS ABOUT THE HYPERBOREANS AND PLACES THEM ON AN ISLAND.

(II 47.1) Since we have deemed worthy of written account the parts of Asia extending towards the north, we think it is not un-

---

[22]   In the surviving fragments of Hesiod's *Catalogue of Women* (seventh or sixth century BC), the tribes of horse-loving Hyperboreans are mentioned along with other non-Greek peoples, including Pygmies, Ethiopians, and Scythians (Hesiod frag. 150.21). A contemporary or later source, the *Homeric Hymn to Dionysus* (VII 28), includes the Hyperboreans along with Egypt and Cyprus as possible destinations of a long-distance sea traveller. The passage from the Homeric *Descendants* on the Hyperboreans has not come down to us.

[23]   See Larson (1995) 118-119.

[24]   In later sources, Abaris the Hyperborean was said to have supernatural powers and to have recognized the philosopher Pythagoras as the "Hyperborean Apollo": Iamblichus *Life of Pythagoras* IXX. See also **V 2 D**, Hecataeus of Abdera reported by Diodorus II 47.5; Aelian *Historical Miscellany* II 26; Diogenes Laertius VIII 1.11; Dodds (1951) 141 and 144 with notes. Like the Pythagoreans, the Hyperboreans are said to be vegetarians (Hellanicus frag. 96 of C. Müller, *Fragmenta Historicorum Graecorum*, Paris 1841-1870).

[25]   On Herodotus' statement about the Hypernotions and his conception of the world, see Romm (1989).

fitting to go through the tales concerning the Hyperboreans. For of those who wrote down the ancient legends, Hecataeus and certain others say that in the territories on the other side of the Celtic land,[26] in Ocean, is an island no smaller than Sicily. And they say that this is in the northern regions, and is inhabited by people called Hyperboreans, from the fact that they are situated beyond the blasts of the wind of Boreas. And the island, since it is fertile in its soil, generates all types of crops, has a remarkably good climate, and bears harvests twice every year. (2) And the legend relates that Leto was born on it; for which reason Apollo is most honored of all the gods among them. And they are essentially like priests of Apollo, since this god is praised with song by them daily and unceasingly and receives exceptional honor. Also on this island is a splendid sanctuary of Apollo and a remarkable temple, decorated with many dedications and shaped like a sphere. (3) In addition, there is a city sacred to this god, and most of those inhabiting it are kithara players who play their kitharas in the temple constantly and proclaim praises for the god in song, extolling his deeds. (4) The Hyperboreans have their own distinctive language and are inclined to be very kindly disposed towards Greeks, especially towards Athenians and Delians, having kept up a tradition of friendliness from a long time ago. And they tell the tale that certain of the Greeks once associated with the Hyperboreans and left with them quite expensive dedications inscribed with Greek letters. (5) And similarly, it is said that Abaris,[27] arriving in Greece from the Hyperboreans a long time ago, restored the friendship and relations towards the Delians. And they relate that the moon appears from this island to be quite close to the earth and that earth-like mounds are visible on its surface. It is said too that every nineteen years, the god arrives on the island, in which years the cyclical movements of the stars are brought to completion. And on account of this, the span of nine-

---

[26]   The Celts were known to live throughout the European mainland but also further west. Herodotus IV 33 states that they live at the mouth of the Danube as well as beyond the Pillars of Heracles. Diodorus elsewhere (V 24, 32.1-3) discusses the Celts (also known as Gauls) of western Europe and the Brettanoi of Iris, i.e., Ireland. It has been suggested that Hecataeus refers to Britain in the passage quoted here (see C. H. Oldfather, trans. [1935] *Diodorus of Sicily* II, 36-37 n2), although Diodorus does not connect this passage to his description of Britain at V 21-22. On Celtic islands of the Blest, see Konrad (1994) 108-109.

[27]   Cf. **V 2 C**, Herodotus IV 36.

teen years is called "Meton's Cycle" by the Greeks.[28] During his epiphany, at frequent intervals during the nights from the spring equinox to the rise of the Pleiades, the god plays the kithara and participates in choral dances, joyful in his own prosperity. People called the Boreadae are kings of this city and govern the sanctuary; they are descendants of Boreas and always inherit their offices by direct descent.

E. HECATAEUS OF ABDERA (*FGrHist* 264 F12) IS ALSO CITED AS EVIDENCE FOR THE HYPERBOREANS BY AELIAN (*On the Characteristics of Animals* XI 1).

> Poets sing of the race of Hyperborean people and their honors to Apollo, but prose writers also praise them, among whom is Hecataeus, not the Milesian, but the Abderite. There seems to be no need right now to invoke the rest of the things that he says,… but the only things that my book invokes are these: the priests of this divinity are sons of Boreas and Chione, three in number, brothers by birth, six cubits tall. Now whenever they carry out the customary religious ceremony at the regular time by prearranged schedule, immeasurably huge clouds of swans fly down from the mountains called by them Rhipaian; these circle the temple as though purifying it by their flight. Then, however, they go down to the precinct of the temple, which is very large in size and exquisite in beauty. Now whenever the singers with their muse address the god in song, and the kithara players accompany the harmonious chorus in melody, then the swans sing with them in agreement and with no discord at all. Chanting in tune even as if they took the key notes from the conductor of the chorus, they sing along with the native inhabitants, who are most skilled in sacred tunes. Then, when the hymn comes to an end, the people retreat, having rendered with honor the customary services to the god, as do also the "winged choral dancers" that I have described, after singing and delighting the god throughout the whole day.[29]

---

[28] Meton, an astronomer of fifth-century Athens, devised a solar calendar with intercalations and months of 29 and 30 days, which came back to the beginning of the cycle after 19 years: *OCD*[3] s.v. "Meton."

[29] On the swans, cf. **V 2 A,** Alcaeus reported by Himerius. Hecataeus also claimed that the Hyperboreans controlled an island called Elizoia (*FGrHist* 264 F 11), as reported by Stephanus of Byzantium s.v. "Elizoia": "an island of the Hyperboreans, no smaller than Sicily, above the river Karambuka. The islanders are called Karambukai from the river, according to Hecataeus of Abdera."

F. Pomponius Mela (first century AD), *On Geography* (*De Chorographia*) III 36-7: Mela came from Baetica, near the Straits of Gibraltar, and wrote in Latin a geography of the world with much attention to coastal regions and mythical traditions.

> The Hyperboreans are the first people on the Asiatic shore, situated beyond the north wind and the Riphaean[30] mountains, beneath the very pole of the constellations, where the sun rises not daily as for us, but first at the spring equinox, and it sets at the autumn equinox. Thus there is perpetual day for six months, and night for the other six months. The land is narrow, sunny, and brings forth produce by itself. Its inhabitants are the most just and live longer and more blessedly happy than any other mortals, ever joyful in festive peace; they do not know war nor quarrels, and occupy themselves especially with rites of Apollo . . . . *Mela paraphrases Herodotus' account of the Hyperboreans' pilgrimages and gifts sent to Delos.* They dwell in sacred groves and forests, and when satiety for living rather than weariness takes hold, they cheerfully crown themselves with garlands and throw themselves headlong from a particular cliff into the sea. That is a distinguished burial for them.

3. The Ethiopians

Ethiopian, "Sun-burnt," was a term used to name dark-skinned peoples, and as early as Homer, distinctions were made between different branches of Ethiopians. Homer (*Odyssey* I 23-24) says that one branch lives at the setting of the sun, the other at its rising, while Mimnermus (X 9-10, cited in Athenaeus *Deipnosophistai* XI 470A) places them in the far east opposite the Hesperides in the far west. Herodotus (VII 70) mentions that the eastern Ethiopians have straight hair, the southern, woolly hair. Later sources usually locate them in Libya. Traditions about them were probably at least partly influenced by reports that had filtered down from historical contacts. Nevertheless, throughout antiquity, attributes are assigned to them that render them counterparts to the Hyperboreans. They are mentioned repeatedly in Homeric epic as hosts of the gods and share with the Hyperboreans the twin virtues of piety and justice, qualities that intensify in emphasis with the proliferation of sources in late antiquity.[31] One way to

---

[30]   A Latin variant spelling for Rhipaian, the Scythian mountains mentioned in **V 2 E**, Hecataeus reported by Aelian, above.

[31]   Homeric Ethiopians appear in the quotation of the *Iliad* (I 423-424) in **V 3 B**, Diodorus Siculus III 2 3 below, *Iliad* XXIII 205-207 (Iris visits them for a feast), and *Odyssey* I 23 (Poseidon goes to their land to receive a hecatomb). See Snowden (1970), esp. chapter 6 (144 ff.), "Ethiopians in Classical Mythology," for the Ethiopians' associations with piety and justice.

understand the pairing of these virtues is to see them reflected in the respect for boundaries, both physical and metaphorical, with incorporation of this respect into their laws and customs (*nomos*; see Introduction §3). Like the Hyperboreans, the Ethiopians are sometimes portrayed as peace-loving and non-acquisitive of their neighbors' territory. In addition, both peoples respect life and limits of the life-span. Mela's tale of Hyperborean suicide is paralleled by Diodorus' claim that kings of Ethiopians once accepted orders of their priests that it was time for them to die (III 6.1-2). Further, under Ethiopian rule, capital punishment was avoided: criminals were employed as civic workers (Herodotus II 137) or killed themselves (Diodorus III 5.2).

 The first passage in this section, from Herodotus, includes the Ethiopians' rejection of worldly riches offered by the Persians, and has been suggested as a possible source used by Thomas More in his *Utopia*.[32] The second selection comes from Diodorus Siculus, who in book III of his work presents not only the idealization of Ethiopians quoted in B below, but also reports of several different tribes of Ethiopians, some of which had been discussed earlier by Herodotus and others.[33] Diodorus claims to have read about these tribes but to have relied in his own work chiefly on what he learned from Egyptians and Ethiopian ambassadors in Egypt (III 11.3).

A. Herodotus III 17-25, on events following the Persian king Cambyses' campaign against Egypt in 525 BC. Having subdued Egypt, Cambyses marched to Sais and tried unsuccessfully to have his men mutilate the corpse of the former king, Amasis. The next step of Cambyses, growing more impious and mad every day, was to march on Libya.

(III 17) After these events Cambyses planned a threefold campaign against the Karchedonians,[34] the Ammonians, and the Long-lived Ethiopians living at the southern sea of Libya. And as he planned, he decided to send off his navy against the Karchedonians, and to divide his army, some of which he would send against the Ammonians, but first to send spies to the Ethiopians with the stated mission of bearing gifts to their king, though actually in order to see if there truly was a "Table of the Sun" reputed to exist among the Ethiopians, and to observe everything else in addition to this.

---

[32]   See Herodotus III 23 (below); Hadas (1935) 113-114; Romm (1992) 56-57 and, on the Ethiopians in general, Romm (1992) 49-60.

[33]   For example, Diodorus says that the Fish-eating Ethiopians hold their wives in common, wear no clothes, cook their food by spreading it upon rocks in the sun, and enjoy a primitive way of life in isolation from other peoples (III 15-17). The same tribe of Ethiopians is said elsewhere in Diodorus (V 5 A, III 53.6 below) to dwell in a sacred city on the island of the Amazons.

[34]   The Carthaginians.

(18) The Table of the Sun is reputed to be as follows. In the suburb is a meadow full of boiled meat of all four-footed animals, in which the men of the villages who are in office take care to place the meats during the night, and whoever wishes comes to feast there during the day. But the natives claim that the earth itself gives forth the meats each time. (19) Such is what is said to be called the Table of the Sun.

As soon as Cambyses decided to send spies, he sent for the Fish-eaters from the city Elephantine, men who knew the Ethiopian language. *Meanwhile, his navy refused to sail against the Karchedonians and thus this part of Cambyses' plan failed.*

(20) When the Fish-eaters arrived from Elephantine at Cambyses' request, he sent them to the Ethiopians, ordering them what to say and to take along as gifts a purple garment, a neck collar of twisted gold, bracelets, an alabaster chest of perfume, and a jar of Phoenician wine.

Now these Ethiopians to whom Cambyses was sending the mission are reputed to be the largest and most beautiful of all people. They have laws and customs different from the rest of humans and in particular in regard to their kingship. They consider worthy to be king whomever of the townsmen they decide is the tallest and has strength in accordance with his size.

(21) And so when the Fish-eaters had arrived among these people, giving the gifts to their king, they said the following: "The king of the Persians, Cambyses, wishing to become your friend and ally, sent us and told us to converse with you, and he gives to you these gifts, things which he himself enjoys most." And the Ethiopian, recognizing that they came as spies, said to them: "The king of the Persians sent you bearing gifts not because he holds an alliance with me in great esteem, and you are not telling the truth, for you have come as spies of my kingdom, and that man is not just. For if he were just, he would not set his heart on a country other than his own and would not try to lead into slavery people by whom he has been done no wrong. Be that as it may, present him with this bow and speak these words to him: 'The king of the Ethiopians advises the king of the Persians that whenever Persians draw a bow of such great size as effortlessly as this, then send an expedition of exceeding magnitude against the Long-lived Ethiopians. Meanwhile, be thankful to the gods for not turning the minds of the Ethiopians' sons towards the acquisition of land in addition to their own.'"

(22) Having said this, he released the bow and handed it over to those who had come to him. And taking up the purple garment, he inquired what it was and how it had been made. After the Fish-eaters had explained the truth about the purple dye and the dipping process, he said that their people were deceitful and so were their garments. Second, he asked about the twisted golden neck collar and the bracelets. And when the Fish-eaters explained that these were meant to be ornaments for him, the king laughed, having thought them to be shackles, and said that among his people, shackles were stronger than these. Third, he asked about the perfume. And after they had explained the manufacture and method of anointing, he gave the same answer as he had concerning the garment. But as he came to the wine and inquired about how it was made, he found extreme delight in the drink, and asked what the king ate and what was the longest life span of a Persian man. They told him that his food was bread, and after explaining the growing of wheat, they set 80 years as the longest span of life for a man. To this the Ethiopian replied that it was no surprise that they lived so few years, if they lived on manure; in fact they would not be able to live even that long if they did not restore themselves with the drink, pointing out the wine to the Fish-eaters. For in this, he said, his own people were inferior to the Persians.

(23) When the Fish-eaters asked the king in turn about his life span and diet, he replied that the majority of his people lived to reach the age of 120 years, and certain people surpassed even this age, and that boiled meat was their food, and milk, their drink. When the spies showed amazement at the span of years, he led them to a spring in which they bathed and thus became smoother and sleeker, just as if it consisted of olive oil, and it smelled as if it consisted of violets. The spies claimed that the water of this spring was so insubstantial that nothing could float upon it, not wood nor whatever is lighter than wood, but everything went down into its depths. And if this water is really as they say it is, their use of this water may be the chief reason why they are long-lived.

When they departed from the spring he led them to the men's prison, where all the prisoners were chained in golden shackles.[35] Bronze is the rarest and most highly valued thing of all among these Ethiopians. After viewing the prison they saw also the so-called Table of the Sun.

---

[35] According to How and Wells (1928) 262, "The whole story is a traveller's tale; but gold was once produced abundantly in Ethiopia."

(24) After this and last of all, they saw their graves, which are said to be manufactured from alabaster in the following way. When they dry up the corpse, whether in keeping with the Egyptian method or otherwise, having coated it with gypsum, they adorn the whole thing with paint, making it as similar as possible to the appearance of the person. They then place it in a hollow column of alabaster; much of this is excavated by them and easy to carve. The corpse is visible in the center of the column, giving off no unpleasant odor nor anything else unseemly, and the whole thing has the appearance of the corpse itself. For one year the closest relatives keep the column in their home, offering it a portion of everything as first fruits, and setting sacrifices before it. After this, bringing them outside, they set up the columns around the city.

(25) When they had seen everything, the spies returned. After they made their report of these things, Cambyses at once became angry and began an expedition against the Ethiopians without ordering any provision for food nor granting a rational thought to himself, that he was going to march to the edges of the earth. And inasmuch as he was in a state of madness and out of his mind, when he had heard the account from the Fish-eaters he began his march, ordering the Greeks with him to remain behind, and leading with him the whole army. Now when he arrived at Thebes along his march, he separated out about 50,000 men of his army and ordered these to make the Ammonians slaves and then to set fire to the oracle of Zeus. But he himself, leading the remainder of the army, proceeded towards the Ethiopians. Just before the army had completed a fifth of the journey, however, all they had of food was completely used up. And after they had eaten their provisions, they devoured even the pack animals. Now if Cambyses had repented when he found out about this and had brought his army back, he would have been a sensible man despite his error in the beginning. But instead, considering it of no importance, he kept going forward. And his soldiers, as long as they could obtain anything from the land, survived by eating grasses. But when they arrived at the desert sand, some of them did a terrible thing: they devoured one man out of every ten, choosing him by lot. When Cambyses heard this, in fear of them eating each other, he gave up the march against the Ethiopians. Journeying back, he arrived at Thebes, having lost many men of his army. Descending to Memphis from Thebes, he allowed the Greeks to sail away.

B. Diodorus Siculus III 2: Diodorus begins his lengthy report of the Ethiopians and their various tribes with a summary of traditions about their general character and history.

(III 2.1) It is asserted that the Ethiopians were the first of all humans to be born, and they claim that proof of this is obvious. For it is agreed by nearly all that they did not come as outsiders, and being native to the land, they are justly called autochthonous. And because they live under the mid-day sun it is believable that they were the first to come to life from the earth; this too is evident to everyone. For in as much as the heat around the sun dried up the earth that was still moist in the genesis of all things and brought them to life, it is likely that the place closest to the sun was the first to carry living and breathing species.

(2.2) They also say that among these people first was introduced the performance of honor to the gods, sacrifices and processions and festivals and all the other methods by which humans honor the divine. For this reason their piety has been publicized among all humans, and sacrifices by Ethiopians are deemed most enjoyable to the divine power. **(2.3)** They offer as testimony for this the perhaps oldest and certainly the most admired of poets among the Greeks. For he, in the *Iliad*, presents Zeus and the rest of the gods with him away from home on a visit to Ethiopia for the sacrifices rendered to them yearly and the feast in common with the Ethiopians:

For on the day before, Zeus went to the blameless Ethiopians for feasting, and all the gods followed together with him.[36]

2.4 And they say that piety towards the divine has clearly brought them grace, since invaders from outside have never succeeded in an attempt to rule them. For they have been for all time in freedom and agreement with each other, and though many powerful people campaigned against them, no one achieved the enterprise.

3.1 *Examples of those who tried to conquer them include Cambyses, Heracles, and Dionysus, but all failed* due to the piety of the men and the difficulty in accomplishing the enterprise.

4. The Continent beyond Ocean

Theopompos of Chios was an historian and orator of the fourth century BC who often included in his works, as in the selection below, digressions concerning ethnography, mythology, and marvels. His imitation of Plato's presentation of Atlantis has been noted by Pierre Vidal Naquet, who

---

[36] Homer *Iliad* I 423-424.

believes that Solon has been replaced by Silenus; the Egyptian priest, by Midas; Atlantis, by Machimos; and Athens, by Eusebes.[37] The following passage is part of the tradition of the Phrygian King Midas, most famous in legend for his touch that turned everything to gold. Midas had captured the satyr Silenus, in order to learn from him about matters unknown to humans. In another conversation reported between them, Silenus tells Midas that the best thing for a human is not to be born at all, the second best, to die as soon as possible. Because Midas treated Silenus well, Dionysus rewarded him by granting his wish that all he touch turn to gold, after which Midas died of starvation.[38]

THEOPOMPOS OF CHIOS (*FGrHist* 115 F 75C) REPORTED IN AELIAN *Historical Miscellany* III 18: THEOPOMPOS TELLS THE FOLLOWING STORY WITHIN HIS HISTORY OF PHILIP OF MACEDON.

> (75C 1) Theopompos describes a certain conversation of Midas the Phrygian and Silenus. This Silenus was son of a nymph, by nature more obscure than a god but greater than a man, since he was also immortal. Now many various things were discussed by them and in addition to these, Silenus said to Midas: (2) "Europe and Asia and Libya are islands around which flows Ocean in a circle, and the one continent that exists is outside of this world." And he related that its size is immeasurable, and it nourishes all the other living things in addition to humans, whose size is twice as large as it is here, and they do not live as long as we do, but twice as long. (3) Many and great are their cities and modes of living; and their established laws and customs are opposite to those observed by us.
>
> (4) And he said that there are two cities which surpass the others in size but do not at all resemble each other. One is called Machimos (*Warlike*), the other Eusebes (*Pious*). Now the Eusebeans live in peace and copious wealth and receive fruits from the earth without the use of plows or oxen, and they have no labor of farming and sowing seed. And he said, "They live healthily, and free of illness they expire, laughing happily and enjoying themselves. And they are so undeniably righteous that the gods do not disapprove of visiting them frequently. (5) But the people of the city Machimos are most warlike and they are even born with weapons, and are always waging war and subjugating hostages, and

---

[37] Vidal-Naquet (1986) 264-265. On the passage quoted here see also Introduction §7 (with a discussion of its connections to Plato's Atlantis; Romm (1992) 67 n51; Dillery (1995) 45-48.

[38] The fullest source of this story is Ovid *Metamorphoses* XI 90-193. See *OCD*[3] s.v. "Midas (1)" for other sources.

this one city rules quite a good number of nations. Its inhabitants number no less than twenty million. They die sometimes because they are ill; but this cause is rare, since they are often struck down in their wars by rocks or wooden sticks; for they are immune to wounds by iron. And they have plenty of gold and silver, so that gold is less valuable to them than iron is to us." **(6)** And he said that they once attempted to travel across to our islands and sailed with ten million people as far as the Hyperboreans. And learning that these were the most prosperous and blessed among us, they deemed them inferior, despising them for faring poorly and wretchedly, and so thought it worthless to proceed beyond them.[39]

(7) But he added something still more amazing. He said that certain humans called the Meropes[40] inhabit many great cities near them, and at the border of their territory is a place named Anostos (No Return); it resembles a chasm, but is covered by neither darkness nor light; instead, air mingled with a turbid redness lies over it. And two rivers flow around this place, the one called Hedones (*Pleasure's*), the other, Lupes (*Pain's*), and beside each of these stand trees the size of a huge plane tree. Those beside the River Lupes bear fruit of such a nature that if anyone tastes it, he casts forth so many tears that he wastes away the rest of his whole life in mourning, and thus meets his end. **(8)** But the others, growing beside the River Hedones, bear corresponding fruit in contrast; for whoever tastes of these ceases from all his former desires, and even if he was in love, he obtains forgetfulness of this, and he soon becomes younger and resumes his earlier age already gone by. For he turns back to the prime of life, casting away old age, and next he goes back to the age of young men, then he becomes a child, then an infant, and after this he expires, utterly spent. And if the Chian who told this story is credible to anyone, let him be believed. But to me he seems to be a clever spinner of fictions both in this and in other tales.

---

[39]   These societies can be compared to Hesiod's Golden Age and Iron races in *Works and Days* and to the myth of the reversal of cosmic cycles in Plato's *Statesman* (268D-274E). The rejection of the Hyperboreans has been compared to the Hyperboreans' rejection of the Greeks (in Herodotus IV 33.3-4): Romm (1992) 67. Dillery (46-47) points out that the rejection of the best people known to the Greeks by the worst of the utopian peoples intensifies the inferiority of the Greeks.

[40]   The word Meropes is sometimes used as an epithet of people to designate their human status, literally, "divided in voice," that is, articulate, e.g., *Iliad* I 250; Hesiod *Works and Days* 109 (LSJ s.v. "merops").

5. *The Amazons, with an excursus on the Atlanteans*

This society of female fighters occurs as early as Homer's *Iliad* (II 814; III 189; VI 186), where we hear that Greek men sometimes killed them in battle. Later literature elaborates on this theme and points out signs of the Amazons' early presence in Greece in the form of tombs (e.g., at Athens, Pausanias I 2.1) and cities named after them (e.g., Sinope, Diodorus Siculus III 55.6). Early sources locate the Amazons on the River Thermodon, on the southern shore of the Black Sea; by the sixth century, they are found in Scythia.[41] An account of these is related by Diodorus Siculus II 44-46. The Amazons of early literature are comparable to the other utopias presented in this collection in their isolated location and their reversal of roles between men and women that might be viewed in terms of the potential for other kinds of societies unrealized in the Greek world. And like Plato's Atlanteans, the Amazons emerge from their isolation to engage in conquests of other lands, and eventually become extinct.

A society in which men were subordinate to women or non-existent was virtually "an un-society, an impossible society"[42] and thus analogous to More's Utopia. We can only speculate on the reasons for the attraction of the impossible world of the Amazons for the Greeks. While literary descriptions and vase paintings reveal that the Greeks admired all excellent warriors, and perhaps found females in this role particularly attractive, modern theories centered on the "Other" link the reactions of discomfort or disdain with pleasure in the notion of "difference," so that the fantasy of Amazons becomes a psychological construct that channels both fears and hopes originating in one's present society.[43]

The Amazons in the selections below live on islands and share additional qualities with other accounts of utopian peoples: the natural fecundity of their land which makes agriculture and technology unnecessary, reminiscent of Golden Age utopias, and their organization of society and laws, including the raising of children. Further, in the tale of the conquests of the Amazons, the first passage (A) reveals the tendency of Hellenistic literature to conflate and combine traditions of mythical peoples at the edges of the civilized world: the proximity of the Amazons to the Ethiopians and the Atlanteans conveniently defines all these peoples as part of the world of primitive "noble savages" and idealized races. Dionysios Skytobrachion

---

[41] See Dowden (1997). On the tombs and worship of the Amazons see Larson 111-116, who notes that the traditions of mainland Greece, but not those of Asia Minor, portrayed the Amazons as foreigners to the Greek world (1997).

[42] Dowden (1997).

[43] See Blok (1995) 67-69. Women of Sparta and of some non-Greek cultures are also portrayed by historians and ethnographers (e.g. Herodotus, Xenophon, Mela) as relatively active members of society.

also wrote on the voyage of the Argonauts, and is known for his rationalization of traditional legends in the spirit of Euhemeros; he was, in addition, highly influenced by ethnographic works such as that of Herodotus.

A. Dionysios Skytobrachion, reported by Diodorus Siculus III 52-56: Dionysios includes this account of the Amazons and Atlanteans in his treatment of Libya.

(III 52.4) There have been quite a few races of women in Libya that were known for battle skills and inspired great amazement for their courage. For we have heard that the nation of the Gorgons, against which Perseus is said to have campaigned, excelled in prowess. That the son of Zeus, the best of the Greeks of his time, performed his greatest struggle in the expedition against these, anyone would accept as a sign of the superiority and ability of the aforementioned women. And the bravery of those who will now be investigated has an incredible superiority when judged in comparison to the nature of women in our time.

(53.1) For they say that there existed in Libya's western regions, at the edges of the known inhabited world, a race under the rule of women and one contentious in their livelihood, unlike our own. For the women's custom was to toil hard at matters of war, and they were obligated to fight in the army for a specific amount of time, while guarding their virginity. But when their years in the military had passed, they went to the men for the sake of producing children. And they administered the offices of government and the whole commonwealth. (53.2) But the men had a domestic life as servants under the orders of their mates, as do wives among us. And they had no share of the military, the government, or any other freedom of speech in the commonwealth, from which they could become proud and set themselves against the women. (53.3) And at the time when children were born, the infants were surrendered to the men and they fed them on milk and other boiled foods suitable for newborn babies. If it happened that a female was born, her breasts were cauterized so that they would not rise up in the time of her prime. For they thought that breasts protruding from the body should not chance to be in the way when it came to war. And because they were deprived of these, they are called Amazons[44] by the Greeks.

---

[44] Literally, "without a breast." The etymology first appears in the late-fifth-century work of Hellanicus (*FGrHist* 4 F107). This and other (including modern) etymologies are discussed by Blok (1995) 21-37. The word may, on the other hand, mean "without bread," perhaps giving rise to the tradition that the Amazons lacked grain, mentioned in 53.5 below.

(53.4) The story goes that they dwelled on an island called Hespera (since it was towards the sunset), situated in Lake Tritonis. This lake lies near Ocean, which encloses the earth, and is named after a river Triton which flows into it. The lake is situated next to Ethiopia and the mountain along Ocean, which is the largest in the region and slopes into Ocean; this is called Atlas by the Greeks.[45]

(53.5) The island under discussion was of a good size and full of all kinds of fruit trees, from which the local inhabitants obtained their food. It had also an abundance of livestock, goats and sheep, from which their owners derived milk and meat for their nourishment. But the people used absolutely no grain, since the use of this crop had not yet been discovered by them.

(53.6) And so, they say, the Amazons, excelling in bravery and with an urge for war, first reduced the cities on the island, except for the one called Mene.[46] For it was thought to be holy, and the Fish-eating Ethiopians dwelled in it; it had huge eruptions of fire and an abundance of stones called *anthrax, sardion*, and *smaragdos*[47] by the Greeks. After this, they made war on many of the nearby Libyans and nomads, and built a great city within Lake Tritonis, named Cherronesos (*Peninsula*) because of its shape.

(54.1) Starting out from this city they undertook great enterprises with an urge that inspired them to march against many parts of the inhabited world. And it is said that the Atlanteans were the first they attacked, men who were the most gentle of those in these regions, and who inhabited a blessed land and great cities. Among these very people, they say that according to tradition, the origin of the gods took place towards the regions along Ocean, in harmony with traditional tales among the Greeks, concerning which we shall go through step by step a little further on. *An account of further conquests by the Amazons follows, concluding at 55.11 with the Amazons' retreat back to Libya after severe losses and repeated defeats, especially against the Thracians.*

---

[45] See Figure 3. Compare Herodotus' report of an island in Lake Tritonis called Phla, associated with Jason and the Argonauts (IV 178-179), and inhabitants on the shore of the lake who worship Athena with military combat of girls (IV 180). Herodotus places this island in North Africa, and Mt. Atlas and its surrounding inhabitants, the Atlantes, further south and west, but his only comment on this people is that they are vegetarians and do not have dreams (IV 184).

[46] *Mene* is a word for "moon" in the Greek language.

[47] On the Fish-eating Ethiopians, cf. **V 3 A**, Herodotus III 19. *Anthrax* is a red stone such as garnet and ruby; *sardion* is either transparent red, comparable to carnelian, or transparent brown, like sardonyx; on *smaragdos* see **V 1 E**, Lucian *True History* II 11.

(56.1) Inasmuch as we have mentioned the Atlanteans, we think it not unfitting to go through their legends concerning the origin of the gods, since they do not diverge much from the legends among the Greeks. **(2)** Well then, the Atlanteans, living in the regions along Ocean and dwelling in a blessed land, seem to surpass by far those of lands nearby in piety and in benevolence towards people from other places, and they say that the birth of the gods occurred among them. They claim that even the most illustrious of poets among the Greeks agrees with what is told by them, in the verses in which he portrays Hera saying,

> For I am going to see the edges of the fruitful earth
> And Ocean the origin of the gods and their mother,
> Tethys.[48]

(56.3) And they claim in their legends that Ouranos was the first king and that he brought the people, who had been dispersed in their dwellings, into a city surrounded by a wall. *There follows a lengthy account of the contributions of Ouranos and his offspring to civilization and how it was spread to the rest of the world. A Golden Age island utopia, Nysa, is presented at 68.4-70, as the place where Dionysus was raised. The island is located in the river Triton, presumably south of the later home of the Amazons described above.*

B. Pseudo-Callisthenes *History of Alexander the Great* III 25: this fictional account of Alexander includes a series of letters between Alexander and the Amazons. In the first letter, Alexander warns the Amazons that he is journeying towards their territory, assuring them that he means to do no harm, but would like to receive permission from them to see their land. They respond as follows.

(25.5) When this letter had been read, they themselves wrote in reply:

The best of the Amazons to King Alexander, greetings. We write to you so that you may know the region before you attack it, lest you leave us ingloriously. Through this letter we shall clearly reveal to you the characteristics of our country and that you must take us seriously. For we are on the other side of the River Amazonikos, and we dwell on an island. It has the circumference of (*the journey of*) a year, and the river is circular, without a beginning; there is only one approach to us. We inhabitants are armed maidens, numbering 200,000. And no male lives with us. But men

---

[48] Homer *Iliad* XIV 301-302. For a discussion of this passage see Diskin Clay (1992) 136-137.

do dwell across the river, inhabiting that land. And every year we celebrate a festival, sacrificing horses to Zeus, Poseidon, and Hephaestus for 30 days. [. . .][49] And whatever men wish to deflower any of us stay attached to those women. And they bring to us all the females born from these unions when they reach the age of seven.[50]

Whenever enemies march against us, the greater part of our 200,000 goes out on horseback; the remaining women guard the island. We assemble at the borders, and the men follow, drawn up in battle order behind us. And if anyone is wounded in war [. . .] is treated with reverence through the day [. . .] there is a crown as an everlasting memorial for her relatives. But if someone falls while fighting on our behalf, her closest relatives receive not a little money. And if anyone brings back the body of an enemy she is served as a reward an abundance of gold and silver and food for the rest of her life. The result is that we each fight on behalf of our own reputation. And if we conquer our enemies or they flee, the disgrace remains theirs for all time. But if they are victorious over us, they will be victors of women. And so, King, see that the same thing does not happen to you. But we shall give you a crown every year, even if you do not order us to. Write back to us when you have reflected on this. You will find our troops at the borders.

---

[49] Gaps in the surviving text are indicated by [. . .].
[50] Age seven is probably borrowed from Spartan tradition, which set the beginning of the *agoge* (education focused on military excellence) at this age.

BIBLIOGRAPHY

Abbreviations

DK   Hermann Diels and Walther Kranz. *Die Fragmente der Vorsokratiker.* Berlin 1979.

FGrHist   Felix Jacoby. *Die Fragmente der griechischen Historiker.* Reprint of the enlarged edition. Leiden 1968.

LSJ   Henry George Liddell and Robert Scott. *A Greek-English Lexicon.* Revised and augmented by Henry Stuart Jones. 9th ed. Oxford: Clarendon Press 1968. With Roderick McKenzie, *Revised Supplement.* Edited by P. G. W. Glare with the assistance of A. A. Thompson. Oxford 1996.

OCD^3 Simon Hornblower and Antony Spawforth. eds. *The Oxford Classical Dictionary.* 3rd ed. New York 1996.

PMG   D. L. Page. ed. *Poetae Melici Graeci.* Oxford 1962.

TAPA   *Transactions of the American Philological Association*

West   M. L. West. ed. *Iambi et elegi graeci ante Alexandrum cantati.* vol. 2. 2nd ed. Oxford 1992.

Texts and Translations

We have used in many cases the Oxford Classical Texts. Exceptions, additional texts, and translations are listed here. Translations of most of the works cited are also available in the Loeb Classical Library.

PLATO, *TIMAEUS* AND *CRITIAS*

Burnet, John. 1901-1907. *Platonis Opera* IV. Oxford.

Clay, Diskin. trans. 1997. "Critias." In Cooper, ed., 1292-1306.

Cooper, John M. ed. 1997. *Plato: Complete Works.* Indianapolis.

Johnson, J. W. 1968. *Utopian Literature: A Selection.* New York.

Rivaud, Albert. 1985. *Platon Œuvres complètes X: Timée-Critias.* Paris.

Taylor, A. E. 1928. *A Commentary on Plato's Timaeus.* Oxford.

EUHEMEROS OF MESSENE

Némethy, Geyza. 1889. *Euhemeri Reliquiae.* Budapest.

Winiarczyk, M. 1991. *Euhemerus Messenius. Reliquae.* Leipzig.

Iamboulos

Oldfather, C. H. 1935. *Diodorus of Sicily* II. Loeb Classical Library. Cambridge, Mass.

Francis Bacon

Spedding, James. R. L. Ellis and D. D. Heath. 1857-1859. *The Works of Francis Bacon.* 7 vols. London.

Vickers, Brian. 1996. *Francis Bacon.* Oxford.

Sir Thomas More

Surtz, Edward S. J. ed. 1964. *Selected Works of St. Thomas More, St. Thomas More, Utopia.* New Haven, Conn.

Surtz, Edward S. J. and J. H. Hexter. eds. 1965. *The Yale Edition of the Complete Works of St. Thomas More.* Vol. 4. *Utopia.* New Haven.

Other Texts

Davis, Herbert. ed. 1965. *Jonathan Swift, Gulliver's Travels.* Oxford.

Dilts, M. R. ed. 1974. *Claudius Aelianus, Varia Historia.* Leipzig.

Gildersleeve, B. L. ed. 1965. *Pindar. Olympian and Pythian Odes.* Amsterdam.

Godley, A. D. trans. 1938. *Herodotus II. Books III and IV.* Revised ed. (1st ed. 1921) Loeb Classical Library. Cambridge, Mass.

Guthrie, Kenneth Sylvan. trans. 1987. "Iamblichus, *The Life of Pythagoras.*" In *The Pythagorean Sourcebook and Library: An Anthology of Ancient Writings which Relate to Pythagoras and Pythagorean Philosophy.* Grand Rapids, Mich., 57-122.

Hudson, H. H. 1941. *The Praise of Folly.* Princeton.

Huizinga, Johan. 1952. *Erasmus of Rotterdam.* London.

Ife, B. W. trans. 1990. *Christopher Columbus: Journal of the First Voyage (Diario del primer viaje) 1942.* Warminster.

Kinkel, G. ed. 1877. *Epicorum Graecorum Fragmenta.* Leipzig.

Kroll, Guilelmus. ed. 1958. *Historia Alexandri Magni (Pseudo-Callisthenes)* I. Recensio Vestuta. Berlin.

Müller, Karl. ed. 1855-1861. *Geographi Graeci Minores.* 2 vols. Paris.

Oldfather, C. H. trans. 1935. *Diodorus of Sicily.* 12 vols. Loeb Classical Library. Cambridge, Mass.

Romer, F. E. 1998. *Pomponius Mela's Description of the World.* Ann Arbor, Mich.

Studies

Altheim, Franz. 1948. *Weltgeschichte Asiens* II. Berlin.

Ashe, Geoffrey. 1992. *Atlantis. Lost Lands, Ancient Wisdom.* London.

Baldry, H. C. 1953. "The Idler's Paradise in Attic Comedy." *Greece and Rome* 22, 49-60.

Bérard, Victor. 1971. *Les Navigations d'Ulysse.* 3 vols. Paris.

Blok, Josine H. 1995. *The Early Amazons. Modern and Ancient Perspectives on a Persistent Myth.* Religions in the Graeco-Roman World 120. Leiden.

Burkert, Walter. 1985. *Greek Religion. Archaic and Classical.* John Raffan, trans. Cambridge Mass.

_____, 1992. *The Orientalizing Revolution: Near Eastern Influence on Early Greek Culture in the Archaic Age.* Margaret E. Pinder and Walter Burkert, trans. Cambridge, Mass.

Campbell, Mary B. 1988. *The Witness and the Other World: Exotic European Travel Writing 400-1600.* Ithaca.

Casson, Lionel. 1991. *The Ancient Mariners: Seafarers and Fighters of the Mediterranean in Ancient Times.* 2nd ed. Princeton.

Clay, Diskin. 1992. "The World of Hesiod." In Apolstolos N. Athanassakis, ed. *Essays on Hesiod II.* Ramus Monographs 21.2, 131-155.

_____, 1997. "The Plan of Plato's *Critias*." In T. Calvo and Luc Brisson, eds. *Proceedings of the Fourth Symposium Platonicum: Interpreting the Timaeus - Critias. Grenada, September 1995* (International Plato Studies 9). Sankt Augustin, 49-54.

_____, 2000. "The Invention of Atlantis: An Anatomy of a Platonic Fiction." *Proceedings of the Boston Area Colloquium in Ancient Philosophy* 15.

Clay, Jenny Strauss. 1980. "Goat Island: *OD.* 9.116-141." *Classical Quarterly* 30, 261-264.

_____. 1985. "Aeolia, or under the Sign of the Circle." *Classical Journal* 80, 289-291.

Cornford, F. M. 1957. *Plato's Cosmology.* New York.

Dawson, Doyne. 1992. *Cities of the Gods: Communist Utopias in Greek Thought.* New York.

Dilke, O. A. W. 1985. *Greek and Roman Maps.* Ithaca.

Dillery, John. 1995. *Xenophon and the History of his Times.* London.

Dobrov, G. W. ed. 1997. *The City as Comedy: Society and Representation in Athenian Drama*. Chapel Hill, North Carolina.

Dodds, E. R. 1951. *The Greeks and the Irrational*. Berkeley and Los Angeles.

_____, 1973. *The Ancient Concept of Progress and Other Essays on Greek Literature and Belief*. Oxford.

Donnely, Ignatius. 1985. *Atlantis: The Antediluvian World* (The Classic Illustrated Edition of 1882). New York.

Dowden, Ken. 1997. "The Amazons: Development and Functions." *Rheinisches Museum für Philologie* 140, 97-128.

Ellis, Richard. 1998. *Imagining Atlantis*. New York.

Farnell, Lewis Richard. 1907. *The Cults of the Greek States* IV. Oxford.

Ferguson, John. 1975. *Utopias in the Classical World*. Ithaca.

Finley, M. I. 1965. *The World of Odysseus*. 2nd ed. New York.

Friedländer, Paul. 1958. *Plato*. Hans Meyerhoff, trans. 3 vols. Princeton.

Gabba, Emilio. 1981. "True and False History in Classical Antiquity." *Journal of Roman Studies* 71, 50-62.

Gibson, R. W. 1950. *Francis Bacon: A Bibliography of his Works and of Baconiana to the Year 1750*. Oxford.

_____, 1961. *St. Thomas More: A Preliminary Bibliography of his Works and of Moreana to the Year 1750*, with a Bibliography of Utopiana compiled by J. Max Patrick. New Haven, Conn.

Grafton, Anthony. 1992. *Ancient Texts: The Power of Tradition and the Shock of Discovery*. Cambridge, Mass.

Griffiths, J. Gwyn. 1985. "Atlantis and Egypt," *Historia* 34, 3-28.

Hadas, M. 1935. "Utopian Sources in Herodotos." *Classical Philology* 30, 113-121.

Harley, J. B. and David Woodward. 1987. *The History of Cartography, Volume I: Geography in Prehistoric, Ancient, and Medieval Europe and the Mediterranean*. Chicago.

Hartog, François. 1980. *Le miroir d'Hérodote: Essai sur la représentation de l'autre*. Paris

Haslam, Michael. 1976. "A Note on Plato's Unfinished Dialogues." *American Journal of Philology* 97, 336-339.

Hedreen, Guy. 1991. "The Cult of Achilles on the Euxine." *Hesperia* 60, 313-330.

How, W. W. and J. Wells. 1928. *A Commentary on Herodotus* I. Oxford.

Howland, Jacob. 1993. *The Republic: The Odyssey of Philosophy*. New York.

Hubbard, Thomas K. 1997. "Utopianism and the Sophistic City in Aristophanes." In Dobrov, ed., 23-50.

Koenen, Ludwig. 1994. "Cyclic Destruction in Hesiod and the Catalogue of Women." *TAPA* 124, 1-34.

Konrad, C. F. 1994. *Plutarch's "Sertorius." A Historical Commentary.* Chapel Hill, North Carolina.

Konstan, David. 1997. "The Greek Polis and its Negations: Versions of Utopia in Aristophanes' *Birds.*" In Dobrov, ed., 5-22. (Reprinted from David Konstan. *Greek Comedy and Ideology.* Oxford 1995, 29-44)

Krappe, Alexander H. 1942. "APOLLON KYKNOS." *Classical Philology* 37, 353-370.

Larson, Jennifer. 1995. *Greek Heroine Cults.* Madison, Wisconsin.

Mace, Sarah. 1996. "Utopian and Erotic Fusion in a New Elegy by Simonides (22 West)." *Zeitschrift für Papyrologie und Epigraphik* 113, 233-247.

Manuel, Frank E. and P. Fritzie. 1979. *Utopian Thought and the Western World.* Cambridge, Mass.

Naddaf, Gerard. "The Atlantis Myth: An Introduction to Plato's later Philosophy of History." *Phoenix* 48, 189-209.

Nagy, Gregory. 1973. "Phaethon, Sappho's Phaon, and the White Rock of Leukas." *Harvard Studies in Classical Philology* 77, 137-177.

————, 1979. *The Best of the Achaeans.* Baltimore.

Negley, Glenn. 1977. *Utopian Literature: A Bibliography with a Supplementary Listing of Works Influential in Utopian Thought.* Lawrence, Kansas.

Nylander, Carl. 1964. "The Disaster of Atlantis." In *The Deep Well.* Joan Tate, trans. New York, 160-174.

Parker, Robert. 1983. *Miasma. Pollution and Purification in Early Greek Religion.* Oxford.

Pearson, Lionel. 1960. *The Lost Histories of Alexander the Great.* American Philological Association (Philological Monograph XX). Oxford.

Rammage, E. S. 1978. *Atlantis: Fact or Fiction.* Bloomington.

Rawson, Elizabeth. 1969. *The Spartan Tradition in European Thought.* Oxford.

Rohde, Erwin. 1914. *Der griechische Roman und seine Vorläufer.* 3rd ed. Leipzig.

————, 1925. *Psyche. The Cult of Souls and Belief in Immortality among the Greeks.* W. B. Hillis, trans. New York.

Romm, James S. 1989. "Herodotus and Mythic Geography: The Case of the Hyperboreans." *TAPA* 119, 97-113.

_____. 1991. "More's Strategy of Naming in the *Utopia.*" *Sixteen Century Journal* 22, 173-183.

_____, 1992. *The Edges of the Earth in Ancient Thought: Geography, Exploration, and Fiction.* Princeton.

Rosenmeyer, T. G. 1956. "Plato's Timaeus: *Timaeus* or *Critias?*" *Phoenix* 10, 163-172.

Schoeck, R. J. 1956. "More, Plutarch, and King Agis: Spartan History and the Meaning of *Utopia,*" *Philological Quarterly* 35:4, 366-375.

Severin, Tim. 1987. *The Ulysses Voyage: Sea Search for the Odyssey.* New York.

Snowden, Frank M. Jr. 1970. *Blacks in Antiquity. Ethiopians in Graeco-Roman Experience.* Cambridge, Mass.

Tarn, W. W. 1951. *The Greeks in Bactria and India.* 2nd ed. Cambridge.

Travlos, John. 1971. *Pictorial Dictionary of Ancient Athens.* New York.

Vidal-Naquet, Pierre. 1986. "Athens and Atlantis: Structure and Meaning of a Myth." In Idem. *The Black Hunter: Forms of Thought and Forms of Society in the Greek World.* Andrew Szegedy Maszak, trans. Baltimore, 263-284.

Waldseemüller, Martin, 1507. *Cosmographiae Introductio.* St. Dié in the Vosges.

Four Island Utopias
Index of Persons and Places